Total Sel

through

Attention Therapies

and

Open Focus

Joel Dames

Joel Dames

ISBN: 9781549986482

CONTENTS

ACKNOWLEDGMENTS

Thank you to my editor, Hiromi Dames. Spelling and grammar applications are a must. But a professional editor takes it from there. Hiromi's acumen,intelligence, and insight about the work enabled me to make the cuts and edits that had to be made, but could never have made without an editor I could completely trust, believe in, and follow.

Thank you to Hitomi Dames for her amazing organizational, layout, and technical skills. It all might have come apart half way through the project without her guidance.

I ask this, that if there be an assassination, I would want 5, 10, a hundred, a thousand to rise. If a bullet should enter my brain, let it destroy every closet door. I ask for the movement to continue. Because it is not about political gain. It is not about ego. It's not about power. It's about the us's out there. Not just the gays, but the blacks, the Asians, the seniors and the disabled. The us's.

Without hope, the us's give up. And I know you can't live on hope alone. But without hope, life is not worth living. So you, and you, and you, you've gotta give them hope. You've gotta give them hope.

Harvey Milk, from the movie, Milk

INTRODUCTION

Our body sends millions of bits per second to our brain for processing – millions – yet our conscious mind processes only 1 to 45 bits per second.We are conscious of only millionths of what is out there.

Our brain, though, is not a computer with bits, but a self-organizing, analogue, parallel processing system. The similarity with digital computing and bits is that neurons are essentially binary: They fire an action potential if they reach a certain threshold and otherwise do not fire. Considering neurons as bit processing offers a close approximation of the information processing capacity of each of our five senses.

We can measure how much information enters our brain through the senses by calculating how many receptors each sensor organ possesses, how many nerve connections send signals to the brain, and how many signals each nerve connection sends a second.

The table below compares the capacity of our sensory receptors with the capacity of our conscious perception.

Sensory System (Receptors)	Total Capacity of Our Sensory Receptors (bits/sec)	Our Actual Conscious Perception (bits/sec)
EYES	10^7	40
EARS	10^5	30
SKIN	10^3	5
TASTE	10^3	1 (?)
SMELL	10^5	1 (?)

Table I-1: Comparison of the Capacity of Our Sensory Receptors With Our Conscious Perception (What We Perceive). Based on Table From "Fundamentals of Sensory Physiology," edited by R.F. Schmidt.

The information available to our sensory receptors is astronomical. By the time we are conscious though, we are missing virtually all of this sight, sound, taste, smell, and touch sensory information out there in the world.

Sensory information enters from our eyes, ears, nose, and skin and travels along sensory (afferent) nerves to the brain. The total capacity for our eyes is 10 to 7th power: The eyes send ten million bits/second to the brain versus the 40 bits/second we consciously perceive.The skin sends a million bits a second to the brain versus 5 bits/sec we consciously perceive. The human body sends millions of bits per second to the brain for processing, yet our conscious mind processes only 1 to 45 bits per second.

Reading silently, our maximum conscious capacity is about 45 bits/sec. Our conscious capacity for spoken speech is about 40 bits/sec. Our conscious capacity for reading aloud is about 30 bits/sec. Our conscious capacity slows to just 12 bits/sec when calculating in our head.

A tremendous compression takes place when 10 million bits per second is reduced to 40 bits per sec. Compression on this massive scale takes time. Research to discover how much time was done by physiologist Benjamin Libbet at University of California, San Francisco. Libbet demonstrated that the brain takes a half second before a person consciously gets this tiny fraction of the total sensory data. The brain discards almost all of the bits of sensory data offering our conscious mind only a few bits, and lets our conscious mind think it is making its own decisions a half second later. But the brain has already decided.

We live in a world teaming with sensory information, but the brain discloses to the conscious mind only what is necessary to move about, procreate, get nourishment, and ruminate. The body gets lots of sensory feedback, but we cannot talk about or share most of what we experience. We are alone in this great solitude.All we have is our conscious internal voice droning on.

We do have some say though, as to what data survives the compression. We can focus our attention anywhere we like, on the light, sound, clothing, itches, odor, posture, or we can focus on the temperature about us. We can use all our senses at once and combine information from them all. We can shut out all of the other senses and focus on listening.

Because from one instant to the next consciousness can switch from one focus to another, it is not perceived as limited in its capacity. One moment we are aware of the lack of space in our shoes, the next moment of the expanding universe. Consciousness possesses peerless agility. But that does not change the fact that at any given moment we are not conscious of much at all.

The flow of what goes through our consciousness is limited only by the scope of our imagination. The limit is the volume – 45 bits of at any given moment, even though the next moment something quite different may be passing through.

Our brain is pulling the wool over our eyes, creating an illusion that we are seeing what is out there. In effect, we are looking with restricting blinders through a pinhole. We are seeing one ten-millionth of what is out there. But no matter how this truth is presented, it runs counter to our intuitive perception of consciousness as vast. Forty-five bits of attention is far from vast.

We are living in a story concocted by our brain. The brain concocts stories to explain to our consciousness what just happened. The brain lies to make things seem right. Even lies that are totally irrational. No way to think our way out of stories within stories. We spend our lives trying, getting tangled in paradox upon paradox. An enormous waste of effort. And a complete waste of therapy if the therapist is unaware of this Alice-in-Wonderland, paradoxical illusion of reality.

Living on a Time Delay

We are on a half second time delay — the kind of delay radio stations use to avoid broadcasting words that might violate Federal Communication standards. What we believe is happening this moment happened a half second ago. Our brain made a half-second calculation of what we require for survival and tossed out the other 99 percent of the data.

David Eagleman demonstrated the concept of this time delay by asking volunteers to press a button to make a light blink. Experimenters programed a slight delay from the time the person pressed the button to the time the light lit. But after 10 or so presses, people caught onto the delay and began to see the blink happen as soon as they pressed the button. Then when the experimenters reduced the delay, people reported that the blink happened before they pressed the button.

Eagleman coined this, "recalibration." Your brain expects your motor actions to produce an immediate effect. So if you were to make the effect happen a tenth of a second after you press the button, the brain recalibrates and makes your pressing the button and the flash of the light instantaneous.

When the experimenter then took away the time delay, the brain recalibrated and made it appear like the light lit before the button was pushed. So you readied to push the button and just before you pushed it, the light came on. So it seemed.

In "Why Time Flies" Alan Burdick went to check this out in person. Eagleman revised his experiment. Now he uses a nine-square cube with one of the squares colored. You press the square where you want the color to move to.

Eagleman programed a 100-millisecond delay between the mouse click and the movement of the colored square. When Burdick clicked the mouse he did not notice the delay.

Then Eagleman removed the delay and to Burdick's amazement the colored square jumped to his chosen destination before he clicked the mouse. It magically knew where he wanted the colored square to jump right before pressed the mouse. Burdick repeated this again and again and each time the computer knew where he wanted the colored square to jump, and it jumped right to that square just before he clicked the mouse.

Burdick tried not to press the mouse immediately after he saw the colored block move to his selected square, but he could not stop himself. It was not possible not to click the mouse, because he had already pressed it. When Eagleman had removed the time delay, Burdick's brain had recalibrated and the colored square seemed to jump before his motor action took place.

Even knowing the reason, it still seemed like the computer magically moved the colored square to his chosen square before he pressed the mouse. And since he had actually already pressed the mouse, he could not stop himself from doing so.

Free will? Who is deciding? What if you shot a man dead and you thought you had just envisioned shooting him, not actually pulling the trigger? But then you could not stop yourself from pulling the trigger, because you had actually already done so and killed the man.

Out of the millions of bits of information our brains process each second, 45 bits give or take are devoted to conscious thought. We can give our total conscious attention to around of one-millionth or 0.000001 of the sensory input available to our brain. We are programmed for virtually total inattention.

Lead With Your Body

During the twenty-five years I worked in Japan I never tired of standing up front, first car, behind the glass door of the compartment with the train engineer standing before his panoramic windshield. Whenever the train approached a signal, the engineer stretched his arm out moving it slowly across his field of vision. As he did so he called out *"Shingo,"* (signal). He would not miss anything obstructing the train's path.

In Japanese psychological theory when you wish to shift your attention, lead with your body. The Japanese train engineer leads with his body, sweeping his arm across his entire field of focus. The Japanese word "Zanchin" literally means "the mind with no remainder." It means the mind completely focused on the task at hand – all 45 bits of your conscious attention. All 45 bits focused on the task at hand.

At one death per 51.4 billion passenger–km and this includes the entire subway system. per passenger-kilometer/year is one of if not the lowest in the world.

I model the Japanese train engineer when I put down my keys or glasses. I point to where I am placing them and I say it aloud. The problem is not forgetting where I put them, but focusing on something unrelated. Not enough bits for sensory input to register, so within minutes I have no idea where my keys or glasses might be. I thought it might be Alzheimers, but I rarely if ever forget where I place anything since I began modeling the Japanese train engineer. All 45 bits focused on where I place my keys or glasses. *Zanchin*.

How we spend our 45 bits of attention is a zero-sum game. For much of my life I squandered my cache ruminating, rehashing, reprocessing thoughts. In high school and college years, my psychoanalyst could not help me stop mental water boarding. He resorted to a series of shock treatments. But it was the explaining to him that unleashed the Narrator in the first place.

Fearful that talk therapy would unleash the inner voice Narrator, after that first dreadful experience, talks with psychiatrists focused on medication. Psychiatrists like med talk. Less stressful than listening to ruminative chatter.

I continued researching therapies and in my sixties began turning my life around with attention-based therapies as opposed to talk psychotherapy. If you care to imagine what life was like before this – and I do not mean to be glib – think "The Hulk." In minutes one evening with my wife locked in the bathroom, I destroyed a living room set of furniture before coming back down to my senses with the police at the door.

AttentionTraining Therapy

Adrian Wells in the UK and Les Fehmi in the US both developed a version of Attention Training Therapy, Fehmi around 1975 and Wells around 1990. Wells focused on sounds, Fehmi on the perception of objectless space.

Adrian Wells introduced Attention-Training Therapy (ATT) as a part of his Metacognitive Therapy (MCT). MCT proposes that psychological disorder involves a style or pattern of recurrent, recycling ideation, fixing attention narrowly on worry and problems. MCT focuses on these recurrent patterns of thinking; cognitive therapy focuses on the thoughts.

ATT involves attending to sounds individually and in combinations. After practicing a few times with an mp3, you practice on your own in natural soundscapes, (such as the classroom if you are teaching as I was), or in the office cubical if that is where you work. You practice shifting from sound to sound, two or more sounds at once, and isolating one sound from others.

When I was teaching I could not filter out sounds in the classroom. If I began talking to the class and heard someone whispering, I could not go on. I was devastated if someone tapped a pencil or crinkled a paper. I devised a system of checkmarks for participation that included minuses for talking to others, even whispering. My classroom was unnaturally silent.

If I forgot my Valium, I could not enter the classroom. I still have nightmares, dreams about misplacing my Valium and attempting desperately to get a doctor to write a prescription so I might return to class unnoticed.

ATT interrupts excessive and inflexible self-focused attention. It strengthens control of attention to help regain flexible control over thinking patterns or styles. Wells considers ATT physical fitness of the mind.

On Wells' 13 minute mp3 or you can use my video in my blog at joeldames.com) you practice the three basic components:
1. Selective attention, 2. Rapid attention switching, and 3. Divided attention.

You move from an internal to an external outward-centered focus. Well's simple scale measures this internal to external shift away from self-focus and ruminating.

Figure I-1: Attention Scale

You rate yourself before you practice ATT and then rate yourself again after each session to check how far you move from internal to external focus.

MCT is a form of Insight Meditation. You note the patterns of attention. Are you aware with reluctance, eagerness, fear, or rejection? Are you aware from the control tower in the head, a cognitive awareness? Or are you aware with a body sense? Is the awareness removed from the sensation, observing, or do awareness and sensations blend together?

As with Insight Meditation, MTC is awareness of harmful repetitive, recycling, brooding patterns of thought without reacting to or judging them. You shift from a focus on the content of thoughts to a focus on these patterns of thinking that maintain disturbance. Rather than becoming enmeshed in unresolvable thoughts, you attend to inflexible focus and perseverative patterns of thinking.

Open Focus
Open-Focus Training shifts attention styles that are often exclusively narrow and objective to attention that is more diffuse and immersed. You shift by focusing your attention on objectless, ubiquitous, space.

From elementary through at least high school we are rewarded for our narrow, objective, focused attention. Most of us have no training in diffuse, immersed attention. I find it hard to sit through a ballet or concert without narrowly focusing and critically taking it apart and evaluating.

With right-brain focus you immerse in experiencing. A right-brain, diffuse, immersed/absorbed focus flows unselfconsciously and inclusively. It's like eating chocolate and you are immersed and absorbed in the experience.

What you don't want to do though, is try too hard, for example trying too hard to experience space. When you try too hard to experience space, you focus narrowly and objectively instead. With Open Focus as well as ATT, you don't try to block out concerns, physical symptoms, mental and physical pain, fear, anxiety, and stress. You include internal and external sensory stimuli without narrowly focusing and without being judgmental.

As you read, experience the space between you and your computer. Then open your focus to include the space of the room. Experience narrow with diffuse focus – Open Focus. This helps with reading comprehension and speed. When you narrowly focus on each word, it slows you down and sometimes you may have no idea of what you just read.

Open Focus asks questions that stimulate objectless experience of space. "Can you imagine yourself reading and experiencing the volume of your whole body? Can you imagine that you can proceed with reading and simultaneously attend to your body feelings? Can you imagine that when you feel a sense of effortlessness about reading with your whole body that you can then gradually expand your attention to include any thoughts, emotions, peripheral visual experiences, tastes, smells and sounds which may be simultaneously occurring as you read? Can you imagine that you need not scan in an effortful or sequential fashion among your various experiences in order to attend to them? Can you permit your attention to be equally and simultaneously spread out among body feelings thoughts, emotions. sounds, etc, while you continue to read?"

By including narrowly focused, physical, mental, and emotional concerns, the tension and stress associated with these concerns is absorbed into a larger diffuse focus. This combination of narrow and diffuse –Open Focus– reduces stress, anxiety, and associated symptoms.

Progress with ATT, Open Focus, and other attention therapies is incremental, much like weight training. Over the short term it may not seem like there is much if any progress. Both ATT and Open Focus need to become habit, a functional part of a daily, weekly, monthly, lifetime routine.

At first, ATT and Open Focus require putting forth extra time. You practice with mp3s, videos, and written exercises until ATT and Open Focus become familiar enough to take out into your world. After the initial work it takes little additional time. You practice anywhere and everywhere. You productively make use of your 45 bits cache to open your focus instead of narrowly ruminating and brooding.

With such a limited cache of attention, any time you find yourself ruminating and brooding, make an effort to switch gears to a more diffused attention. It takes effort to pull away from internal dialog. Ruminating and brooding are a magnetic draw and once it clicks it is hard to let go.

Release narrow immersed focus on internal dialog; allow it to become a smaller part of a diffuse Open Focus. Pay attention to sensations throughout the body: fullness and warmth, heaviness and lightness, hardness and softness, pulsing, tingling, vibration, pain, fear, stress, and anxiety.

Dissolve pain by diving inside the body with a narrow focus on the pain, then out to include the spaces within the body and expanding and dissolving into a wider and wider focus beyond the body. The narrow awareness of pain becomes smaller and smaller against this diffuse, widening attentional focus. With Ki Breathing Meditation, I take the pain down to my one point deep in my abdomen on the in-breath and out to infinity on the out-breath.

Narrow-objective focus works for income taxes. Listening to music or watching dance performance requires a shift to diffuse-immersed focus. An ability to shift at will between narrow-objective and diffuse-immersed focus counters stress, depression, anxiety, and emotional and physical pain.

Ki Breathing Meditation

Though I no longer practice Aikido, Ki Breathing Meditation is my go-to therapy. It slows breathing and heart rate, lowers blood pressure and counters stress-related symptoms. It is a challenge to Ki Breathe and keep the four basic principals of ki in your forty-bit cache. I do this with both ATT and Open Focus. Ki Breathing Meditation, ATT, and Open Focus become one consolidated training.

Four Basic Principals Unify Mind and Body

1. Relax Completely – The way to approach this is to relax your shoulders.

2. Keep One Point – As you relax your shoulders, let your weight fall naturally to a point low in your abdomen.

3. Let Your Weight Fall Underside – As you relax your shoulders and relax completely, your weight falls to a point low in your abdomen and to the underside of your arms. If you are sitting, your weight falls under your thighs, feet, and arms.

4. Extend Ki – Rather than narrowly focusing inside your mind, breathe out, extending ki infinitely.

We get the sudden urge to punch our boss and we react with a polite smile. We cannot respond in the animal way that nature intended. While humans are equipped with the same automatic stress response as cavemen, most situations fail to provide the outlet for the surge of chemical energy zapping through our bodies.

Ki Breathing Meditation slows breathing and heart rate, lowers blood pressure, and counters stress related symptoms. It is a physiological response to a physiological stimulus. Ki Breathing Meditation improves circulation and restores your own self-healing power.

We can replace rumination with mindful meditation on our breath. When we begin to ruminate, we note rumination, returning to a focus on our breath. Breathe in breathe out. Each time you start to ruminate, think "ruminate." The same with feelings, emotions, and bodily sensations. Be aware. No judgement. No clinging.

It comes down to a choice: ruminate or Ki Breathe. Rumination is destructive to mind and body. Ki Breathing is healing to mind and body. When you ruminate, almost by definition you cling to what you are thinking about. It takes effort to shift your mind and body to Ki Breathing Meditation. But this is what you need to do. You focus on Ki Breathing. After you make this shift you are in Ki Breathing Meditation Mode. When you begin to ruminate, note it and continue on with Ki Breathing Meditation mode.

Reminding yourself non judgmentally is the core of Insight Meditation. You can combine Ki Breathing Meditation and Insight meditation. Download the mp3s from http://www.insightmeditationcenter.org and Ki Breath as you listen.

Stress affects the heart, endocrine system, and immune function and diminishes the body's natural capacity to heal. Mind-body practices can reverse the harmful effects of stress and restore the body's natural capacity to heal.

The reversal is far from instantaneous and it is tempting to try one of the mind-body practices and give up thinking it is a waste of time. I practice Ki Breathing Meditation throughout the day, whenever I become aware of my breathing. When I get angry or upset, I begin again, and remind myself of the half-life effect of adrenaline, cortisol, and other stress hormones released at the start of the upset. Half life means the emotion lingers on after the upset is over.

What you want to avoid is thinking because you still feel angry or upset, you need to ruminate and get more angry and upset. Ruminating reignites the upset releasing stress chemicals in a destructive cycle. Though you still feel angry, upset, and stressed, you want to keep on with Ki Breathing Meditation, Attention Training Therapy (ATT), Open-Focus, Metacognitive Therapy (MCT), or Cognitive Self Talk. The effects of these therapies are not instantaneous.

Our sense of self is encapsulated in a thought-generating module, aka Narrator, in the left hemisphere of our brain, the focal point of billions of parallel-processing, networked neurons, communicating within 45 to 50 bits what the brain decides we need to know to keep the story intact. Without the Narrator we would be lost in the brain's chaotic processing. The Narrator puts it together into stories we accept as reality; stories that blind and bind us with false limits.

I ran track and cross country all four years of high school. I was a skinny kid and those were the only sports accepting the skeletally emaciated. When I walked into the gym the coach took one look at me and burst into laughter. But show up for practice and take part in meets and you were on the team. I came in last in every race. In a mile run, I was lapped twice on a quarter mile track by at least the first three placers. Fortunately no one showed up to watch the meets.

At the start of the season in my senior year, we raced a mile on a much smaller indoor track high above a large gymnasium. I had no sense of the distance around the track, but that distance looked manageable. I kept up with the leader the entire race, knocking almost two minutes off my outdoor track time.

I overheard the same coach who laughed at me three years before ask someone who I was. He said I had the ability to be a top competitor. I had just come in second in an indoor track meet, coming close to overtaking the first place runner. But when the race was at an outdoor track, I knew I would look at the huge quarter mile track and come in last. And that is what happened. I went back to coming in last and getting lapped by the first three placers, usually more.

That indoor track meet might have woken me up to the fact that we are bound by false limits. It might have been impact for change. In words attributed to Winston Churchill, "Men occasionally stumble over the truth, but most of them pick themselves up and hurry off as if nothing had happened." Finally, I know what I might have learned after that run; that you can change beyond conceivable limits, and bits of that change can be as instantaneous as it was on that indoor track high above the gym.

My race was over as soon as the outdoor quarter mile track narrowly filled my fifty-bit cache. The other runners became background. I was condemned like Greek mythical boulder-shlepping Sisyphus, trudging four times around a seemingly infinitely distancing track.

When we narrowly focus our attention we limit our beliefs. These beliefs at the center of our attention become expressed by our inner speech. This inner speech (a.k.a. Narrator) strengthens our limited beliefs. Our beliefs limit our perception. Round and round it goes.

Wisdom comes when you discover you are not what you believed yourself to be and you move to a deeper reality. This new depth becomes another surface, and all that appears on this new surface vanishes and discloses a depth beneath. This happens again and again throughout your life as long as you go on exploring deeper and deeper layers of your being.

This does not mean probing into deeper and deeper layers of problems, but with accepting and living with paradox. Paradox is with us along with death and taxes. Much of it comes from the division of right and left brain and the corpus coliseum highway between that ironically serves to block as well as enhance communication between the hemispheres. Over the centuries, it seems the left hemisphere has become dominant over the right.

We are convinced of the veracity of the left brain hemisphere's specious arguments over a right hemisphere with no voice at all. We have given up freedom and are trapped in a maze of words, concepts, and the mental and emotional states that reflect back the only world we know. Mental illness is remaining trapped in the Narrator's left brain hemisphere hall of mirrors. Freedom is learning to move freely from one hemisphere to the other, leaving the prison of left-brain concepts and states.

Life's Irresolvable Problems

Albert Einstein said significant life problems cannot be solved from the same consciousness that created them. I translate that as you can't think your way out of chronic, impassible, wordy, left-brain paradox. Flexible patterns of attention such as Open Focus, Attention Training Therapy (ATT), and Ki-Breathing Meditation help move beyond impasse to a state of flow between the hemispheres of the brain.

To make changes, rather than focus on perceived problems, thoughts, and beliefs, it can be more productive to deal with the patterns of thinking that maintain disturbance and postpone living. Rather than become entwined in irresolvable problems, a metacognitive stepping aside is effective in dealing with the chronic perseverative patterns of thinking that cause the suffering. (You don't do the problem solving and healing. Mind-body heals you.)

Rather than focusing on irresolvable problems, it is more productive to work on replacing patterns of ruminative, perseverative thinking with Open Focus Attention that includes narrow and diffuse, and objective and immersed focus. Inner strength requires disengaging from rumination, rigid mental control, and inflexible patterns of thinking.

You begin life in a state of open focus, experiencing the sights, sounds, smells, and haptic sensations of the world. The educational process dampens open focus as you learn to "pay attention," forcing you to into a narrowly defined band of focus. Unable to shift from this narrow, objective band of attention, a brilliantly performed ballet or concert leaves you intent on the mechanics, unable to open expansively and diffusely into the aesthetics.

Life presents us with irresolvable paradoxes. But focus on irresolvable paradoxes blocks us from a valued life. Most of us live our lives narrowly focused, unaware of our ability to dissolve physical and emotional pain and live more expansive lives. Few tap into the potentials of the three-pound blob of gelatin within our skull, but some who have suffered and survived learn to dive in deepest.

Alfred Adler, considered by some to be the father of individual psychology, believed that understanding of human nature lies not with psychologists and psychiatrists, but with those of us who have suffered and survived. Nothing compares with this depth of understanding. Values are shaped and actualized by our suffering and limitations.

Victor Frankl, German death camp survivor:

> Suffering and trouble belong to life as much as fate and
> death. None of these can be subtracted from life without
> destroying its meaning. To subtract death, fate, and
> suffering from life would mean stripping it from its form
> and shape.Only under the hammer blows of fate, in the
> white heat of suffering, does life gain shape and form.

Paul Tillich, twentieth century American influential philosopher and
theologian:

> Truths, once deep and powerful, discovered by the greatest
> geniuses through profound suffering and incredible labor,
> become shallow and superficial when used in daily
> discussion. How can and how does this tragedy occur? It
> can and does unavoidably occur, because there can be no
> depth without the way to depth. Truth without the way to
> truth is dead; if it is still used, it contributes only to the
> surface of things. "The Shaking of the
> Foundations" (p55).

Tillich compares the scholar who knows the content of the one hundred
most important books to the uneducated worker who searches deep inside
her/himself for meaningful questions about her/his life. The uneducated
woman/man may know nothing of the truths of the past that the scholar
possesses, yet because of her/his suffering may get beneath the surface to a
depth of truth.

Scholars who dwell on the surface and accept themselves as they appear
on the surface, may never attain any depth of truth. It is only when this
image falls apart and shakes the surface self-knowledge, that the scholar is
willing to explore beneath this shallow surface of her/his life into a deeper
level of being.

Most of the vast neural processing network occurs well beneath a
conscious level of thought. Decisions are made before you consciously
decide. Rational problem solving that works for day to day issues fails with
psychological problems you have struggled with for years. The mind does
not work in the conscious rational way you might think it should. The mind
is nowhere to be found in this vast twisted network of billions of neurons.

Focusing on psychological issues that have been with you for a lifetime and expecting to solve them with normal problem-solving methods is getting trapped in quicksand and attempting to get out by struggling, but instead sinking deeper and deeper. Normal problem-solving methods become an integral part of the problem.

You need to accept the reality of irresolvable problems that are a part of your life; to look at your pain, but not see the world from the vantage point of your pain. Focusing on irresolvable pain amplifies and entangles, sometimes to the level of trauma. Accept the pain and not place your life on hold until you resolve painful issues. Free yourself of the illusions of language and cognitive filters and see there are other things to do in the present moment than focusing on irresolvable issues. Focus that puts you in a state of mind-healing flow fosters psychological well-being.

In his two books Harvard cardiologist and author of "Relaxation Response" and "Relaxation Revolution," Herbert Benson discusses how mind-body techniques lower blood pressure, calm brain activity, and balance healthful emissions of nitric oxide in the body's cells.

Next he wanted to determine whether mind-body techniques might alter gene expression (https://hms.harvard.edu/news/genetics/mind-body-genomics-5-1-13). Which, if any, of the body's 54,000 genes were "turned on" or "turned off" by mind-body techniques. Epigenetics is the turning on or off of genes by life situations.

His team discovered 2,209 genes that are in fact affected by mind-body techniques. These genes affected by mind-body training are associated with stress-related medical problems involving immune response, inflammation, aging, thinning of the brain's cortex, and oxidative stress causing damage to physical tissues by the release of destructive oxygen molecules known as free radicals.

Mind-body practices take a bad gene and make it better. The benefits of mind-body practices include healthful regulation of the immune system, lowered psychosocial stress levels, less destructive oxidative stress, and a reduced tendency toward premature aging. These benefits are associated with healthful gene activity, the opposite of that found in cardiovascular diseases and other medical conditions.

Benson was aware that his relaxation response was due at least in part to the placebo response. But all medication and treatment effects are at least thirty percent due to the placebo effect. The placebo response is the body using its own resources to heal, and healing without medication or surgery is the most natural way of healing.

Rather than discard the placebo response, Benson established the Benson-Henry Institute for Mind Body Medicine (BHI) at Massachusetts General Hospital in Boston. Ongoing research employs evidence-based techniques to strengthen the natural healing capacities of the body and mind. BHI clinicians serve as a resource in the areas of mind-body and integrative medicine available to all departments of the hospital and community.

In all the psychotherapy I received over the years, the body was left out of the equation. I was never asked how I felt about my body and I never thought of bringing it up, even though body image was a huge issue from early on. Too skinny, hairless, no muscular development; I hated my body. I could not stand touching my body. My nose slanted downward like all of the evil comic book characters. Dumbo ears, thin upper lip and rolling lower lip, weak chin. I was conscious of all this mirror to mirror, reflection to reflection.

The body is the container of feelings and emotions, source of security and self-confidence; insecurity and lack of self-confidence. Mind/body, somatic/psychic are inseparable dimensions. It is essential to come to terms with a somatic body — the body that simply is — and a body image that can sometimes be unrecognizably apart.

When I say "Total Self Renewal" I mean exactly that. I have come forth from a schizoid violent man. I truly believe you can do the same, whatever point you are starting from. I hope it is not where I started out, but if it is you will do the same as me.

Don't take this book as a quick once-through read. All the strategies replace poisonous rumination with movement forward. Pick one or more self-therapies and make it yours, as it fits you. I will be eighty on my next birthday. I am writing this to pass the baton to you. You may be one of the few readers. Take the baton and run with it. Renew your life! Pass the baton on.

1 ATTENTION ROBBERS: PIT OF DESPAIR

Though I am not a fan of psychotherapy that indulges in discussions of the past, it is important to be aware of issues robbing us of our attention in the present. Childhood stress and trauma can affect the immune system, the architecture of the brain, turn some genes off and others on, and bring about a lifetime of physical and emotional suffering.

Most people say I am different and perhaps in not a very positive way. I usually respond, if at all, with we all different. To which most recently my aunt replied, "But you are really different, different from everyone."

What I would have liked to say is never judge anyone without knowing their trauma and suffering. You have no idea how far someone has come without knowing where they started out. We can never fully understand the extent of their trauma and suffering, so let's leave it at that and refrain from dispersing judgement.

Pit of Despair

I gained insight–not solutions–into my problems sometime in the 1960s when I read Harry Harlow's experiments with macaque monkeys. I had virtually experienced his Pit of Despair for the first several years of my life. The stress was intense, incessant and at some point mid childhood, I was aware that it must be doing damage.

Having lived from 1905-1981, Harry Harlow grew up during the time when psychologists, psychiatrists, even the US government warned of the dire consequences of affectionate, coddling and mothering. Harlow's research with rhesus macaque monkeys set out to disprove the steely behaviorists' thinking and end an era. He set out to show that an expressed loving relationship is important between a mother and her infant child.

Out of context this sounds absurd. But through the 1920s, 1930s and 1940s, most psychologists and pediatricians denied a beneficial relationship between mother and child other than offering food. Many professionals in the field of child development were saying that a physical demonstration of motherly love was harmful to the young child's emotional development. This view held strong through the 1940s.

Attempting to show that motherly love was needed in child rearing was a hard stance for a psychologist starting his career in 1930. After one year at Stanford University, Harlow relocated to the University of Wisconsin in Madison and was given a small office in the basement of a building with no lab for his work. He finally persuaded the university to give him a lab in an old building and spent twenty-five years working with the learning abilities of rhesus macaque monkeys.

In the 1950s Harlow began his iconoclastic experiments, the ones that would show the world that mothers are not seen by their offspring as mere food sources. He took a group of newborn rhesus macaque babies and put them in a cage with two surrogate mothers. One of these substitute mothers was constructed of wire mesh and the other of wood covered with sponge rubber and covered again with tan, soft terry cloth. Hidden behind the terry-cloth mother, a 100 watt light bulb radiated warmth. Both the wire mesh and terry-cloth mothers were the same height and width.

For one of the experiments, one group of monkeys received milk from the wire mother and the other group received milk from the terry-cloth mother. According to the theories of the time, the wire fed babies should have bonded to wire-mother surrogate and the terrycloth fed babies should have bonded to the terrycloth-mother surrogate. But both groups spent the most time with the warmer terry-cloth mother whether or not she was feeding them. So something other than the milk they were receiving attracted them to the warm, cuddly terry-cloth mother.

Harlow's experiments showed the mother child relationship has more to it than just feeding. Babies or baby monkeys in his experiments cannot live by milk alone. And though of course babies need milk to survive, there is a primary need for frequent and intimate warm body contact with the mother. The baby needs cuddling, touching and loving. These experiments are what Harlow described in his talk at the Annual Convention of the American Psychological Association on August 31, 1958 and first published in American Psychologist, 13, 573-685.

At this APA meeting, however, Harlow did not report the experiments he conducted that involved isolating and abusing the monkeys. Harlow referred to these experiments as "The Pit of Despair." This was a vertical chamber apparatus with a stainless steel trough and sides that sloped to a rounded bottom with a wire mesh one inch above the bottom. Waste material fell through the wire mesh and drained out of holes drilled in the stainless steel. The top of this pit was also covered with wire mesh. A small mirror allowed experimenters to look in, but the monkey could not look out.

After allowing the rhesus monkeys to bond with their natural mothers, Harlow placed monkeys between three months and three years old into the Pit of Despair alone for up to ten weeks. The monkeys would spend the first day or two trying to climb up the cold slippery steel sides. Within a few days, they stopped moving about and remained huddled in a corner. The monkeys were found to be psychotic when removed. Even the happiest monkeys came out damaged. Most never recovered.

Figure 1-1: People Pit of Despair

Other monkeys were placed in these steel containers soon after birth and left there from thirty days to a year. After thirty days in the container, they were incapable of having sexual relations. When placed with other monkeys for a daily play session, they were badly bullied. Two of them refused to eat and starved themselves to death.

Other of Harlow's experiments involved taking the terry-cloth mothers the monkeys bonded with and turning them into evil mothers. Some had the terry cloth mother's breast area that held the milk bottle rigged to shoot blunt spikes at the clinging infant monkey. Some of the terry-cloth moms shook so violently the infant was severely shaken up. Other terry cloth mothers were spring loaded and violently threw the clinging baby away.

What happened when the spikes stopped shooting or the violent shaking stopped was that the babies kept coming back to cling to the mother. They had been comforted by and bonded with this terry-cloth mother and this was their only source of refuge. So the terry-cloth mother was now loving and evil by turns.

Harlow and his researchers concluded that the impact of early maternal deprivation could possibly be reversed in monkeys only if it lasted less than 90 days. He estimated that the equivalent for humans was six months. After these critical periods, no amount of exposure to mothers or peers could alter the monkeys' abnormal behaviors and make up for the emotional damage that had already occurred.

Throughout his life Harry Harlow experienced bouts of depression. At school he did not fit in. He (and I) grew up when psychologists discouraged "an overly loving" mother. His mother, he wrote in his partly finished autobiography, was not a warm woman. In the early 1970s around the time his wife died of breast cancer, he had a series of electroshock treatments.

2 ATTENTION ROBBERS: ATTACHMENT ATTACHMENT ATTACHMENT

Harlow was an experimental psychologist and John Bowlby a clinical child psychiatrist. The publication of Harlow's research with monkeys helped John Bowlby's Attachment Theory gain acceptance. The two were introduced to each other by British ethnologist Robert Hind who realized how close the men were in their views and willingness to challenge prevailing Zeitgeist. They corresponded and attended some of the same scientific meetings from about 1957 through the mid-1970s when Harlow retired. Harlow provided the experimental research, the controlled laboratory studies that Bowlby needed to document his theories.

Their exchange of ideas led to a break from Freud and to an understanding of developmental psychology that strongly influences therapists and researchers today. Harlow and Bowlby's work center about the premise that much of present resentment, anger, and hostility stem from past mistreatment at the hands of a significant other, most often the mother, very early on.

By the nineteen-forties, a number of psychologists were conducting studies and writing about the ill effects of children neglected under institutional care, but Bowlby was the most influential. In 1949 the Chief of the Mental Health Section of the World Health Organization (WHO) asked Bowlby to do a report on the needs of homeless children. Bowlby spent six months researching and meeting with clinicians in the field.

His report, published in 1951 in the form of a WHO monograph entitled "Maternal Care and Mental Health," chronicled the adverse affects of inadequate maternal care during early childhood on personality development. During the next few years, his report was translated into twelve languages and gave birth to the field of Attachment Theory. Bowlby's report was not well received by clinicians, but the publication of

Harlow's work helped to authenticate his findings.

Like Harlow, Bowlby concluded that what is essential for mental health is that the infant and young child experience a warm, intimate, and continuous relationship with her/his mother (and/or permanent mother-substitute) in which both find satisfaction and enjoyment. Bowlby called this "secure attachment," the first of his three basic attachment patterns.

And the corollary, that even limited deprivation of three to six months during the the first three or four years can produce "affectionless and psychopathic character." He reported that early maternal deprivation results in dramatically lower IQ scores and poor physical development. Infants observed in institutional studies showed listlessness, emaciation, immobility, unresponsiveness, failure to gain weight properly, poor sleep, an appearance of unhappiness, and an inability to love or enter into relationships. (So much for free will.)

Not only do threats of abandonment create intense anxiety, they arouse anger, often of an intense degree. Acute anxiety and powerful feelings of revenge result even from partial maternal deprivation. But the most violently angry and dysfunctional responses of all are elicited in children and adolescents who not only experience repeated separations, but are constantly subjected to the threat of being abandoned.

Maternal deprivation is any situation where the mother or permanent mother-substitute is unable to offer the loving care small children need. Of course, maternal deprivation exists when the mother or mother-substitute is absent. At age seven, Bowlby was sent off to boarding school. He later said, "I wouldn't send a dog away to a boarding school at age seven."

Bowlby's development of Attachment Theory began soon after his graduation from Cambridge University, when he was employed in a home for maladjusted boys. He observed that boys who were separated from their mothers suffered intense distress, though they were adequately fed and cared for. And what followed this distress were angry protests and then despair.

After leaving the boys home, he conducted a study with forty-four adolescents in a child guidance program in London who were convicted of stealing. As a control group he selected the same number of children who had not committed crimes. He interviewed the parents from both groups about whether their children had been separated from them. The conclusions were published in his seminal work, "Forty-Four Juvenile Thieves: Their Characters and Home Life" (Bowlby, 1944). More than half of the children convicted of theft had been separated from their mothers for longer than six months during the first five years of their lives.

The belief at the time of his work was that the bond between mother and infant emerges because of the feeding relationship. Bowlby believed in a primal need for the infant to emotionally bond with the mother. This rational concept was challenged by the psychoanalytic community predominant at the time. It was not until the publication of Harlow's rigorous controlled experimental studies that Bowlby's attachment theory gained a wide acceptance within the scientific community.

Basic Attachment Patterns

Understanding the three basic patterns of attachment are necessary for the treatment of infants and toddlers, but also for the treatment of youth and adults. Bowlby details both the evidence base and treatment for Attachment Theory in a trilogy of books: "Attachment" 1969, "Separation: Anxiety and Anger" (1972), and "Loss: Sadness and Depression" (1980).

The second pattern, anxious-resistant attachment, is when the mother is available and helpful only some of the time, and the parents threaten the child with abandonment as a means of control. There are some separations of parent and child. The child is always prone to separation anxiety, tends to be clinging and is anxious about exploring the world.

Third and worst of the three patterns, anxious-avoidant attachment, is when the mother rebuffs the child whenever she/he approaches for comfort or protection. The child has no confidence at all that the parent will be there for her/him. In severe cases, the child is constantly rejected, ill-treated, or institutionalized. The child has no confidence he can get help from anyone, and attempts to live his life without the love and support of others. Needless to say, this results in personality disorders and suffering. And today we are aware of the physical, neurological, and even genetic damage.

An unhappy past cannot be changed however understandable the suffering may be. Bowlby would say that to continue fighting old battles is unproductive. Even with attachment so dependent on early years, Bowlby broke from Freudian therapy with its roots in the patient's past. As with Cognitive Therapy, Attachment Therapy focuses on the here and now and only brings up past events when the events might shed light on the patient's present way of dealing with her/his current life.

Attachment Therapy

In clinical practice as set forth by Bowlby, the therapist attempts to establish a secure attachment the patient never had. The therapist provides the patient with a secure base by taking the role of a parent providing the child with a secure base from which to explore the world. The therapist strives to be reliable, attentive, and sympathetically responsive. She/he tries to see the world though the patient's eyes and be empathic.

Patients are helped to understand that much of their present resentment, anger, and hostility stems from past mistreatment at the hands of others. But however understandable their anger may be, the therapist now helps to see that to continue fighting old battles is unproductive.

Patients consider the ways they engage in relationships with significant others in their lives. What are their expectations of their own feelings and behavior? What are their expectations for the feelings and behavior of others? What unconscious biases do they bring to a relationship? What are those biases in relation to why and when things go badly?

Patients consider the ways they engage in relationships with significant others in their lives. What are their expectations of their own feelings and behavior? What are their expectations for the feelings and behavior of others? What unconscious biases do they bring to a relationship? What are those biases in relation to why and when things go badly?

The overlaying ongoing relationship with the therapist will be influenced by the perception and expectation of how an attachment figure is likely to feel and behave towards them, which is influenced by the models they hold of their parents and themselves. The patient considers how his/her current expectations, feelings, and behavior may be the product of events, situations, and what he/she has been told about him/her self during childhood and adolescence.

They are encouraged to recognize that their image of themselves and of others that often emanates from a parent, may not be appropriate or justified. They can work on imagining and developing a more positive and helpful alternative image to replace the unreasonable image of their past experiences, to stop being a slave to old and unconscious stereotypes, and to feel, to think, and to act in new ways.

Bowlby's goal for the therapist to provide the patient with a secure base is not an easy task and Bowlby acknowledged this. The therapist must be aware that the patient's adverse experiences may make it difficult for him to believe the therapist can be trusted to behave kindly, or understand his situation. On the other hand, the unexpectedly attentive and sympathetic responses the patient receives may lead him to think the therapist can provide more than is realistic. And the therapist comes to the relationship with his own views of himself and others, developed during his own childhood and adolescence.

Bowlby has left us with both an understanding of Attachment Theory and the ingredients of a good therapist. In his last book, "Secure Attachment," he presents both Attachment Theory and attachment therapy. That makes it possible to design a self-therapy with mental scripts constructed with an understanding of the unhealthy messages constructed during childhood and adolescence.

Many beliefs about ourselves and the world are formed during the first thousand days of our lives and are truly hard to shake. John Bowlby spent a lifetime researching and developing Attachment Theory that deals with beliefs formed during these early years as a result of mother child relationships. Many therapies today have roots in Attachment Theory and it has become a pop psychology buzzword.

The Ultimate Secure Attachment

Figure 2-1: Ultimate Secure Attachment

Lee A. Kirkpatrick, author of "Attachment, Evolution, and the Psychology of Religion," says that for many people, in many religions, Bowlby's Attachment System is fundamentally involved in their thinking, beliefs, and reasoning about God and their relationship to God.

Kirkpatrick's therapeutic approach presents God as the ultimate parent of secure attachment. While humans are always fallible and limited attachment figures, God can be a protective and caring parent available and reliable whenever you are in need. Many people relate to God in terms of this parent-child relationship.

Kirkpatrick lists five characteristics of an attachment figure:

1. Child seeks proximity to the caregiver, especially when frightened and alarmed.

2. Caregiver provides care and protection.

3. Caregiver provides a sense of security.

4. Threat of separation causes anxiety in the child.

5. Loss of the attached figure would cause the child grief.

He concludes that an attachment figure who is simultaneously omnipresent, omniscient, and omnipotent, would provide the most secure of secure bases. The five characteristics of an attachment figure apply fairly well to the concept of a supreme being. Not quite so obviously, perhaps with numbers 4 and 5. But in many religions, in some way there is a threat of some sort of separation or even excommunication if you stray too far from the dogma. If this were to happen and you still were with the program, grief would ordinarily follow.

3 ATTENTION ROBBERS: ACES

There Will Be Blood

Matthew Lysiak fit together the puzzle of massacre shooter, Adam Lanza, in his nonfiction book "Newtown, an American Tragedy." On December 14, 2012, Lanza shot his way into Newtown public elementary school and slaughtered the principal, school psychologist, four other educators, and twenty-six seven-year-olds. Before the massacre started, he shot and killed his mother at their home.

Adam was a loner from the start, rarely ever playing with other children,and reacting blankly to approaches by adults. He was a frail child and was mostly silent. He suffered anxiety attacks, hyperventilated, and. threw tantrums. He could not sit still and constantly fidgeted. Some kids taunted and teased him, and in middle school he became the target for class bullies. Then in high school the students, aware that he was uncommunicative, different, and that something was wrong, ignored him. He was obsessed with germs and wiped things down with a disinfectant, especially before he would eat. And if someone were to touch his food, no matter how hungry he was, he would not eat.

James L. Knoll IV, psychiatrist and Director of Forensic Psychiatry at SUNY Upstate Medical University in Syracuse, NY, offers a basic list of factors to keep watch for to prevent mass shootings. He defines mass murder as the killing of four or more victims at one location within one event. Common factors include extreme feelings of anger, social alienation, rumination on violent revenge, feelings of persecution, and destructive envy.

Most of my life I've lived with all of these attributes. Each time I read of a mass murderer, or any murderer, I think "if not for fortune." I am lucky not to have murdered. When I was five or six I planned to kill my mother and father. I would make a long fuse out of gunpowder from firecrackers. During the night I would turn on the gas, wait till the apartment was filled with fumes and then light the fuse from outside of the house.

In researching for his book "Far from the Tree" concerning the Columbine massacre in Littleton, Colorado in 1999, Andrew Solomon said that he had spent hundreds of hours with the Klebolds, parents of Dylan Klebold, one of the teenaged perpetrators. In an NewYork Times interview, he said that in all that time he could find nothing about the parents that might have in any way contributed toward the mass murders. In fact, he said they were "admirable, intelligent and kind people whom I would have gladly have had as parents myself."

He might have been describing my parents. My father devoted much of his time as a volunteer first aide instructor for the Red Cross. He taught classes to firemen, police officers and many other civic groups. He was friendly, listened to others, and got along with everyone. Everyone except me and my sister.

My mother too, was friendly, a good quiet listener, and got along well and was loved by everyone. She looked as warm and caring as a story-book mother, and took good care of my sister.

Earliest memory: My father was driving on an isolated country road, my mother up front with him, and Zan and I in back. Zan, eight or nine years old, did not agree with something my father said, (or perhaps she began to sing). He stopped the car, got out, opened the back door, shoved Zan out, got back in and we drove away. I don't know how long he drove before he turned around to go back and pick her up.

Even early into my fifties–as I write this, I'm months now from 80–I thought of killing my mother. (My father had already died.) I would take an airplane back from where I was teaching in Japan. I would get a gun and come to her apartment and kill her. I did not want to kill my sister. But she was mentally ill and depended on my mother for her survival. I would have to kill her. I struggled with this and perhaps that is what kept me from carrying it out. In the meantime I continued to wake up screaming from nightmares about my mother.

A Test You Don't Want to ACE

The Adverse Childhood Experiences (ACE) study, a collaboration between the CDC and Kaiser Permanente Health Appraisal Clinic in San Diego, examined the link between childhood stressors and adult health. Over 17,000 adults participated in the research, making it one of the largest studies of its kind. Each participant completed a questionnaire that asked for detailed information on their past history of abuse, neglect, and family dysfunction as well as their current behaviors and health status.

The research identified basic Adverse Childhood Experiences (ACEs) that included physical abuse, emotional abuse, sexual abuse, incarceration, mental illness, separations, and bereavement. These adverse experiences cumulatively increase a gamut of later-occurring negative events including attempted suicide, alcohol and drug abuse, depression, and the list goes on and on.

With his Macaque monkeys, Harry Harlow had already demonstrated the life-long impact of infant trauma and distress. If maternal depravation lasts more than three months, no amount of exposure to mothers or peers reverses the harm done. John Bowlby demonstrated much the same with human children. So the best thing to prevent making monsters is to establish a warm, loving, caring, bond during infancy and early childhood.

For a long while I was envious, resenting anyone who seemingly born with the proverbial silver spoon. Then I chanced upon a 2010 article published in the Journal of Personality and Social Psychology by a Mark D. Seery, professor at University of Buffalo, titled "Whatever Does Not Kill Us: Cumulative Lifetime Adversity, Vulnerability, and Resilience." As expected he found that that high ACEs are "associated with higher global distress, functional impairment, PTS symptoms, and lower life satisfaction."

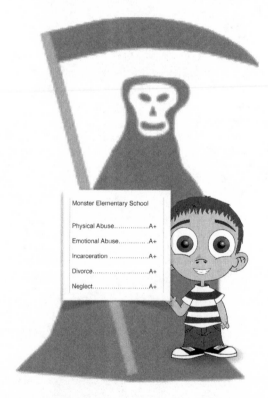

Figure 3-1: ACEs

He also discovered that having some ACEs can benefit us by making us resilient.

And having no ACEs can be sometimes be as bad as having high ACEs!

Having some ACEs fosters subsequent resilience later in life. People with some ACEs were actually the least affected by recent adverse events. In the words of German philosopher Friedrich Nietzsche "That which does not kill us makes us stronger. "

Epigenetic Loops

Early adversity alters the chemistry of DNA in the brain through a process called methylation. The epigenome or methyl groups are tiny markers attached to the DNA. The DNA code remains fixed for life, but the epigenome is flexible. Epigenome chemical markers provide a link between our environment and how our genes are expressed. These markers react to signals from the outside world such as smoking, diet, stress, and exercise.

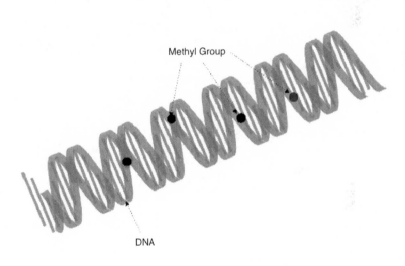

Methyl Group

DNA

Figure 3-2: Epigenetic Loops

The epigenome adjusts strands of DNA to our rapidly changing environment, causing them to scrunch down and become inactive, or relaxed and active. DNA contains all of the instructions for building the parts of the body. But that tells only half of the story. The epigenome effects a change of expression of the genes. Our genes plus our epigenome together determine our fate.

So if a child is constantly confronted with abuse or neglect, he would have epigenetic markers on his DNA determining how appropriately and effectively, or rather inappropriately and ineffectively, he will respond to stress later in his life. Once these markers do their business and the stress system and ability to recover is damaged, he will over respond to stress and will always be over-responding to stress. His anxiety sensors are constantly on and he has no idea how to turn them off.

Not all ACEs are equally damaging, though. The most damaging are deeply personal, chronic, and perpetrated by someone you love and depend upon for your survival.

Countering ACEs takes at least one reliable adult who knows what is happening and is openly supportive to the child. Teachers are already overburdened. But one supportive, reliable teacher can make a difference in a child's life. I took a tremendous amount of class time away from instruction whenever I was disciplined and I was disciplined throughout each school day from kindergarten through seventh grade.

I never bonded with a reliable adult, but because of my background I bonded with and was supportive of my students who were labeled disruptive or odd. I was one of them. I think I might have rescued a few from impending demise.

My students, fellow educators, and most people saw calm and rational Dr. Jekyll. They could not possibly imagine Mr. Hyde. My wife's friends told her how lucky she was to have married me.

I would never put a woman through what she suffered with me. Legally binding myself to a woman was a brutally selfish act.

4 BURNT TO A CRISP

If you want to deal with stress, the place to start is Hans Selye's 1974 book, "Stress without distress." In the 1930s he began publishing about general adaption syndrome (GAS). It is helpful to become familiar with GAS in working with stress in any form.

If something is wrong physically and you go to the doctor, most people want their doctor to explain exactly what is wrong in terms you can understand. Then you can learn and consider the options available to you.

Since stress has been a major problem in my life, I want to know the physical roots of this debilitating discomfort. Understanding the physical side of stress is the start of a plan for dealing with it.

But in all my years of therapy, stress had never really been discussed. If I brought up stress with a psychiatrist, it would be dealt with as a symptom of OCD with medication. I had a dresser drawer filled with color-coded pills of all shapes and sizes. But at fifty-six years old, I burnt out of teaching before I dealt with stress head on. (Actually, I burnt out from the ongoing stress of dealing with administrators.)

A familiarity with the physiological basis of stress helps in understanding how the brain affects changes throughout the body and in behavioral changes.

Hans Selye coined the word "stress" and in "Stress Without Distress," is his comprehensive, but digestible overview.

General Adaption Syndrome (GAS)
Three Stages of Stress: Alarm, Resistance, Exhaustion

Selye divides the way our body reacts to stress into three time periods or phases:

Phase one – Alarm reaction.

Phase two – Resistance (or adaption).

Phase three – Exhaustion.

Phase One – Alarm

1. The hypothalamus releases corticotrophin-releasing hormone (CRH).
2. CRH nudges the pituitary gland to release adrenocorticotropic hormone (ACTH).

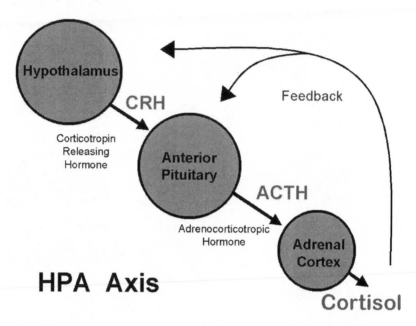

Figure 4-1: The hypothalamic-pituitary-adrenal (HPA) axis

The hypothalamus activates the pituitary gland, which in turn activates the adrenal glands atop the kidneys. When the adrenal glands release adrenaline and cortisol, the sympathetic nervous system activates. Pupils dilate, heart rate increases, and muscles tense. You may tremble as respiration quickens. You are proverbially ready for a fight or to take off in flight.

The autonomic reactions in your body to a remark or event that angers you come on at lightning speed, but are slow in recovery back to baseline. This is what makes it so difficult to get a hold of yourself and take back control. You feel the unpleasant autonomic changes and it feels like it requires a reaction. Road rage and other seemingly irrational acts are examples of this high speed escalation.

Worked for cavemen, but when you get into a hassle with your spouse or partner, not a good idea to fight, and not so good to take off running. So you stand there as cortisol and adrenaline stress hormones race through your system egging you on to attack or run away – awful feeling triggering stuff that occasionally ends up news.

Phase Two – Resistance

If stress is prolonged after the initial shock of alarm, your body is still on alert, but at lowered intensity. During the resistance stage, your body adapts to stress.

If your body is starved, it may adapt to this stressor by maximizing the digestion of food and extracting more of the nutrients. Or you may lose the desire to exercise or move about, so as to conserve energy.

Phase Three – Exhaustion

Harm comes if the stress persists after the resistance stage and the body no longer has the strength to adapt. A stressful job or family situation continues for a prolonged period of time and you are no longer able to adapt. Your body's ability to resist becomes depleted as physical wear and tear takes its toll. If you don't learn to manage stress, it may lead to high blood pressure, heart attack, and stroke. Even severe infection may come about due to lower immunity.

Stress can be an especially serious problem for children. The HPA stress response can get programmed to rev up inflammatory stress hormones for the rest of their life. This can result in irritable bowel syndrome. High ACE scores are associated with headaches, diabetes, asthma, ulcers, chronic fatigue, even cancer.

Eustress/Distress

Not all stress is bad. Seyle coined the term "eustress" for good stress (Greek "eu" means good.) Eustress is determined by the perception of the stressor, rather than the stressor. Athletes and actors get motivated and energized from pre-performance stress.

Stress motivates and energizes me to research and try out hopeful self therapies. It motivates me to get up each morning. Increasing stress causes increase in performance, general well-being, and a state of eustress. At the perfect stress level both performance and well-being peak. At this level you feel energized, focused, and creative. You are in the zone; a state of flow.

Beyond this point it is downhill and you feel fatigued. As stress is increased it becomes excessive and debilitating. Performance declines and may come to a halt. You feel exhausted, in a state of distress. Burnout.

Seyle writes, "Activity is a biological necessity." We need to exercise our minds and body. We need activities with some kind of aim or goal. We need activity that spurs our "innate urge to create." It does not matter whether this is work or relaxing play.

Inactivity leads to suffering because of the lure of focusing on unpleasant people/events, looming deadlines, catastrophic future, and irresolvable problems. If you are religious "Idle hands are the devil's workshop." Proverbs (16:27) That has many renditions: "An idle brain is the devil's workshop," and "If the devil finds a man idle, he'll set him at work."

Countering stress is all about attention and focus. Ki Breathing Meditation is my first line of defense.

5 ILLUSION OF SELF

The Big Picture Looks Dark

How can therapists tag us with a DSM (Diagnostic and Statistical Manual of Mental Disorders) label that sometimes stays for life when we are a state of flux; when there is no center of self? When you peer inside the skull with brain scans, all you can hope to see are areas lighting up from neural or metabolic activity. But we can change this pattern of neural activity and alter lives, while the DSM label is resistant to change.

Figure 5-1: Illusion of Self

When you look inside a computer you see hardware; nothing of the myriad universes that unfold to you with clicks of the mouse or taps on a screen. When you open a skull you see three pounds of semi translucent meat; none of the visual, auditory, perceptual, and tactual imagery. Billions of on-off neurons firing and creating an illusion of self, but this self is nowhere to be found.

No homunculus. No self or consciousness in any specific area of the brain. Neuroscientists cannot comprehend this concept of consciousness. Yet psychiatrists and psychologists give out DSM tags and have us pegged.

Our internal universe parallels the external universe. The Milky Way, contains from 200 to 400 billion stars. The stars of the Milky Way spread across 100,000 light years. Of the 86 billion neurons in our brain, about 70 billion are contained in the cerebellum, a small structure at the back of the brain involved with motor control. The entire six-layered cerebral cortex with an average thickness of 3 millimeters, less than a quarter inch thick, responsible for human thought, has 16 billion neurons. The remaining few billion neurons are spread throughout the rest of the brain.

Stretched out, the cerebral cortex would be about the size of a large cloth dinner napkin that would not easily fit back into a human skull. So our cortex is squished together until if fits into the skull, looking like a walnut blob with its hills called gyri and valleys called sulci.

While the stars are isolated light years apart, every neuron makes about ten thousand connections or synapses with other nerve cells making a total of about one quadrillion synaptic connections. Specs of neurotransmitter juice flow at these synapses and there are around a hundred and fifty identified neurotransmitters, maybe more at the time you read this.

There are ten times as many glial cells as there are neurons in the brain. Glial cells make up almost 90 percent of the cells in the brain, but up until recently scientists knew nothing about them. They thought they were just insulators between neurons. They do act as insulators, but glial cells are the dark matter of our internal universe. They speak in a chemical language all their own that scientists have yet to understand. Einstein had an unusually high ratio of glial cells to neurons in the inferior parietal lobe, an area of the brain known to be associated with mathematical and spacial reasoning.

The most abundant of the glial cells are the astrocytes, named for their starlike rays. A single astrocyte can connect with its rays to more than a million synapses. The total number of these astrocyte synapses is astronomical. But what these starlike rays do at these synapses, no one has a clue.

We cannot fathom the chaos of our internal universe, so the brain creates stories about us that give a 45 bit illusion of self. We rehash these stories day by day, hour by hour, minute after minute. The stories start from the time we are born when a mother responds in a positive, negative or neutral way. The stories morph through our early years of life. We believe in the stories. We believe in a self that is strong, weak, scared, liked, hated, or popular, or oner. We are trapped in illusions of language. We expand words with modifiers: big nose, skinny, fat legs, stupid, brilliant, feminine, masculine, ugly, handsome, pretty.

The narratives we create about our internal universe are much like stories we created of the external universe. Up until recently we believed that we were at the central point in the universe. Nicholas Copernicus changed that viewpoint somewhat with the publication of "On the Revolution of the Celestial Spheres" just before his death in 1543. He waited until just before he died, because he would have been in trouble with scientists and with the church had he published his work earlier his lifetime.

Copernicus said we were not the center of the universe. The sun was the center and earth was just one of the planets that revolved around the sun. We humans were no longer at the center of the universe, a giant step in the right direction. But since the sun was the center of the universe, we were not that far off from the center.

That belief held sway into the 1920s when Harlow Shapley realized the Milky Way Galaxy was much larger than previously believed. He declared that the Earth is not at the center of our Solar System, our galaxy, or the Universe. But he believed there was only one large galaxy and our sun was off from the center. He believed the center was somewhere off toward the direction of Sagittarius. We were still not that far off center.

Later in the 1920s Edwin Hubble discovered other galaxies in the universe besides the Milky way. Hubble discovered the universe was expanding. This is a difficult concept to get your head around. It is not like the air expanding inside of a balloon. It means the entire universe is expanding. As the universe expands it is creating new space.

Einstein pointed out that if you live in this expanding universe in the fabric of space and time, no matter where you are it will look like you are at the center. Every center is an illusion. Everyone who looks at the universe sees themselves at the center with all of the other galaxies receding from them. This is how an expanding universe looks from every point of view.

We see ourselves at the center and think we are made up of the same stuff as the universe. The universe is made up of hydrogen and so are we. Next abundant is oxygen and the same with us. Next in the universe comes carbon and nitrogen, and again the same with us here on earth. It continues on and on like this.

All this looks consistent and good. Then comes the discovery that the universe has stuff that doesn't shine or reflect or back. This dark energy that we can't see takes up 73% of the universe. And dark matter makes up an additional 23 % of the universe. Both dark energy and dark matter are a mystery to us. We only know about the remaining 4 percent, the stars, planets , and people and stuff here on earth. That leaves us metaphorically and literally pretty much in the dark.

In his 1995 book, "The Astonishing Hypothesis," Francis Crick, who received the Nobel Prize for his work breaking the DNA code, said that our feelings and thoughts were nothing more than the movement of currents from neural synapse to neural synapse in our brains. This defines materialism. The brain is a material, physical device, and the mind is a construct of the material neural pathways of the brain and does not exist independent of these material neural pathways.

We know the physical, material structure of neurons and we know of neural pathways though the brain. We have no idea, though, how this creates a sense of consciousness and self. Mind or self cannot be found anywhere within these neural pathways. Self and consciousness may be an illusion, much the same as the illusion of looking out at the universe and seeing so clearly that we are the center.

So many large and small questions remain unanswered. How is information encoded and transferred from cell to cell, or from network to network of cells? Science found a genetic code but there is no brain-wide neural code; no electrical or chemical alphabet exists that can be recombined to say "red" or "fear" or "wink" or "run."

Kleck and Strenta studied a person's perception of being stigmatized. They painted a hideous scar on the subject's face and had the subject look at his face in the mirror. In an instant the he-she was stigmatized with an ostensible facial scar; ostensible because it was not really there. Pretending to moisturize the scar to prevent it from cracking, the lab assistant actually wiped it away leaving no mark at all.

The subjects were then videotaped as they conversed with a partner. They were shown the video in which the camera had focused solely on their partner and they were asked to comment on how their partner was reacting to their scar. The subjects pointed out that their partner was staring at the scar, looking away in disgust and reacting nervously.

Kleck & Strenta demonstrated that when subjects believe themselves to be physically stigmatized, they attribute neutral behavior of others to a negative reaction to their stigma. In fact, during a normal conversation people glance away frequently. Without the influence of the stigma, glancing away is hardly noticed.

The left brain Narrator Interpreter module searches for pattens to fill in to make a contextually coherent story. The Narrator takes the facts it has available and creates the most plausible narrative. You have a hideous scar. The person you are talking to cannot but help from reacting with disgust to the scar. He constantly looks away in disgust and acts nervously.

Narrator

The Narrator constructs stories on the fly with whatever fits, eliminating anything that might contradict the story. At the same time, the right hemisphere sees things literally, with no attempt at interpretation. The right hemisphere sees the person glancing away now and then without a trace of stigma consciousness. The right brain perceives without filling in and creating a story.

Michael Gazzaniga, professor of psychology at UC Santa Barbara and author of "The Ethical Brain" and "Who's in Charge: Free Will and the Science of the Brain," is credited with coining the name "cognitive neuroscience." He did a series of experiments isolating the location of the Interpreter or Narrater module to the left hemisphere of the brain. His subjects were split-brain patients whose corpus callosum had been surgically severed to minimize the spread of seizure activity. The corpus callosum is the bundle of neural fibers connecting the left and right hemispheres of the human and some other higher animal brains.

With the corpus callosum severed, the right and left hemispheres cannot communicate with each other. It is as if the person now has two entirely separate consciousnesses. When only the right brain sees the event, the left brain is driven to concoct explanations or causes for the event. The Narrator in the left hemisphere has all the words and is the explainer or BSer.

When Gazzaniga presented images to the right visual field (left hemisphere), the patients described the image presented to them. When the same image was presented to the left visual field (right hemisphere), they said they did not see anything. Even though they said they did not see anything, when asked to point to the object, they did. The right hemisphere saw the image and could mobilize a nonverbal response, but could not put the image into a verbal description. Only the left hemisphere connects the image to a narrative.

Figure 5-2: Super Highway Connecting Hemispheres

In another of Gazanniga's experiments with a split-brain patient, the experimenter triggered a negative mood in the right-hemisphere by presenting a frightening video about a man getting pushed into a blazing fire. When asked what she saw, all she could describe was seeing a white flash. The right hemisphere saw the video but could not talk about it or draw inferences. The subject reported feeling nervous and jumpy.

For some reason, she felt afraid of Dr. Gazanniga who was in the room during the experiment. Her left-brain Interpreter or Narrator attempted to fill in the blanks as to what caused the autonomic emotional response. But her left brain had not seen the video. The only fact it had to go on was that Dr. Gazanniga was in the room asking her questions. So it created a narrative to make sense of what she was feeling by connecting her feeling to a fear of Dr. Gazanniga.

With another split-brain patient, the experimenter flashed a picture of a pinup girl to her right hemisphere and the subject responded by laughing. When asked what she saw that made her laugh, she said that she saw nothing, but she was laughing at the funny machine they were using. The left brain with all the words, again created a story to make sense of the funny feeling.

Our brain has no central command system other than the Narrator creating a fictional self, a self that is based upon implicit, buried-deep-beneath-the-surface, for the most part core beliefs. The Narrator is a part of the conscious brain, so a part of the brain is a tiny real estate of consciousness. It is difficult to comprehend that our brains are a mind-boggling neural system composed of virtually countless decision-making points and centers of integration that operate 24/7 under our radar. It is impossible to comprehend in any real sense the billions of neurons and modules organized into specialized circuits for specific functions, multiple modules flashing parallel processes throughout the brain. If not for the Narrator offering a simplified, fictional illusion, the chaos would be incomprehensible insanity. So we live ensconced within the Narrator's fifty-bit cache.

We "know" who we are from the Narrator and the Narrator makes up whatever it needs to come up with . No one is behind the curtain pulling levers. No center of consciousness that we know of. The Narrator takes all of the input, meaningful and things with no intrinsic meaning, spinning it all into a narrative that makes a lot of sense and becomes a unified story line; our concept of self, of "me-ness." It is this concept of self based on unconscious, implicit beliefs that causes many of us a tremendous amount of suffering.

We accept, we believe in the cohesive and fictional self and world created by the Narrator. We give irrational, harmful thoughts authority because they are intimately connected with this fictional self. Ironically, when these thoughts are most judgmental is when we are convinced they must be true. And when a desire is there, we think the desire is there to be fulfilled, instead of corps of brain modules firing away.

It is the interpretive power of the left brain that gives us the illusion of self. The left-hemisphere Narrator takes myriad neural modules firing throughout the brain and creates an on-the-fly conscious experience and sense of self. This interpretive power of the left brain offers an illusion of unity and control and accounts for much of our feelings and behavior, while denying and rationalizing at the same time. Without this left-brain Narrator we would be lost in the fierce, firefly chaos of billions of neural modules and their unfathomable interconnected pathways firing throughout the brain.

But the left-brain narrative creation is a slow process and what the Narrator weaves for us has already happened, only appearing to be happening at that instant. We are on a taped delay similar to the few second delay of call-in radio stations used to screen calls before they come on air. The Narrator gives us the illusion that we are making decisions. In fact, the massive, powerful networks of the brain have pooled together and decided for us at least a half second before we believe we are deciding.

What an enormously difficult concept to grasp, even difficult for the scientists who have proven it so. It is like trying to conceive of where we fit into infinite space that expands forever out in all dimensions. But some grasp of this internal reality can set us free. Knowing that our Narrator spins messages and stories, we can determine what is in our best interest and work at disregarding messages and stories that do us harm. We cannot stop the brain from interpreting and spitting out story narratives, but we can work to create less harmful narratives of who we are or want to become. Our brain does not perceive the difference.

It is a Sisyphean task to change attitudes and behavior. I majored in psychology both in undergraduate and graduate school. I've published in professional journals and wrote a self-help psychology book with a forward by Albert Ellis that was published in Japanese while I was in Japan. It was in all the major bookstores throughout Japan. It sold out two twelve-thousand printings. All that had virtually no affect at changing the way I thought or behaved. While writing a book on rational-emotive behavior therapy, I was in counseling for domestic violence.

Most of us assume we think logically and make rational decisions. Albert Ellis believed otherwise. I listened to his weekly Friday night workshops many times over and can still hear him saying, "We are all fucked up fallible human beings, every one of us." His theory and therapy was grounded on the many thousands of clients he saw over more than fifty years. Research documents he was right. We are not the rational thinkers we think we are.

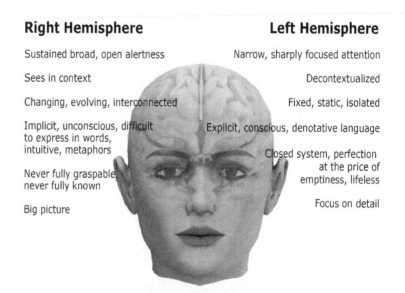

Right Hemisphere	Left Hemisphere
Sustained broad, open alertness	Narrow, sharply focused attention
Sees in context	Decontextualized
Changing, evolving, interconnected	Fixed, static, isolated
Implicit, unconscious, difficult to express in words, intuitive, metaphors	Explicit, conscious, denotative language
Never fully graspable never fully known	Closed system, perfection at the price of emptiness, lifeless
Big picture	Focus on detail

Image 5-3: Right Brain Left Brain Image

The right side of the brain engages more with the intuitive and the left side with the rational. Actually, though, the left side of the brain is not rational, since it is home of the Narrator. The Narrator creates and weaves stories to fit with our belief system. It is difficult to question and more difficult to change this narrative that colors everything we perceive. The greatest B.S.er we will ever encounter, the Narrator, resides within our own skulls and most of us don't know, understand, or believe it is there.

Gazzaniga describes how the left-hemisphere is not only a master of belief creation, but it will stick to its belief system no matter what. He illustrates this with a description of a patient with brain damage resulting in "reduplicative paramnesia." The patient believed that the New York Hospital where she was staying was her own home. When the doctor pointed out that this could not be her home since there was an elevator in the hall, the patient said that she had gone through a great financial sacrifice to install this elevator.

The left side of her brain was still functioning and kept generating stories to keep her belief system in tact no matter what facts it was fed. With other parts of her brain damaged, she had no way of questioning the stories fed to her by her brain. Though an extreme example, her case offers a picture of how the left-brain Narrator-Interpreter module works to keep a belief system intact on a moment to moment basis. We have an image of ourselves and the world, and the left hemisphere of the brain generates patterns that tie in with this image and belief system. Our sense of self gets attached to and confused with these often deceptive messages, stories, beliefs, and feelings.

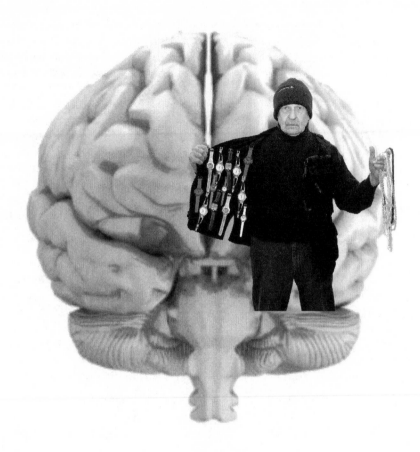

Figure 5-4: The Greatest BS Artist Ever Resides in Our Brain

Francis Crick, discoverer of the DNA double helix puts it this way: "You, your joys and sorrows, your memories and your ambitions, your sense of personal identity and free will, are in fact no more than the behavior of a vast assembly of nerve cells and their associated molecules. As Lewis Carroll's Alice might have phrased it: 'You're nothing but a pack of neurons.' "

The three-pound gelatin mass of neurons is divided into a left and right hemisphere. A surgeon can anesthetize each hemisphere separately and the awake hemisphere is conscious and will respond to questions. If one hemisphere is sacrificed life will go on   pretty much as usual. So in the future, what if you donate one of your hemispheres? Which one is you?

It's the Neural Circuits, Stupid!

Much of what we know today about how neurons communicate to

form circuits and neural pathways stems from the work of Santiago Ramon y Cajal who in 1906 was awarded the Nobel Prize in medicine for his work on the structure of the nervous system. Considered by many to be the father of modern neuroscience, he pioneered microscopic investigations of neurons, drawing hundreds of illustrations of these brain cells. We learned from his drawings that a neuron consists of a cell body or soma with treelike branches called dendrites bunched more toward one side and a tube called an axon extending from the other side with a one-way transmission of electrical information from the dendrites down to the axonal tip. At the tip the electrical current becomes a chemical discharge of neurotransmitters into the space called the synaptic gap.

Cajal is popularly known for the phrase "neurons that fire together wire together." When two neurons fire at the same time, chemical changes occur and they get linked together in circuits. Each time you repeat a behavior or thought, you strengthen neural circuits that become habits and patterns of thinking.

We make ourselves miserable to a large degree because of an illusion of self that is constructed by these linked neural circuits. Over the years we add to this illusion by repeating and building upon these narratives. We are puny and weak and we have the desire to be rich and powerful. We are too feminine and we put up a front of machoness, or too masculine and put up a front of femininity. After years of building neural pathways, our brains have an arsenal of these linked neural chains from which to jog our memories on a minute to minute basis. A neural circuit is a neural circuit and our brain does not distinguish between what is real and what is illusion and what is beneficial and what is harmful to us.

Psychotherapy and counseling involving endless discussions of childhood trauma can strengthen associated neuronal pathways and build revised memory networks on top of them. Friendships where you constantly share and relive an unfortunate past also serve to strengthen and build upon these pathways. It does not help to constantly reinforce negative images of self and strengthen already powerful neural circuitry.

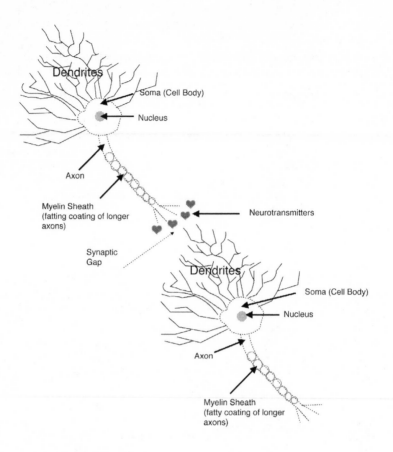

Figure: 5-5 Neural Intercourse

You alter linked neural pathways by allowing networked modules harmful to you to lose strength, while at the same time building and reinforcing networked modules that are beneficial to you. Building healthy networks of the mind can be harder than body building though, and body building takes years of concentrated workouts and diets. But I come from absolute suicidal ground zero and assure you there are no limits. At seventy-nine, I am a work in progress.

Alfred Adler, co-founder with Freud of the psychoanalytic movement, believed it is extremely difficult to deviate from the patterns of behavior developed in early life. He observed that few individuals have ever been able to change their childhood behavior patterns, even though in adult life they may have found themselves in entirely different situations. Even a change of attitude in adult life need not necessarily lead to a change of behavior. Adler said we select the most expedient error to describe the world as we perceive it and we call this error truth. Everything we perceive is subjective and fictional.

Extremely difficult to deviate from childhood patterns of behavior, but doable. Adler, of course, did not know of Metacognitive Therapy (MCT) or other attention therapies. With a combination of these therapies, starting at insane suicidal ground zero, I have risen from the stifling patterns of behavior formed in early life and am living a pretty decent life.

6 KI LIFE FORCE

If therapy is to be effective with rage and violence, you had better be able to call upon it and put it into practice instantly when you are headed for trouble. Many psychotherapies and self-help systems are logical and seem like they should be effective. But when you are about to erupt and become violent, you need something that works in an instant.

Lots can be packed away under the hood, but a therapy needs to pass Keep it Simple Stupid (KISS) in terms of a basic understanding and instant applicability. I cannot call upon REBT in an instant at these volatile times. REBT is an ongoing long-term project that gradually builds in effectiveness and power. I need an arsenal of weapons. I take medications and do Ki Breathing Meditation as part of an ongoing day to day routine.

I detest violence. I dislike being around hot heads. After I erupt I want to crawl under a rock. I feel I have no right to exist. Surely, I don't want to be this way. My frontal cortex shuts down and subcortical regions take reign. I am not able to rationally decide not to react violently.

Years back I could not convince a spouse-abuse counselor this was so. Had I murdered someone in this distressed state, I would not be around to tell this story. Back then there were no selective serotonin reuptake inhibitors (SSRI).

Though a black belt in aikido, I no longer practice the martial art I studied in Japan, but incorporate Ki Breathing Meditation into my daily life. Ki Breathing Meditation affects body, mind, and emotional state.

Breathing That Fights Stress and Disease

Ki Breathing techniques developed by Koichi Tohei slow breathing and heart rate, lowers blood pressure, and counters all stress-related symptoms. Breathing comes naturally, yet most of us never master the technique, not even close to our fullest potential, and breathing seriously impacts physical and mental health.

Though the average adult's lung capacity is 3,000 cubic centimeters, during an untrained normal respiration, we inhale an average 300 to 500 cc of air. Tenseness, sickness and anxiety produce states of even shallower breathing. An adult trained in Ki Breathing fills the lungs to between 5,000 and 8,000 cc capacity.

At the base of the windpipe air enters bronchial treelike branches and travels down thin tapering ducts terminating in air sacs called alveoli. About 300 to 700 million alveoli cover an adult lung. This alveoli rainforest serves as both entranceway for oxygen and exit for carbon dioxide. Yet the average adult uses less than ten percent of this life-giving arena.

Ki Breathing Meditation involves relaxation and positive visualization. At least during the time that you Ki Breathe, let go of negative thoughts and accentuate the positive. You will need to try different approaches and see what works for you. Sometimes I say to myself "Feels so good!" At other times I say, "Plus." Most times I say nothing. Just relax and breathe. You will notice a powerful mental and bodily effect of positive emotive Ki Breathing.

Let your shoulders drop, let go of tension in your gut, and allow your body weight to fall naturally to a point low in your gut. As you inhale, picture oxygen transported by the blood to every organ, cell, and body extremity. At the end of the inhalation, relax for a couple of seconds while holding this image. As you exhale, picture all of the wastes transported back to the lungs and carried out like an exhaust fan from the mouth. Relax while holding this image at the end of your exhalation.

Tilt your neck down at a 45 degree angle toward the end of the exhalation and feel the flow of air and Ki continuing to flow even after the physical flow of air has stopped. Inhale and at the end of the inhalation allow your neck to lift naturally back to the level starting position and feel ki flowing out through the back of your head at a 45 degree angle skyward.

Except for oxygen, you can survive for days without any of the other essential nutrients, including water. Cut off oxygen and you turn livid blue and get a complete and final shutdown. Inadequate supplies of oxygen affect your health from head to toe. Irritability, insomnia, anxiety, aches and pains, depression, memory loss, arthritis, impotence or frigidity, and the gamut of organ dysfunctions more often than not reflect a deficiency in the functioning of oxygen and glucose and the concurrent buildup of oxidants and wastes.

Add job and domestic stress and you've got karoshi, sudden death through overwork and fatigue, a phenomenon coined in Japan. Actually mislabeled Sudden Death Syndrome, karoshi results from prolonged stress, cellular starvation of nutrients, and a concurrent buildup of toxic wastes. By severely cutting the supply of nourishment as well as limiting the elimination of poisonous wastes, some people commit a prolonged, painful, and highly effective suicide.

By breathing deeply, keeping one point and relaxing completely, all the capillary vessels open and oxygen is sent to every organ of the body and carbon dioxide is carried away. Ki Breathing Meditation helps to control high blood pressure. Ki Breathing is an elixir of life. If we continue practice unfailingly, we will be able to cultivate an invisible but powerful undercurrent of strength and healthy organ functioning.

The effects of Ki Breathing Meditation are incremental both over each session and over a period of time. During a session you may not notice results instantly. To feel the full effect it may take twenty or thirty minutes. But if you begin soon after getting up in the morning, and continue if possible through your commute to work, you will arrive at work feeling balanced and alert.

Over time, your lungs stretch and you are able to take in much more oxygen. When I had an ultrasound echocardiogram, my doctor noted the expanded size of my lungs.

Vagus Nerve Stimulation

Beyond oxygen intake and carbon dioxide release from the body, there is a neurological calming with Ki breathing. Breathing from low in the abdomen stimulates an extremely long pair of nerves, referred to as the vagus nerve running from the brain stem down through the neck and chest and into the abdomen.

Vagal nerve stimulation (VNS) treats extreme cases of depression. A pulse generator is inserted in the chest and a wire is threaded under the skin connecting the pulse generator to the left vagus nerve in the neck. The pulse generator sends out electrical signals along the vagus nerve to the brain. These signals affect mood centers of the brain, which may improve symptoms of depression.

A jelly-bean size microprocessor can be clamped onto the vagus nerve in the neck in about a twenty-minute surgery. Once in place it is like a pacemaker, giving a short electrical stimulation to the vagus nerve. It provides pain relief to a rheumatoid-arthritis patient, who no longer will require medication.

You can stimulate the vagus nerves without surgery. Ki or low abdominal breathing stimulates the vagus nerve and triggers a relaxation response. The parasympathetic nervous system is set in motion, slowing the heart and calming the body. In the brain, the vagus nerve affects the limbic system, a group of midbrain structures affecting mood, motivation, sleep, appetite, and alertness.

Perhaps babies and young children are more relaxed because they breathe deeply and fully with a relaxed belly. Their abdomen moves in concert with their breathing. It is the natural way of breathing. As we grow older and become more tense, we tighten our stomachs and breathe more shallowly and higher up. This breathing pattern is perceived by the body as a stress response and reinforces the sympathetic fight or flight nervous system. Stress hormones like cortisol are released and we feel stressed and uncomfortable.

Shinshin Toitsu Aikido

Shinshin toitsu aikido, introduced in the early 1970s by Koichi Tohei, means "the way to harmony with Ki," placing emphasis on the Ki principal that mind moves body, and that by the coordination of mind and body we can perform to the best of our ability in all aspects of life. It is not necessary to learn aikido, Ki training provides skills for relaxation, calmness, and concentration.

Take care in pronouncing shinshin toitsu aikido. I meant to say *shinshin toitsu* aikido, but when the entire dojo broke out in uncontrolled laughter, I knew I pronounced it wrong. Shinshin toitsu means mind and body coordination. I was saying *chinchin toitsu* which means coordination of the penis.

The Four Principals of Ki Enhance and Maximize the Benefits of Ki Breathing

According to John Bowlby's attachment theory and Harry Harlow's experiments with rhesus macaque monkeys, I passed the point of no return in the first two years of my life. Later in life, everyone and everything bothered me. I became distracted by a barely audible whisper in the classroom when I was teaching. Ki Breathing Meditation helps to lower my irritation trigger point.

Keep one point.
Relax completely.
Keep weight underside.
Extend Ki.

These four principles work together. To keep one point low in the abdomen, you need to relax completely and keep your weight underside. When you get angry and lose it, your energy radiates from top side. If you were to encounter an opponent in aikido with this top-heavy mindset, your opponent would easily throw you for a literal loop. With shoulders relaxed and weight underside low in your abdomen, you are immovable. Extending Ki creates a 360 degree buffer zone.

Keeping weight underside is a challenge to beginners. But it is simple. Gravity causes the weight of objects to naturally settle at the lowest point. If you relax completely, the weight of your body will settle low in your abdomen. Weight will fall to the underside of your arms when held extended and relaxed. All you need to do is relax your shoulders and stomach, and breathe in and out slowly and deeply.

In the West we are brought up with the concept of physical strength. Aikido requires no physical strength. Aikido requires relaxing, keeping one point, weight underside and extending ki. You learn to calm yourself, remain focused, and allow the breath and life force to flow naturally.

Think of every action originating from low in your abdomen. Life energy radiates infinitely outward on the out-breath and infinitely down into the one point low in the abdomen on the in breath. When Ki flows, attackers fall as if by magic.

On the bare, hard, tatami mat, we practiced ki meditation for the first hour of every practice to unify mind and body. No student reaches first degree black belt or *Shodan* without "mastering" *shinshin toitsu*, mind-body coordination. My wife Hitomi weighs 85 pounds, but the test for black belt is the same no matter gender or size. She fended three attackers, all considerably taller and heavier.

It seems a paradox to stand completely relaxed facing charging attackers. Yet, this is the way to tap into a well flowing with power. Before beginning a session in the dojo, *sensei* (teacher) reads from a tiny black book of Ki Sayings written by Koichi Tohei. "Breathe out so that your breath travels infinitely to the ends of the universe; breathe in so that your breath reaches your one point and continues infinitely there. The Ki breathing methods are an important way of unifying the mind and body."

Imagine your breath going out infinitely on your exhalation. If you are alone, make a *haaaaaaaaaa* whispering sound on the exhale. This keeps focus on the breath. When you breathe in, feel as though you are taking Ki of the universe deep inside, infinitely down into the point low in your abdomen and out to organs and extremities.

If you are sitting, sit comfortably with your lower back straight, shoulders relaxed, and weight falling low in the abdomen. Open your mouth slightly and exhale with a whispering *haaaaa*.

Figure 6-1: Open your mouth slightly and exhale with a whispering *haaaaa*.

In that straight, but relaxed position, at the end of the long relaxed breath, lean forward as you let out the remaining breath.

Figure 6-2: Lean forward as you let out the remaining breath.

Tohei says the exhale should last thirty or forty seconds. That is a really long exhale. Start out wherever you are and progress slowly and comfortably. Exhale about ten to twenty seconds. After exhaling completely, close your mouth, lean forward and pause for two or three seconds before starting to inhale. Inhale through the nose, in-breath flowing down into your lower abdomen. A flow of oxygen courses into your blood and throughout your body.

Figure 6-3: Inhale

Straightening, inhale a bit more and hold for a few seconds before the next exhalation. Use your body in this way to breathe in and out completely. Tohei says the inhalation should be a bit shorter than the exhalation, but let it come naturally.

If you are having difficulty, most likely you are not fully relaxed. When you are calm and relaxed, your breathing will be smoother and deeper. As you progress through the session, you will become more and more relaxed.

With each breath, oxygen is taken in by the capillary vessels that cover the air cells of the lungs and placed into blood vessels supplying the entire body. On the exhalation, carbon dioxide is carried to capillary vessels of the lungs where it is exhaled. When you practice Ki Breathing, you practice relaxed, deep, internal breathing where the whole body inhales and exhales.

Over time, you want to gradually and naturally increase the in-breath and the out-breath. It takes about twenty seconds for blood to distribute oxygen throughout the body. If you get up to about twenty seconds on inhalation and exhalation, you give the blood time to distribute the oxygen and time to carry away carbon dioxide from the entire body to the lungs where it is exhaled.

Don't be discouraged if you find this difficult at first. Almost surely, you will find it difficult. It is difficult overcoming inertia and getting started. It is difficult staying with the breath and returning to a focus on breathing each time you get carried away in thought. And it is difficult practicing the four principles of Ki. Your breathing may at first be rough and choppy, but as you practice with the four principles of Ki, it will get smoother. You can practice the four principles of Ki and Ki Breathing Meditation anywhere, at any time of day or night, standing, walking, sitting, or lying in bed.

Time for sleep can offer time to practice Ki Breathing and meditation. If you breathe shallowly, CO_2 collects in the bloodstream and can result in anxiety or panic attacks. Trying to fall asleep in this condition is like a pitcher worrying about throwing a good pitch, or like struggling to get aroused sexually. The more you try, the worse it gets. You breathe even more shallowly and take in even less than 300 to 500 cc. CO_2 collects in the bloodstream and a sleepless cycle filled with anxiety gets progressively worse.

Increasing CO_2 by even a very small fraction can have a noticeable impact. CO_2 is a trace molecule in our atmosphere, at a low 0.3 mm. But CO_2 levels on the International Space Station (ISS) were found to be between 2.3 and 5.3 mm. This resulted in headaches, irritability, insomnia, intense mood swings, and difficulties in performing on-board activities. CO_2 is a vascular dilator and so can increase intracranial pressure. When CO_2 levels were adjusted, all of these negative effects went away.

When you Ki Breathe, you double the oxygen, and as you become experienced you can breathe many times more deeply. You nourish every cell in your body. If you experience insomnia, the time spent Ki Breathing will strengthen you and likely help you to sleep. Insomnia offers extra time for your practice.

Though effective on so many levels, Ki Breathing Meditation is not an end, aim, or goal. It is not an outlet for our perhaps innate urge to create. In no way do I sit around Ki Breathing. Inactivity would slip me headlong back into rumination. I am virtually never inactive.

When I interviewed Albert Ellis, world-famous psychologist, I asked him if he would ever think of retiring. He responded, "What, and lie around on a beach in Florida? I'd go out of my fucking mind." Ellis worked more than seventy hours a week counseling patients, ten to twelve hours a day, six days a week. On Sundays he wrote. It seems he was in a state of flow right up until the end, at the age of ninety four. What more could you want out of life?

7 FINDING FLOW

Mihaly Csikszentmihalyi, who coined the term "flow," said that the natural state of the mind is chaos and this is why we need to constantly work at flow.

Csikszentmihalyi came up with the term flow, thinking of a river. When we are left alone with no demands on attention, entropy is the normal state of consciousness, a condition he says is neither useful or enjoyable. Flow Entropy is a state of disorder, deterioration, randomness; not a place we want to be. This, too, important to keep in awareness.

Alone in our heads, the brain moves like a digital radio in rapid-search mode. With the radio, we stop on something that gives us pleasure. But unless we actively attend, the brain may seek pain, grudges, and real and imagined upsetting conversations and events.

Csikszentmihalyi describes flow as the antidote and breaks activities offering flow into seven components.

1. Completely involved in what we are doing – focused.

2. A sense of ecstasy –of being outside everyday reality.

3. Great inner clarity – knowing what needs to be done and how well we are doing,

4. Knowing the activity is doable – that our skills are adequate to the task.

5. A sense of serenity – no worries about oneself, and a feeling of growing beyond the boundaries of the ego.

6. Timelessness – thoroughly focused on the present; hours seem to pass by in minutes.

7. Intrinsic motivation – whatever produces flow becomes its own reward.

Habits and strategies offering a sense of flow are activities you are so into that you lose a sense of time. Writing, drawing, painting, sports, nature, yoga, meditation, music, and gaming are some activities that can transport you into this state of flow.

Daydreaming and imagining can be a source of flow. Playing out a sequence of events as mental images create emotional order by compensating for unpleasant realities. Imaginary situations are a positive way for children to rehearse and test out strategies and consider various optional behaviors. A well-timed book inspires the imagination and creates a state of flow. We need to provide kids with reading that targets personal needs early on. Once they tap into a sense of flow from reading, they are on a path to self-discovery. Both fiction and nonfiction offer flow when personal needs are targeted at the right time.

Figure 7-1 Finding Flow

Flow requires a delicate balance between skill level and challenge. A good video game is programmed so that the level of challenge stays just ahead of skill level. If the skill level is set too low you get bored. If it is too high you get frustrated. The precise balance between challenge and level of skill contributes to flow.

Gaming offers a world with immediate feedback so you know how well you are doing moment to moment. You enter into a world where the activity is intrinsically rewarding, concentration is deep, problems are forgotten, and control and a feeling of mastery is possible. Self-consciousness disappears and it is possible to transcend the limits of ego, self, and time, lifting you out of a powerless state of ennui or chronic stress.

Once you have entered this effortless, spontaneous state, whatever you are doing is worth doing for its own sake. It is a state in which you are doing something that you really like to do and are totally involved. You lose track of time and may not notice when you are hungry or tired. It is a state when both the skill level and challenge are higher than average, with the challenge slightly higher than the the skill level. You can be doing practically anything, riding the balance between the challenge and skill level, constantly working a bit beyond your comfort zone to reinforce and advance from each level of skill.

Csikszentmihalyi searched for ways to make flow accessible to more people. It comes to artists, gamers, and athletes naturally. But many people rarely experience flow, so the challenge is to incorporate it into our educational system from the earliest grades. All of us should be able to shift into a flow activity offering a sense of serene clarity and focus.

Work Flow

The fortunate achieve flow from their work, even though their work may be ordinary or hard. Freud said:

> Laying stress upon importance of work has a greater effect
> than any other technique of living in the direction of
> binding the individual more closely to reality; in his work
> he is at least securely attached to a part of reality, the
> human community . . . As a path to happiness, work is not
> valued very highly by men. They do not run after it as they
> do after other opportunities of gratification.

If a job offers variety, flexible challenges, clear goals and immediate feedback, by its very nature it can offer flow. It fits the definition of autotelic or inherently satisfying. If a person is autotelic, they are internally driven as opposed to externally driven by such things as comfort, money, or power. Some people will not find flow in the most satisfying job, while an autotelic person may find flow in an otherwise common, boring, and even stressful work environment. People who know how to find flow are able to enjoy situations where others find only despair.

Csikszentmihalyi says in theory any job could be changed so as to make it more enjoyable by adjusting it to fit the seven components of flow. If you can view difficult aspects of the job as a challenge, the very attempt at adjusting these aspects of the job to fit components of flow can be a source of flow. For example, if stress is a difficult aspect of the job, the challenge of working with stress can offer a sense of flow.

The process involves linking it together into an all-encompassing set of components that gives a higher purpose to the challenges of work. Csikszentmihalyi wrote:

> To gain personal control over the quality of experience,
> one needs to learn how to build enjoyment into what
> happens day in, day out.

Research has confirmed the obvious, workers are more productive when they are happy, so some companies have begun to introduce fun and flow into their work environment. According to Nic Marks of the New Economics Foundation in the UK, the difference in productivity between happy and unhappy workers ranges between 10 and 50 percent. Huge in terms of business revenues. When work is enjoyable and goals are clear and achievable, motivation is intrinsic and people come in and work on their own.

To get employees as absorbed in their work as when playing a good game, you need to program in at several of the seven basic components of flow. Clear goals need be highlighted at each stage of the task and workers' skills matched to the challenge of the task, keeping challenge just beyond skill set. The challenge needs to be realistic and achievable, with little or no fear of failure. If skills and challenges are matched with ongoing feedback, it is possible for employees to take control of the situation and meet challenges with some of the joy of gaming.

Companies are challenged to bring the workplace out from the last century where the time clock marked a clear division between work and play. With an array of mobile devices and interconnectivity, work bleeds into evenings, weekends and vacations, while personal tasks, social life and play become a part of the work day. But some offices are designed for an antiquated work ethic where clocks set the time for breaks and lunch, with clear boundaries between work and play. That leads to boredom and stress.

Companies most highly rated by employees, retirees, and spouses of retirees are attuned to Csikszentmihalyi's seven basic concepts of flow. Google and Bain Capital have been at the top of two of the largest company rating sites. Employee comments include: lots of reward, smart people, great values and respect, open transparent communication, passionate about job, constantly being pushed to improve and expand skills, clear goals and objectives, stimulating, challenging , fast paced work with deep and lasting impacts, a fun learning environment where you can have impact right away.

Flow is Flow

Flow is much the same across a wide scope of activities. What could be further apart than researching and writing at a computer, and competitive track and field? It seems both potentially offer a somewhat similar sense of flow. Here is a collage of interviews with world class track and field athletes.

From a high jumper:

When I take off and when I climb in the air, it all goes

pretty fast, but once I hit that apex of the jump and my hips are up over the bar, time really slows down. I mean you can just feel this rotation. It feels as though someone has grabbed a hold of your hips and really is giving you a push, a boost up in the air.

From a runner:
In that moment when they say, take your mark, I become the gun. So when that gun fires, it's almost like I'm the bullet being fired out of the pistol. When I hear that sound it's almost like there's a firing pin smacking me on my butt and pushing me. I'm the bullet and it's only me in the chamber.

From another runner:
When you're running and you're so relaxed in what you're doing, a song can just pop into your mind (at) about thirty meters. That is the ultimate point an athlete wants to be, because that's when you get that peak performance. It's almost like everything is moving in slow motion and you are watching the birds slowly fly by, and you hear that song just whistling in your ear.

Survival Flow

Some survive, even thrive the ravages of mental illness by escaping into a sense of flow. Tom Harrell is composer, trumpet player, internationally known musician, suffering with paranoid schizophrenia.

Flow starts the instant he puts trumpet to lips and blows. Devoid of cliches, intricate notes flow from deep inside. Each of his solos a communion with the soul, his means of reaching out to the world. Though he cannot hold the simplest conversation, from the first notes floating from his horn, the slouched, disturbed looking old man morphs into supreme maestro, leader of the Tom Harrell Quintet. When he stops and mumbles, "Don't worry, don't worry, don't worry . .be positive . . .believe in yourself," he morphs just as instantly back into the tragic, mentally ill old man.

Schreber's Memoir

Flow within a state of mental illness is documented in, "Memoirs of My Nervous Illness," by Daniel Paul Schreber, published in 1903. Sigmund Freud read Schreber's memoir and in 1907 he published, "The Schreber

Case." In a letter to Jung, Freud remarked that Schreber ought to have been made a professor of psychiatry and director of a mental hospital.

Mental hospitals today are not a great place to end up, but the asylum that housed Schreber at the start of the twentieth century was a classic insane asylum. If you were not insane before entering the asylum, you would be after a short stay. Physical restraints of straps, railings, padded cells, and drugging were the treatment. Female patients might have their ovaries removed. Come to think of it, it wasn't that different when my sister Zan was hospitalized in the 1940s and 50s in the state hospital on an isolated island connected by a bridge to Harlem, NYC.

Schreber wrote
> Completely cut off from the outside world, without any
> contact with my family, left in the hands of rough
> attendants with whom the inner voices said it was my duty
> to fight now and then to prove my manly courage, I could
> think of nothing else but that any manner of death,
> however frightful, was preferable to so degrading an end.

Perhaps it was Schreber's focus on documenting his tragic ordeal that made him one of the few inmates who were ever discharged from the institution. In the 1955 translation, the editors describe Schreber's Memoirs:
> The "Memoirs" are an account of what it is to be forsaken
> by everything familiar and real and of the delusional world
> that gets invented in its place. The complicated mythic
> universe that Schreber in his captivity created, an affair of
> rays and miracles, upper and lower gods, souls and soul
> murder, voices of nerve language, struggles against the
> "Order of the World," concerned itself with issues of
> realness and unreality, identity and fusion, power and
> passivity. His own identity having been invaded,
> fragmented, distorted, and annihilated, a story had to be
> found that made sense of it. The more massive the
> violations, the more grandiose the explanations.

Schreber, had been a lawyer, judge, and at the age of 41 the chief justice of the Supreme Court of Appeal in Saxony. There he presided over five judges, most of whom were considerably older and more knowledgeable about procedures of court than him. He and his family being new to Dresden had no social life (which he said would have been good for him.) He was overtaxed mentally and was taking more and more powerful sedatives for insomnia. He describes the onset of the schizophrenia when he and his wife heard a "recurring crackling noise in the walls of our bedroom." His wife thought it was mice, but it kept him up more and more of the night and he came to recognize this as divine messages.

He kept notes during his entire stay at the asylum and organized them into a manuscript in the later years of his initial nine-year confinement. He wrote the book both to describe the nature of his psychosis and as a message to the world of his divine revelation. His hospital chart noted:

> Constantly under the tormenting influence of his hallucinations. Sleep at night mostly poor. Moans, stands in bed, stands rigidly in front of the window with eyes closed and an expression of listening on his face. From time to time the tragic patient would scribble words on scraps of paper: 'miracles' -- 'tomb' -- 'not eat.'

Besides his escape into the fantasy world of his brilliant narrative, his love of music and the piano helped him gain freedom back with his family for a few years. Somehow a piano was put in his room for his sole use. When he saw it, he quoted from Tannhauser:

> I could only remember that I had had lost all hope of ever greeting you again or ever raising my eyes to you.

And reflecting the same change as Tom Harrell as he lifts the trumpet to his mouth and begins to blow heavenly notes:

> During piano-playing the nonsensical twaddle of the voices which talk to me is drowned . . . Every attempt at representing me by the creation of a false feeling and suchlike is doomed to end in failure because of the real feeling one can put into piano playing.

And while playing an aria from The Magic Flute:

> Oh, I feel it, it has vanished, gone for ever.

Biblio-Flow

Though my writing obsession nearly ended in suicide early in life, it has continued to this day and offers the intense moments I live for each day. I have not lived if I don't sit with a cup of coffee or plum wine and popcorn and escape into my research and writing. I had no idea writing offered this sense of flow and release until years after my formal education.

Bibliotherapy can be a mix of reading, writing, and research. Motivated by what he describes as blinding depression and crippling anxiety, Andrew Solomon, author of "Noonday Demon" set out reading, researching, and writing about his own recovery and the range of treatments for depression.

One world opened into another, into another, like biting off chunks of Alice's magic mushroom. He researched everything from experimental brain surgery to hypnotherapy. His quest took him to Cambodia and to rural Africa, where he very literally immersed himself in a tribal exorcism.

The biggest part of my biblioflow is reading. Actually, I listen to novels on mp3s. When I get into a story I am transported to another life, place, and time. It gets me through exercise and household chores. In fact, I look forward to exercise and household chores for the chance to "get away." And I spend time each day researching for books, and when I find one it is almost like hitting the jackpot. Although I don't travel, for me it is almost the same, without the packing, airports, planes, and hotels. It is a flow experience without the hassle.

STEM Flow

Perhaps the key to some of societal problems is to help children discover their source of flow. Kids are dreamers and we can make daydreaming and fantasy a part of their academic lives. We can introduce them to characters like Nobel Prize winner Paul Dirac, for whom math was his source of flow keeping his demons at bay for most of his life. We need to help kids explore things they might never explore on their own. Most textbooks don't open into worlds that flow.

Too many kids in elementary, high school, and college are turned off by science and math before they know what it holds. Math and science can be infused with a search for meaning and flow. String theory, multi and parallel universes, astrophysics, and gazing out into the country sky on a dark clear night can all be a part of a lifelong quest.

I had no idea during my formal education from elementary school on that science could do anything for me. Now it is a part of my reading every day. I subscribe to Smithsonian, Science Bulletin, and a bunch of cell publications online. I love to read not-so-technical books on theoretical physics, like "Hyperspace" and "Parallel Worlds" by Micheo Kaku.

Paul Dirac

Characters with stories like Paul Dirac draw us in and imbue facts with meaning and flow. Up until the 1920s we knew about matter. Then in 1933 at age 31, Paul Dirac won the Nobel Prize for his discovery of antimatter. He was the youngest theoretician to ever win the Nobel Prize in physics. Through the power of his imagination, he used quantum mechanics and Einstein's theory of relativity in the form of an equation to describe the electron.

For all of his life Dirac was known for his equability, reserve, and logical, rational, and genius mind. His contributions to quantum physics were on par with Albert Einstein. He was a leading player on the international stage of science and moved among the elite.

But he was like Harrel or Schreiber. The source of his flow was in the equations of theoretical quantum physics. For almost all of his life he was operating at a peak or optimal flow level of experience.

So it was stunning to his colleague Kurt Hofer at Florida State University, when in 1980 Dirac suddenly opened up to him about his animosity to his father. Up until that time, even to this closest of colleagues, Dirac spoke only sparsely about some of his private loves: Chopin's waltzes and Mickey Mouse. Hofer said that he sat there feeling embarrassed as Dirac, whose voice was normally neutral and balanced in tone, began in a voice tinged with a deep sorrow saying that he never knew love or affection as a child.

His father was French and insisted that Dirac and his brother speak to him in French. Dirac was poor in languages and his father demanded that his French was grammatically perfect. He refused to let him leave the table if he made a mistake. Since he could not express himself in French, he would sit still and vomit.

Dirac went on like this, confessing to Hofer nonstop for more than two hours. Dirac was obsessed with his father. He told Hofer that his father was even stricter and meaner to his older brother. He said that his father constantly bullied and frustrated all his brother's ambitions. His brother committed suicide. And his father treated his mother like a doormat. Dirac ended the conversation by blurting raspingly, "I owe him absolutely nothing!"

We have no idea what is in a man's heart, the pain he is suffering. The past competes for a voice in the present moment within our 50 bits of attention. For most of his life, Dirac's focus was the inscrutable. The equations of quantum physics were his passion, the essence of his being, his open faucet of flow.

When Dirac unburdened his sole, he was in his eighties, no longer productively involved with his mathematical theorems. The flow turned off. The past bubbled up, filling his focus to the extent that he lost the discreteness of social niceties, causing Hofer to become aghast at what he was suddenly privy to.

Finding Your Own Meaning

Though we stay in flow when the challenge slightly exceeds our skill level, Csikszentmihalyi says we need to eventually take this to a higher level where activities are linked to one another in a meaningful way. This involves an overarching goal where all of the unrelated activities merge into an all-encompassing set of challenges that give purpose to everything we do.

Whoever achieves this state will never really lack anything else. A person whose consciousness is so ordered need not fear unexpected events, or even death. Every living moment will make sense and most of it will be enjoyable.

Few achieve this state. Many people are stuck in the day to day rut of personal survival. They need to focus psychic energies on themselves with little or nothing left for the goals of wider community, no less for family. But they still have a need for flow.

Juvenile delinquents get flow from car theft and vandalism. Way back, I got flow from setting fires, calling in bomb scares, and shooting huge ashcan and cherry bomb firecrackers out my back window with a Whamo slingshot as cursing policemen scurried from garage roof to roof, unable to discover the source of the blasts riling upset neighbors all about them.

It is not necessary to achieve goals in order to bring meaning to your life. You bring meaning into your life when you put intent to reach the goal into action. What matters is that psychic energy is expended to reach the goal, not wasted on doubt, regret, guilt and fear.

The activities that bring us to optimal experience are not all fun and games. The best moments can be when the mind or body is stretched to its limits in an effort to accomplish something difficult and worthwhile. Optimal experience is a process of attempting to gain mastery, sometimes over mind or body. The key is a constant "attempting." When you get there, the challenge is over. So maybe fortunately, we never really get there.

Putting intent to action and working toward your goal takes more resolve than most people have. Climbers and runners go through excruciating pain to experience the rewards of optimal experience. Working toward goals leads to blocks, dead ends, and troubles, and it is far easier to give it up when faced with barriers than plodding on.

If you maintain focus on putting intent to action despite pain and failure, Csikszentmihalyi says that life is felt to be meaningful and can become extended episodes of flow.

Victor Frankl said the meaning of life is finding your own meaning. Personal meaning may change completely at different stages of life. It may be concrete and external like total commitment to a job, a cause, a sport; or internal, as the quest for self knowledge and mental health. But it is important to think through the consequences of any long-term commitment. If I commit all my resources to my job and sacrifice my family, is it worth it? In the best of all worlds, we would have balanced commitments.

Our commitments can fit the rules of family and society or they can be an expression of what we truly feel and believe. The more intrinsically motivated, the more authentic; the more externally driven, the more inauthentic.

As important as an intrinsic, authentic life style, Csikszentmihalyi says the optimal condition is when you no longer see yourself in opposition to the environment, insisting that your goals and intentions take precedence over everything else. The optimal condition is when you are in tune with and feel a part of whatever goes on around you, and you attempt to do the best within the system in which you operate. Goals may have to be subordinated to a greater entity and you may have to play by a different set of rules from what you might prefer.

Though you don't want to lose sight of your intents and goals, you need to hold them with an Open Focus, processing information from within your surroundings. People who function at an optimal level don't expend all of their energy trying to satisfy what they believe are their needs, nor do they attempt to conform to all that society might expect of them. It is possible to work toward developing an Open Focus that includes both inward focus and an awareness of myriad alternate possibilities.

8 OPEN FOCUS

In 1982, Les Fehmi and George Fritz self-published 150-page spiral-bound 8 1/2 x 11 "The Open Focus Handbook." I found the information too tightly packed to understand, no less put it into practice. Then in 2007 Les Fehmi and Jim Robbins published a full-length book that is easy to understand and put into practice, "The Open-Focus Brain: Harnessing the Power of Attention to Heal the Mind and Body." In 2010 they expanded on what had been a chapter in their 2007 book with "Dissolving Pain: Simple Brain-Training Exercises For Overcoming Chronic Pain."

Most of our formal education encourages narrow focus of attention. "Pay attention," a phrase most of us have heard through grade school, meaning focus narrowly on what I am saying or on what you are doing. But constant narrow focus in managing experiences leads to gradual accumulation of physical and mental stress, distress, even burnout as it did for me, long before I understood enough to use Open Focus in my job as a counselor, school psychologist, and teacher.

Open Focus is a mix of narrow and diffuse focus.

Figure 8-1: Serious Cat (Narrow Focus)

If you are narrowly focused on a book you are reading, in Open-Focus mode you take in the music playing and conversation around you. If you are engrossed in an internal dialog, you open up and experience the world all around. You alternate attention between narrow and diffuse focus, sometimes paying attention simultaneously in both modes.

Figure 8-2: Daydream (Diffuse Focus)

Most of us live our lives predominantly in the left side of our brain. The left hemisphere completely convinces by cutting from its dialog whatever does not fit. The left hemisphere is convincingly consistent and believable because it allows no counter argument. Most of the time the left hemisphere has complete control of language, while the right hemisphere has no linguistic functionality. The left hemisphere is a world of its own denotative language and manipulates what we "know" to be true by reflecting back to us what we know in an endless matrix of mirrors. Everywhere we turn it reflects back a specious, but utterly consistent "truth." Most of us never exit this hall of mirrors.

We single out experiences for attention and focus, separating ourselves, excluding body experience, emotions, and sense modalities. A narrowly objective left-brain attentional style controls, excludes, and is judgmental.

Fehmi says that people who were abused physically or emotionally often suffer from extreme narrow focus. They constantly feel a need to protect themselves from getting stabbed in the back. They become hyper vigilant in this narrow, objective focus-mode of attention and are under constant stress.

It is the difference between a unidirectional microphone and an omnidirectional mic. The unidirectional, narrow-focus mic picks up what you are pointing at. This might be good in an interview where you want the focus on the interviewee and shut everything else out. Sometimes you had best use an omnidirectional, diffuse-focus mic that picks up everything around. It offers a wider, open sound with birds chirping in the background, planes flying overhead, children playing, and dogs barking.

Left-brain narrow attention excludes peripheral perception from our awareness. We can have narrow auditory perception, narrow visual perception, and a narrow focus of thoughts, sensations, and urges. Extremely narrow perception becomes obsessive-compulsive where we focus on a small piece of the puzzle and blow that piece up, so that we are unable to take in a gestalt whole. This tiny segment becomes a reality and behavior in this altered reality may seem bizarre and offensive to someone outside this narrowly focused field.

In addition to narrow versus diffuse, Open Focus includes remote/ objective versus immersed focus. With right-brain focus you are immersed in what you are experiencing. If you are tasting something and get totally into the tasting experience, this is immersed attention. An immersion style of attending is associated with mindful meditation where we attend to the body, emotions, sense modalities, and passing thoughts. Remote attention is when you create a distance between yourself and the object of attention.

A right-brain diffuse immersed/absorbed attentional style would be one of flow, unselfconscious and inclusive. An Open-Focus that integrates narrow and diffuse attention is positive, creative, flexible, even loving. Opening up our right brain to the world allows us to see things in context and adapt to a world that is constantly changing and evolving, never fully graspable, never fully known.

EEG Neurofeedback

At his clinic in Princeton, New Jersey, Les Fehmi hooks clients up to an electroencephalographic (EEG) feedback device, but Open-Focus exercises can be done with or without EEG feedback. If you want to experiment with EEG feedback, more and more companies offer reasonably priced neurofeedback hardware and software.

Electroencephalography records brain waves from sensors placed on the scalp. Though the technique of measuring brain waves has been around since the very early 1900s, it was only used for experiments with animals until the early 1920s. In 1934, German physiologist and psychiatrist Hans Berger invented the electroencephalogram, giving the device and the field its name and initials EEG.

Each neuron has its own electrical charge or voltage. An EEG graphs brain voltage from huge populations of neurons, hundreds of thousands firing together in patterns or frequencies. EEG sensors placed on the scalp pick up these electrical signals from the brain right through the skull and are translated into an EEG wave graph.

Brain waves are described by their frequency and amplitude. Frequency of a wave is measured in Hertz (Hz) or cycles per second (cps). Each cycle is measured from the top of one wave to the top of another or peak to peak.

Scrunched tightly together, gamma are the fastest brain waves ranging from 31 to 90 Hz or cps with an average of 40 Hz. Gamma have the smallest amplitude (peak to peak waves), ranging from 3 to 5 microvolts (uV). One microvolt equals 0.001 millivolts.

Long-term Buddhist meditators enter into a state of gamma. Gamma waves are thought to reflect the integration of complex stimuli into a coherent whole.

Delta deep sleep waves are spaced far apart, ranging from .5 to 3.5 Hz or cps. Delta amplitude ranges from 20-200(uV). Ironically, ADD/ADHD kids fall into this slow range of brain waves and even lower theta waves.

Alpha waves, 8 to 13 Hz or cps, range between gamma and delta, with the same huge amplitude range (20 to 200 uV) as delta waves.

You can experience alpha state by closing your eyes and relaxing or meditating. The Open-Focus exercises are an effective way to move quickly from high, fast waves of stress, to a relaxed alpha state.

Beta waves of alertness, attentiveness, and mental effort, range from 13 to 30 Hz or cps with a low amplitude of 5 to 10 uV.

Open Focus shifts between narrow and diffuse attention styles. The brain waves associated with Open Focus attention include both high amplitude synchronous waves of diffuse and immersed attention and the low and asynchronous waves of narrow and objective attention.

Fehmi's EEG neurofeedback sessions move the client toward relatively large amplitude, synchronous, alpha brain wave activity with a frequency range between 8 and 13 cycles per second. Alpha brain waves are associated with relaxed wakefulness.With the amplitude, phase-synchrony of alpha activity, trainees report feeling less tense, timelessness, energy, unity or integration, and unselfconsciousness.

Normal Adult Brain Waves

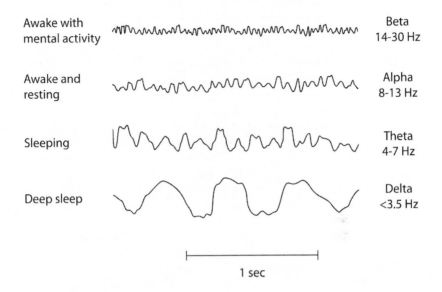

Awake with mental activity		Beta 14-30 Hz
Awake and resting		Alpha 8-13 Hz
Sleeping		Theta 4-7 Hz
Deep sleep		Delta <3.5 Hz

1 sec

Figure 8-3: Cycles per second (Peak to Peak)

Open-Focus exercises are designed to promote greater brain-wave synchrony by opening and merging self with outside, other than self. A diffuse-immersed style of attention dissolves the separateness and isolation resulting from overuse of narrow-objective attention. Fehmi says attention bias and attentional rigidity are the principal causes of human misery and suffering. Chronic use of narrow-objective focus separates us from the outside world. An Open-Focus mix of narrow and diffuse attention allowing us to merge inner thoughts with outside experience is optimal.

ADD/ADHD

Initially when working with ADD children, sensors were placed on their head and they watched a monitor displaying their brain waves and were instructed how to shift into a target brain wave. Not a captivating task, especially for kids with ADHD.

In the next generation of ADD/ADHD neurofeedback, the child wears a headset with sensors and plays a video game. Studies suggest that brains of children with ADHD generate too many lower-frequency theta waves of daydreaming or drowsiness. If the EEG records a higher percentage of these theta waves, the computer program lowers the top speed the car can travel in a car-racing game. To increase the speed of the car, the player's brain must decrease theta and increase beta waves. This task is embedded in the game and the child's brain becomes the player.

The EEG sensors record her/his brainwaves. She/he doesn't have to do anything other than play the game. The brain computes what to do to succeed. When her/his brain waves are in the target range, the car travels at top speed. When the brain waves slip out of target range, the car slows down. The brain learns to remain longer and longer within the target brain waves.

The goal of the training is for increased attentiveness and focus playing the game to carry over into daily life activities such as paying attention in class and focusing on homework. After a child goes through forty hours or so of these sessions, there is documentation of such carryover, though there is a need for more random, double blind studies.

EEG Neurofeedback is safer than medications which have side effects and long-term unknowns. Neurofeedback rewards the brain as it fires within target brain waves and withholds reward when the brain fires outside this range. This method of training the brain to make adjustments in brain waves is much the same as the operant conditioning done with rats pressing a lever for food or monkeys learning a trick for a squirt of juice. Unlike with medications, improvement is likely to endure beyond treatment because the brain has learned to function more effectively. When neurofeedback is effective, improved attention and reduced hyperactive/impulsive behavior is reported.

During the first couple of treatments with ADD/ADHD clients, the theta-beta ratio will tend to shift in favor of beta waves, but this may be due more to the novelty effect when the brain is experiencing something new and exciting. Since it doesn't stay new and exciting, the trend may not look as good on the eighth or ninth session. It usually takes twenty or so sessions for real improvement and forty sessions for lasting change.

Neurofeedback works even with cognitively impaired infants who have absolutely no inkling of what the objective of the training is all about. The brain is attracted to anything that engages it. It quickly figures out without conscious interpretation that it is part of an interactive system in which it is playing an active role. The brain plays the game on its own without conscious perception.

Consumer Hardware and Apps

On the cover of the original 1982 Open-Focus Handbook, a woman stands next to several interconnected electrical consoles with a tiny monitor. One headband holds sensor plates to her forehead and the back of her head, the other atop her head. Dangling from the ear facing us hangs a sensor with a wire connecting to the consoles. From the back of her head, a braided pack of wires hangs over a shoulder, connecting to the consoles.

That was Fehmi's state-of-the-art-electroencephalography (EEG) technology in 1982 when Fehmi's handbook was published.

His two basic Open-Focus books supply the exercises and all you need to know for Open-Focus meditation without EEG training. In Dissolving Pain, Fehmi says you can experience all of the benefits of Open-Focus exercises without use of an EEG.

A growing number of companies offer Blue Tooth wireless headsets with apps that train the brain to function within a specific brainwave state. Most sets monitor a state of either beta or alpha waves. Alpha waves accompany a state of diffuse focus and beta waves a state of narrow focus.

Neurofeedback apps improve focus and concentration, enhance cognitive skills like memory, concentration and attention, reduce negative thoughts, maintain composure in high stress situations, increase memory, enhance or change mood, and engage in the world of brain-operated, flow-generating video games.

3D surround, virtual reality headsets can take neurofeedback to another level where a patient can experience a trauma again in a virtual world under safe and controlled conditions. For example, BraveMind VR Exposure Therapy Software was created at the University of Southern California Institute for Creative Technologies (ICT) for the treatment of combat-related PTSD.

Currently found at over 60 sites, including VA hospitals, military bases and university centers, ICT's Virtual Iraq/Afghanistan exposure therapy approach has been shown to produce a meaningful reduction in PTS symptoms.

Exercise One: Open-Focus Reading

The perception of space is the foundation of open focus exercises. Once you grasp the concept of focusing on space, you are able to shift from narrow to diffused and immersed focus, between foreground and background, and into a relaxed and synchronous space of alpha brain waves.

As you read this page soften and relax your focus to include the space between your eyes and the print on the page or screen. Become aware of the three dimensional space between your eyes and the words. Allow this to happen as you continue reading. Once you are aware of this space, pause for a few seconds to maintain this awareness. Focusing on space is at the heart of Open Focus.

Increase your awareness of space to the borders around the left and right sides of the page, gradually allowing your perceptual field to expand to include more of this space. Continue to relax and expand awareness to include whatever is in the foreground and background. If you are sitting at a desk, you might take in your lap, your hands and arms, laptop, and desk. Expand your peripheral field to include space near in the foreground and then beyond this space.

Allow your visual background equal importance with the foreground. Move back and forth between foreground and background. You likely don't usually give foreground and background equal focus and interest. It takes practice to develop this open style of attention. Become aware of your attentional style. If it is mainly narrow focus, practice including background and space around this narrow target of focus. An ability to switch between narrow and diffuse focus mitigates stress.

As you do this reading exercise, you take in more in a glance, increasing your reading speed as well as comprehension, without attempting to do so. You can create this same relaxed alpha state while driving or while talking with someone, or in front of a classroom, by alternating from narrow to diffuse focus, taking into attention a more spacial and inclusive view. Of course, you want to relax as you do this. It may take a little time to get the hang of it. Don't stress on whether you are doing it correctly. It will just start to feel natural.

Exercise Two: Internal-External Focus

Think of the space around your brain, between your skull and brain. As you take in deep relaxed breaths, breathe in to fill the space between your skull and brain. Visualize the open pathway from the nostrils to the brain. As you begin to relax into deep breathing and diffuse focus, become aware of the space outside your skull. Think of the space outside the skull and the space inside the skull and the skull between these two spaces. Breathe into and fill the space between your brain and skull.

Think of the space outside of your skull and let that expand to include the space in the room. Continue breathing into the space surrounding your brain with a rich supply of oxygen. Expand the space outside your skull to include the space in the room, out beyond the room, out into deep space.

Don't stress with these exercises. Adapt them to fit your unique style and tempo. The goal is a relaxed alpha state.

9 BIBLIOTHERAPY

Healing Power of Reading

The voice of literary narrative narrows and expands attention like a camera lens blurring background so you can focus on the foreground and blurring the past so you can focus on the present. I listen to mp3s wherever I am throughout the day. Tedious workouts at the fitness center become my story time.

Though none of my therapists tapped the therapeutic power of bibliotherapy, the right book at the right time is transformative. Without the help of a therapist, though, it takes considerable sleuthing to match the right book for the right time. I subscribe to blogs like "Literary Hub," "Brain Pickings," "The New Yorker Fiction," and PRI's "Selected Shorts.". If I like the reading I check out novels and short story collections by the author. Another two of my resources are the Pulitzer Prize for Literature and Nobel Prize for Fiction. I work back through winners and runner ups including Pulitzer Prize biographies and autobiographies. Later I enter empowering books into Goodread's database and get related recommendations.

Art As a Framework for Bibliotherapy

As an undergraduate student at Rutgers University in downtown Newark, New Jersey, I made the acquaintance of an itinerant bum who roamed the "campus" area. We would sit and talk in the YMCA lounge and he shared how he would stand in front of paintings at the Newark Museum in rapturous awe. Years later I discovered literature holds that power for me.

> There is no better way of coming to be aware of what one
> feels oneself than by trying to recreate in oneself what a

master has felt. In this profound effort, it is our thought itself that we bring out into the light, together with his.

Marcel Proust

Framework for Self-Renewal

In "Art as Therapy" philosopher and essayist Alain de Botton and John Armstrong present seven areas art can help to become better versions of yourself. I find these seven areas serve as a framework for self-renewal through literature as well.

1. Remembering – Winston S. Churchill is purported to have said, "Men occasionally stumble over the truth, but most of them pick themselves up and hurry off as if nothing ever happened." Literature has the power to rekindle transforming but evanescent epiphanies.

2. Hope – A clear hopeful focus is essential to chart a path of self-renewal. You cannot achieve self-renewal if you do not believe in the possibility of renewal. Literature edits down complexity helping to focus on what is meaningful and doable. In "Self-Renewal," James Gardner writes:

> In a society capable of renewal, people not only welcome
> the future and changes it brings but believe they can have a
> hand in shaping that future, that man can improve his lot
> by making an effort. In fact, the view that humans are
> helpless to alter their fate is probably the more common
> view and has been throughout history. Such fatalism is a
> grave obstacle to renewal.

3. Sorrow - Not only are we not alone in our sorrows, they are central and universal to life. Yet in our everyday lives when someone asks how we are doing so many glibly reply, "Great!" That can make us feel so all alone. Literature unveils the suffering behind the facade. Our loss, disappointment, frustrated hope, and despair are acknowledged and made meaningful through this shared experience.

4. Rebalancing – I listened to the biography of Steve Jobs. The first ten disks are smudged with finger prints. As you near disk twenty, the condition of the disks get more and more pristine. But even when a book gets boring, I often get something from it. I was motivated by a description of Tim Cook, Apple CO who successfully worked for "a boss from hell." Cook was up at 4:30 a.m., exercised, and was at the office working by 6:30 a.m. This helped me rebalance some priorities. Modeling is a potent and direct force for self-renewal.

5. Self-understanding - We are a narrative of selves and as we meet some of the better and challenging selves through literature, we explore our potentialities, our capacities for sensing, wondering, learning, understanding, and loving. Through self-understanding we can break out of our rigidity, opening a path to renewal. Without self-understanding we may not even imagine the extent of our imprisonment.

6. Self-Growth – Too often we reject experiences with people and places that might have something to offer the growth of one of our selves. I have found these experiences with in the world of literature.

Internal-growth parallels external physical development through weight training. One session shows no results. Both internal and external growth come with time when you fall into a consistent day to day routine. Looking back a decade, I am not the same person. Physical growth is apparent to others. Mental, emotional, and spiritual growth are perceptible to me.

Fiction allows readers to participate in lives other than their own and this sets it apart from other art forms. Literature allows you to view life through the eyes of the character. Good literature allows you to enter that characters's soul, a powerful tool for self-renewal no therapist can offer.

7. Appreciation - Literature helps us to see the value of a life we're forced to lead. Not only books, though, even a newspaper article can offer enough of a portrait to glimpse the complex cross currents of human psychology. I read of the man who took a gun from his glove compartment and shot and killed a teenager because of the loud music he was playing on his car's speakers. The thought of him imprisoned for life connects with a violent past that casts a dark shadow on my own life. At the same time I feel he deserves every minute of his life sentence, I connect with him for giving up his existence, albeit unknowingly, for me to live.

Literature defines what we feel. It opens our eyes, it sensitizes and empowers us. It has power to sharpen attention, enabling us to perceive what we might never have considered.

But just as the best of therapists disappoints, so will the author. Neither the therapist or author is who we are. With both therapist and author a little something feels not quite right. With a book we take whatever works and move on to the next read. Not so easy with a therapist.

Healing Power of Writing

Though I'll describe how I used clustering with my high school juniors, clustering is effective for many purposes. I've used it in writing poems, fiction, articles, and nonfiction manuscripts. You can use clustering, brainstorming for ideas or to expand on a piece after an initial draft. It is amazing how it unlocks the mind. And though I taught high school English, my goal was always to help kids with self-discovery and self-healing.

Students call out words, any words. I write them on the board as fast as I can, branching off and interconnecting related words with lines and arrows.

Thoughts, images, ideas, pictures, even emotional states flow outward and form patterns and clusters. Where linear thinking comes to a dead end, branches of clusters sprout in all directions, growing shoots of their own.

At the board I write all of their words, even though some might not seem to fit. Clustering overrides the censor. Surprising words pop into mind, branching out in all directions. I keep going until I feel the urge to say something, then start writing. I keep writing without censoring, glancing back at the cluster whenever it helps. Kids who never thought about writing are captured by this display.

Clustering helps students open up, explore and share themselves. Thoughts and feelings spill onto the page without worry about shocking, disappointing, spelling, grammar, punctuation and readability. When students write freely with little or no censorship about their needs, desires, conflicts and fantasies, they find their unique voice, something difficult in a linear, left-brain way.

I got to know my students in a new light. Most were more than willing to open up and share their lives. No "Discipline Problems;" just individuals, each with their own story. Here is a cluster and writing by an eleventh grade girl:

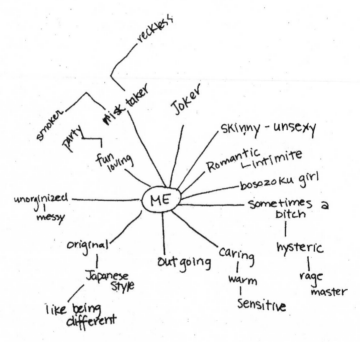

Figures 9-1 Student Cluster

77

For some people who look at me

they think I'm a little different from

everyone else. I don't think of it as

different, I think of it as original

as me. I'm pretty out going, but at times

I get really pulled back. I'm a real

romantic, I think life should be like

the movies. I'm a real bitch too, I've been

told. I don't think I'm mean, I just

speak the truth very bluntly. I think

I'm pretty, people also tell me that, but

then I have my bad days. I do things

that make adults and good kids push

me away - like smoke, and drugs.

But I don't mind, I've got my

group. I like myself most of the time,

but if others don't like me, then

they're missing something good.

I allowed them to open up without restricting or censoring their use of language. This can lead to trouble and eventually it did with one of their parents. But I would do it again if I were teaching today.

Throughout the process, students read each other's work and at times read their own work aloud before the class. If you thought someone was a dork or thought you had them pegged, you got to see their multifaceted selves. Sometimes what you had been seeing was a facade. We did blind readings where I read the paper without telling them who wrote it and more often than not they had no idea who it actually was.

Powerful Therapy

Of course, graphic sex and violence are a part of what teenagers choose to write about. Some of their stories were first person accounts of their friends and family. Their stories dealt with stealing, rape, domestic violence and incest. Only one time I felt the need to bring something to the attention of the school nurse and that was when I felt the student was seriously contemplating suicide.

I sat through sometimes painful revisions. I vividly recall a girl who wrote detailed accounts of incest with her father. Though I was not the school counselor at the time, I felt competent helping her work through her trauma by allowing her open up and to share with an adult who cared about her life and listened and empathized in a way that helped her to sort it out. Apparently it was not going on at the time but without her permission, I would not have reported this to authorities. My relationship with my students was one of unspoken but absolute confidentiality.

This was powerful therapy for me. Listening to kids with problems let me know that I had not been suffering alone. I would have had no idea of some of their horrendous problems if it were not for their writing. Incredible bonding is a bene of a relentlessly stressful occupation.

Recovering from Trauma and Emotional Upheaval

It wasn't until I had left teaching and was researching trauma, that I came across the work of James W. Pennebaker. "Opening Up: the Healing Power of Expressing Emotions," published in 1997 and "Writing to Heal: a Guided Journal For Recovering From Trauma & Emotional Upheaval," published in 2004. Pennebaker began his work in the late 1970s. His research of traumatic experiences included death of spouses, natural disasters, sexual traumas, divorce, physical abuse, even the Holocaust.

He divided subjects into three basic groups: no trauma, trauma talked about, and trauma kept inside. He found that people who were not able to confide in someone about their trauma later visited physicians almost 40 percent more often than those who had a chance to openly discussed their trauma.

Other research labs later confirmed his studies. One related study with gays and lesbians who were out verses those who kept their sexual orientation a secret found the ones who were out had fewer major health problems. Overall the studies confirmed a positive immunological protection of being open with yourself.

These encouraging findings about talking versus not talking about trauma sparked the idea to see if the effects would be the same with writing. So in the mid 1980s Pennebaker conducted a study with fifty freshman college students. When they signed up, all they knew is that they would be writing for fifteen minutes a day for four consecutive days. Depending on a flip of a coin, they would be writing about traumatic or superficial, non emotional topics.

Students writing about traumatic experiences made 43 percent fewer doctor visits for illness than the control group who wrote only about superficial topics. They had significant beneficial immune function, including T helper cell growth. T helper cells are a type of white blood cells that play an important role in the immune system. Systolic blood pressure (upper number) and heart rate dropped significantly lower than before the writing began. And when tested four months after the writing, diastolic blood pressure (lower number) remained lower than their initial baseline.

There were other effects unrelated to the immune system. The students that wrote about trauma reported feeling happier and less negative in the long term than before writing. Reports of depressive symptoms, rumination, and general anxiety tended to drop in the weeks and months after writing about emotional upheavals. Other studies confirmed these results and went much farther, reporting better performance at school and better social relationships.

More recent studies found that when people first write about a trauma, they see and understand from their own perspective. But the most dramatic change comes when they are encouraged to switch perspectives. They benefit most when they see and write about events from another person's perspective.

The benefits of a self-distanced perspective was shown by Ethan Kross, Professor of Psychology at the University of Michigan. His research deals with a paradox in therapy. On the one hand it is helpful to analyze and understand one's feelings. On the other hand, people's attempts to do this are often counterproductive leading to rumination and/or avoidance.

His research addresses this paradox by having the client take a self-distanced or third-person perspective. Both Pennebaker and Kross found a self-distanced perspective was shown to cut down on rumination. Basically, self-distancing is at the core of Metacognitive Therapy and Insight Meditation.

Simple Guidelines

Pennebaker found that people benefit most from expressive writing by following simple guidelines:

1. Acknowledge your emotions openly.

Feel and label both the negative and the positive feelings that take place during and after the trauma.

2. Construct a coherent story.

The traumatic experience almost by definition is a mix of chaos and terror before and after the trauma. The goal of writing is to take disconnected events and put them back together into a meaningful story of what happened and how it is affecting you.

It brings to mind the ending paragraph of David Mean's short story, "Two Ruminations on a Homeless Brother." The piece was a sad and chaotic story of his homeless and mentally ill brother. As he drove away from visiting him at Rockland, now called Blaisdell Addiction Treatment Center:

> It's the fact that when you left him behind, speeding down the road past the old Rockland buildings, boarded up and unused now that most of the mad and crazy are outpatients, medicated, wandering the streets and the homeless shelters, you felt a keen elation. It's the fact that once again you were joyfully facing the harsh limitations of reality, admitting that it all had to be taken and turned into a story of some kind. Otherwise, it would just be one more expression of precise discontent. And expressions of discontent—you think in the car, sitting in front of your own house now—no matter how beautiful, never solve the riddle of the world, or bring the banality of sequential reality to a location of deeper grace.

3. Switch perspectives.

I found that effective when I took my mother's point of view. Up until then I hated her for being cold and unaffectionate with me. But taking her perspective, I saw that she was under terrific pressure and anxiety. She had no life preparation for the traumatic situation she was thrust into.

My father was unable to see and accept that my sister had a mental illness and needed kindness and acceptance, not hostility and alienation from the family. He wanted to be king on the throne, an accepted paternal role when he grew up. Whatever he said and believed was beyond challenge. With no counseling or prior knowledge of mental illness, my mother was in charge of my sister while satisfying my father's strict orders and commands, while keeping the family from falling, at least not completely, to pieces.

Taking her perspective helped to dissipate some of the trauma from chronic memories affecting my life, especially in my relations with other women. I was irrationally angry, hurt, and violent with most of them, but I had no way of preventing my violence. I was truly like Dr. Jekyll and Mr.

Hyde. If you only knew me as Mr. Hyde, the monster I would become as Dr. Jekyll was unthinkable.

At least a part of childhood adversity is recorded and stored in a part of the brain apart from the rational frontal cortex and inaccessible to the conscious mind. It took medication to stop the violence. Prozac does that for me and I doubt I will stop taking it.

4. Find your voice.

Impressive writing is not the point of expressive writing. Those who benefit the most are able to express themselves in their own words openly and honestly. You are writing for yourself. You can be open and honest with no fear of censorship. You can come out in the open with your most hidden secrets. You can express exactly who you are without pretension. Even though it is for your eyes only, it can be difficult to hang everything out there.

Unless you are comfortable sharing your writing, though, put this writing somewhere absolutely out of anyone's curious eyes. To avoid an uncomfortable confrontation, it might be best to have your own computer access password. I say this, yet leave my file on my desktop. But my wife sometimes does not even read the things I email to her to read. (Yes, we communicate in the same house by email.)

Studies compare the effect on health of using positive words (happy, joy, pleasure, laugh) versus negative words (sad, cry, angry, hate) when writing about traumatic or negative emotional experiences. The more positive words used in the writing, the more the health of the person improved as evidenced by the drop in physician visits in the months after writing. One interpretation is that using positive words reflects a reappraisal of the trauma in a broader life sense that may reflect a change in perspective. But I never attempted to use positive words in my writing and I did not encourage my students to do so.

Writing shapes the chaos of trauma, failure, disappointment, emotional hurt, and pathology into an exploration and search for a more meaningful and purposeful well being. And that is the goal, a more meaningful life, not to eliminate problems that will always be with us.

10 METACOGNITIVE THERAPY (MCT)

Metacognition

The first time I heard the term was when I came to Seattle in 1992 and took graduate educational psychology courses. Metacognition had become a buzzword. In its simplest definition, metacognition is about understanding your thinking process. The term metacognition was coined in 1979 by American developmental psychologist John Flavell. Flavell defined metacognition as knowledge about and control of cognition.

Metacognitive Therapy (MCT)

(http://joeldames.com/metacognitive-therapy/)

Metacognition had little or nothing to do with psychotherapy until 1994 when Adrian Wells of the University of Manchester, UK described Metacognitive Therapy (MCT) in a series of research papers.

MCT steps back from perceived problems rather than attempting to solve them head on. It shifts from a focus on problems to a focus on thinking style. It involves a cognitive shift from what you are thinking to how you think.

The content of what people think can be virtually anything. The thought process, though, involves a constant pattern of worry and rumination. MCT focuses on this recurrent, recycling, ideation of worry and rumination. MCT involves the process or pattern of thinking, rather than the cognitive content. Psychological disorder occurs principally as a result of extended thinking which prolongs emotion. Of importance is not the belief or thought, but the way you respond to the belief or thought, the pattern by which you process thoughts and beliefs.

Cognitive-Attentional Syndrome (CAS)

Rather than focusing on the thought, MCT steps back to look at the thinking process. Is this an old repeated thought pattern? Biased, repetitive patterns of worry, rumination, fixation of attention on threat, and coping behaviors, feed the monster and keep emotional problems alive and well. Wells named this maze of thinking the Cognitive-Attentional Syndrome (CAS).

This maze of worrisome behaviors keep emotional fires burning by increasing the sense of danger, creating a vicious cycle of escalating fear and anxiety. Worry and rumination disrupt a built-in recovery process. Instead of top-down control via the frontal cortex executive brain center, a bottom-up surge from the deep, emotional limbic brain takes control.

CAS is an attentional strategy of threat monitoring. Attention gets fixed on threatening stimuli. A person with OCD monitors forbidden thoughts, feelings, and behaviors. A paranoid monitors people's suspicious behaviors. The hypochondriac monitors the body for signs of disease. Threat monitoring increases access to negative information and maintains the sense of threat.

Patterns Over Problems

A cognitive therapist works with perceived problems. A metacognitive therapist works with CAS patterns of worry, rumination, fixation, and other unhelpful self-regulatory problem and coping strategies. The core principle of MCT is that psychological disorder is linked to unhealthy patterns of thinking that maintain emotional disturbance and strengthen negative ideation.

MCT deals with the way you think, the inflexible, recurrent styles of thinking in response to negative thoughts, feelings, and beliefs. You cannot think or ruminate your way out of chronic mental problems. Mental problems are the inflexible, recurrent, ruminating, perseverating thinking style.

The cognitive behavior therapist asks, "Where is the evidence?" The metacognitive therapist asks, "What is the point in evaluating your worth?" The answer is there is no point. It takes you spiraling in unending harmful patterns of thought and behavior.

Some people believe they are ugly and put their energy into getting an education and working hard at whatever they do in life. Others believe they are ugly and slip into a chain of thoughts, brooding about unsolvable problems that become paradoxical Zen koans.

Instead of questioning and reality-testing thoughts, feelings, and beliefs, MCT focuses on how you respond to thoughts, feelings, and beliefs. MCT steps back, examining thought processes and patterns. Most people think the thoughts about themselves and the world are reality. But thoughts and beliefs are filters for viewing oneself and the world, each of us with our own unique filters.

Attention Training Therapy (ATT)

ATT is a Metacognitive (MCT) method of working on reducing Cognitive Attentional Syndrome (CAS) patterns of thinking and behaving. These sound exercises parallel the visual Open-Focus ones. Wells developed ATT to reduce perseverative thinking, increase attentional flexibility, reduce self-focused attention, and respond more appropriately to events in the external world.

On his mp3, you listen to sounds individually and in combinations while focusing your gaze on a fixed mark ahead. You can find instructions in his book, "Metacognitive Therapy for Anxiety and Depression." I would add OCD to the title.

You first monitor or assess the extent of self-focus, which is considerable when you are obsessing about your body. Wells devised a simple scale from -3 to +3 where -3 is entirely self-focused on thoughts,feelings, and behavior and +3 is entirely focused on task or environment. Task includes something as basic as having a conversation and focusing on the other person rather than self. The environment means everything going on outside you.

Wells developed sound-based exercises similar to open-focus exercises. His recorded ATT exercises run for a total of eleven minutes and thirty seconds. You focus first on the voice of the narrator, ignoring all distracting sounds.

You focus on a ticking clock, church bells, traffic sounds, birds singing, running water, and insects chirping. You focus on sounds outside of the recorded sounds, sounds from the space about you. You focus on the spaces to your left and right, then back to a focus on the sounds on the recording, shifting focus among the different sounds and areas of space, as guided by the narrator. You focus on the sounds away from the recording, on the spaces around you, shifting back to the sounds of the recording, away from the recording, and back. Finally, you focus on sounds in as broad a scope as you can.

It is difficult to sort out and isolate some of the sounds on the recording, but listening to these sound exercises is practice for ATT Open-Focus in the real world. Sounds are a distraction in the workplace. You can work with these sounds as you would the recorded exercises, moving and shifting from sound to sound, background to foreground, space to space, selecting your focus, moving on to another focus. You can listen to all sounds together, seeing how many you can hear and focus on, sounds to the space on your left, right, background, foreground, above, below.

When I was teaching, one or two students would try to distract me with tapping and crinkling paper sounds. If I were not heavily drugged on some form of diazepam, I could not focus on what I was saying. The classroom is a perfect on-the-job training for these exercises. The exercises begin by focusing on the tapping sound and expanding from there. With practice, I would have been able to function in the classroom with less, maybe even without diazepam. But I missed that chance and the opportunity to share the training with my students. But I have successfully used the technique now outside of the classroom.

MCT shines a light on CAS. You recognize patterns of thinking and coping that lock you into states of emotional distress. You work on replacing them with more productive ways of focusing.

Most psychotherapy is content based, focusing on what you think and believe are your problems. This drives an obsessive thinker deep into content-based-ruminations, dwelling on unresolvable problems. It is far more productive to step back in a flexible, mindful way and attend to patterns of thoughts and feelings.

Body Dysmorphic Disorder (BDD) & Gender Dysphoria

A core principle of MCT is that psychological disorder is linked to unhealthy patterns of thinking that maintain emotional disturbance and strengthen negative ideas. These patterns, the Cognitive Attentional Syndrome (CAS), consist of worry, rumination, fixated attention, and unhelpful self-regulatory strategies and coping behaviors.

CAS is the problem. You cannot think or ruminate your way out of Body Dysmorphic Disorder (BDD) and Gender Dysphoria. BDD and Gender Dysphoria are inflexible, recurrent, ruminating, perseverating, CAS patterns of thought.

I have found MCT to be effective with BDD. In Diagnostic and Statistical Manual of Mental Disorders (DSM)-2 era of my high school and college years, obsessive compulsive disorder was obsessive compulsive neurosis. It wasn't until DSM-3 in 1980 that "neurosis" became "disorder." That actually made a difference. I could not have found employment early on had I disclosed an obsessive compulsive neurosis, not that I would have disclosed this to anyone.

DSM 5 removed OCD from anxiety disorders, giving it a chapter of its own that includes body dysmorphic disorder (BDD). Dys for bad and morphic, form, so dysmorphic ironically means badly formed. One criteria for BDD in DSM 5 is a preoccupation with perceived defects or flaws in appearance that are not observable or appear slight to others. A significant change is the word "perceived." In DSM 4 it was "imagined." DSM 3 used the word "delusional." "Perceived" is a step toward recognizing and legitimizing BDD.

Though it is thought to affect 1-2% of the population and 29% of those with BDD have attempted suicide, BDD is a neglected disorder, first appearing in DSM 3 as dysmorphophobia and renamed Body Dysmorphic

Disorder with the release of DSM-3-R. In 1987, most people with this disorder experienced shame and would never discuss it, even with their doctor. In 2013, DSM 5 brought BDD under the umbrella of OCD, cracking the closet door open a slit on BDD. I was into my mid seventies and still that meant a lot to me.

In high school I could not stand my body. Dumbo ears, my nose had a sharp, evil slant, my lips and chin unacceptable. At puberty my body did not develop muscularity. I was thinner than any of the girls in my class. I spent hours standing naked before the mirror, detesting what I saw.

At Rutgers, I sat deep in the library stacks with William Sheldon's collection of four thousand male nudes photographed from every angle. Sheldon devised a standardized numerical measurement classifying body types into ectomorphs, mesomorphs, and endomorphs. I lifted weights and looked for indications I might be morphing into a mesomorph. I spent so much time in the stacks with Sheldon, I flunked most of my first-year pre-pharmacy classes, ending up on probation. I solved that by changing my major to psychology and receive college credit for my obsessions.

DSM-5 includes a subtype of BDD called Muscle Dysmorphia, belief one's body is too small or insufficiently muscular. I am not alone. I cherish the thought that some of my fellow body builders grunting and groaning with pain as they push heavier and heavier iron, may too be motivated by Muscle Dysmorphia. Shadenfreude!

Cognitive Therapy for BDD

Cognitive therapy is a part of BDD therapy, an adjunct at least for metacognitive therapy (MCT). You can enjoy life if you are the weakest, ugliest person on this planet. You can enjoy movies and reading books. You can enjoy learning new things, playing an instrument, learning a language, learning how to get the most out of life. If you are the ugliest person on the planet you may likely not do as well as you might desire attracting a mate, but this is not a disaster.

Cognitive therapy helps to see you don't have to be loved by significant people who you select in your life. You do not need to be loved all of the time or feel that somebody must love you completely and give you approval. The more of a needy person you are, the more boring you are to others who are also into themselves.

Conquering the Dire Need for Love

Healthy people have a positive slant, viewing themselves as more rather than less attractive. They view themselves as a whole, whereas people with BDD focus on the parts of their face or body they consider ugly and ignore the features that are more attractive. They do the opposite of viewing the world with "rose-colored glasses." So a cognitive goal is to shift in the direction of a more self-serving, positive bias.

Both Cognitive Therapy and Metacognitive Therapy for BDD involve a shift of focus away from appearance, e.g., I am my nose, my legs, my body. Attention in healthy individuals is more on tasks. So you work on shifting focus from the body to tasks and the environment. In terms of dividing a pie, the endgame goal might be a complete reversal to 10% self and 90% to include education, family, friendship, learning new things, expanding one's horizons, etc. It is a shift from internal to external focus and from narrow to diffuse focus. It involves working towards thinking of yourself without self-rating or self-judgement.

It is a shift away from the idea that if my nose or ears or eyes or legs were acceptable to me, life would be better. It is an understanding that my appearance does not have to be acceptable before I can enjoy life. It is a shift from the view of the self as an object keeping me from enjoying life. "Felt impression" is at the heart of BDD, imagery that has become fused with negative experiences resulting in extreme self-consciousness and bias. BDD thrives on self-focus and ghosts from the past. Cognitive therapy assists the shift from the belief that if I am ugly or defective, I cannot enjoy life and life is not worth living.

Change will likely not come about by attempting to convince someone with BDD they are not ugly or that they look okay. They are 100% convinced that they do not look okay. It is more than an appearance problem. They spend their lives looking in mirrors and comparing themselves with most everyone. Their preoccupation with an appearance together with an uncomfortable past makes life a painful challenge.

The goal is to view the problem as BDD and to decrease "safety behaviors" that include self-focused attention, comparing, mirror gazing, and cosmetic surgery. The goal is letting go of an unproductive focus on appearance that blocks or detracts from the enjoyment of life now.

MTC and Cognitive Therapy for Gender Dysphoria is much the same as for Body Dysmorphic Disorder (BDD).

Gender Dysphoria

I might never have thought much about Gender Dysphoria had I not come across a young woman in her twenties on a site called PsychForums. The title of her post was "Some days I feel insane." She starts off by saying that her Body Dysmorphic Disorder became apparent from puberty, but her gender identity since birth. Her blog was written two years before DSM-V changed the category from gender identity disorder to Gender Dysphoria. She views herself as having a very beautiful androgynous face, though from her photo, I don't detect the androgyny.

She swaps back and forth between genders, injecting herself with testosterone to become more masculine, since her body is normally thin. As a guy, her BDD centers around her small overall size and her face, neck, eyes, and midsection, which she perceives to be feminine.

When she takes estrogen, her BDD centers around her lean muscular shoulders, toned back, arms and legs, and what she calls pectus excavatum, a slight dip in the chest, causing the rib cage to flare out. She admits her pectus excavatum is very mild, but it is there and that is enough to upset her.

She contemplates surgery to make her body more feminine at times, and surgery to make her body more masculine at other times. Her condition seems to be stable 60-70% of the time and then all of a sudden she is anxious, stressed, depressed, and ambivalent in regards to her appearance and gender. At these times she focuses on her perceived flaws, obsessing, searching the internet to see others with the same problem to try to make herself feel better.

I wanted to reach out to her, but she was no longer posting on the site. I guess I would tell her that though I am 80 and she is 28 and we are different genders, I understand what she is experiencing. I experienced the pain of a male caught in a body I perceived as too feminine. I hated my body every day of my life since puberty. I compensated by body building, obsessively. I lost the chance at becoming an executive of a large company early on, because I had to leave at 5 p.m. each day to go to the YMCA and lift weights for three hours. Including the commute and showering after the workout barely left time other than preparing for and eating supper, then sleeping.

Ironically, I would go out on a date and resent a girl for admiring and feeling my muscles. If I got into a relationship I felt a weird jealousy. It was as if she were being unfaithful to me. I was not the muscular man she was attracted to. In my mind, I was slender and completely non muscular. I longed to find a girl who would love me for who I was. But if I continued to body build, I would never be able to know that. And if I stopped body building, I could not walk into a bar or dance and pick up a girl. The answer was a never-ending series of extremely short-time affairs.

Too fat, too thin, too muscular, not enough muscle, too much hair, too little hair, too ugly, too masculine, too feminine. Thoughts pop into your mind like garish, uninvited guests. You mostly hear about body image problems with girls and women. But it starts with men early on.

I think it took root with me back in the 1940s when I spent much of my time reading comic books. At the back of these comic books, Charles Atlas's Dynamic Tension advertisement first appeared early in the 1940s. The "97-pound weakling" sits on sits on the beach, his girlfriend beside him. Along comes this hunk who laughs and kicks sand in his face. He is helpless to defend himself and sits there humiliated. That potent, emotional image got reinforced and layered with comments like, "Why are you so skinny?"

BDD and Gender Dysphoria are a life centered on safety-seeking behaviors of weight-loss, weight-gain diets, workouts, mirror viewing, and constantly comparing bodies. Weight lifting creates a shield, my first psychoanalyst said. But not only is body building a safety-seeking behavior, it sets up a condition for preconditioned self-acceptance. You accept yourself when you look in the mirror and appear buff, but when the body building comes to an end, so does conditional self-acceptance.

Therapy for BDD and gender dysphoria had best include working on unconditional self acceptance. This means accepting yourself fat, skinny, ugly, old, masculine, feminine, as you are. Precondition sets you up for trouble. It is irrational not to accept yourself unconditionally. Why would you do otherwise? You are the decider. But we are not rational and it is not easy to accept ourselves unconditionally. I never could give up weight training. At least it gets me out and very occasionally interacting with people.

11 COGNITIVE "RATIONAL" THERAPY (CT)

Counseling 0.0000005 – Fifty Bits– of Brain

I read Albert Ellis's books and listened over and over to his tapes, yet I was a raging monster. I felt a part or maybe most of my brain was not rational and could not be reached by CT.

How do you give 50 bits of attention to Rational Emotive Behavior Therapy (REBT)? I can focus on my breath in tough times. But when I try focusing on REBT, there is nothing to give my attention over to. Nothing substantial comes readily to mind.

I can give my attention to REBT or Cognitive Therapy (CT), though, by reading books by Albert Ellis, Albert Beck, or Adrian Wells. I can give full attention then for several minutes. Little by little, bit by bit finally starts to take hold unconsciously. For me, that was over a period of many years.

REBT and Attachment Therapy

On the surface, differences between Attachment Theory and Rational-Emotive-Behavior Therapy (REBT) are irreconcilable. Attachment Theory attributes adjustment/maladjustment to mother/child relationship very early on; warm, loving, accepting, supportive mother versus cold, neglecting, rejecting mother.

The focus of Albert Ellis's REBT is on what you are telling yourself now. The Activating Event (A) is not the main cause of Emotional-Behavioral Consequences (C). Emotional-Behavioral consequences are more directly affected by (B), beliefs, rational or irrational. Somewhat oversimplifying, rational beliefs (rB) serve self-interest and goals; irrational beliefs (iB) work against self-interest and goals.

According to Ellis, your early childhood experiences and past conditioning do not originally make you disturbed. The Activating Event

(A) does not directly cause Consequences (C). Your beliefs cause C. If your mother was cold and rejecting (A) and you felt miserable (C), it was your beliefs about A that caused you to feel miserable at C. Though A contributes to C, it never really causes C. In an interview with Ellis, he said he realized early on that his mother was crazy and after that he was not bothered by her words and actions.

Though Ellis appears to be contradicting the core principal of Bowlby's Attachment Theory, surely, he could not have meant that a one or two year old child can control his feelings of parental rejection. Ellis is offering a perspective to look back on childhood. If the child were able to think rationally, he would realize that although it would be much better if mother acted warmly, he does not need her to do so. He would realize that her coldness (A) is not what is causing him to feel miserable. It is his irrational belief (iB) that she must treat him warmly that is the major cause of his distress.

This perspective helps to stop reliving your childhood. To stop saying that is why I am who I am today and I can't do much to change that. Because I never felt the love of my mother as a child, I will go on in this screwed up painful state now as an adult. Ellis would want you to challenge memories of past events as they apply to your present adult life, so that you can choose not to keep these beliefs vibrant today.

iB: You are saying you not only want your mother's approval, but you need it. You must have it. Because you never felt the love of your mother as a child, you will go on in this screwed up painful state now as an adult.

rB: I want my mother's love, but I do not need it.

Ellis is saying you need to stop actively holding on to childhood beliefs. Rethink and react against these iBs until you no longer use them to upset yourself today. You can acknowledge your mother's cold behavior and at the same time accept that you are now creating your miserable feelings.

This does not blame the child for having these beliefs. It is an admission of irrational thinking today holding you back. It is about exploring what you are doing now to cause your upset feelings and to work to make changes in thinking right now that will better serve your interests and goals.

Counseling the Child Within

This involves convincing him/her that he/she is making her/himself miserable. Your mother/father was cold, unsupportive, and non nurturing. At the same time, it is your iBs that you can't stand her/his coldness and absolutely need and must have his/her love and nurturance.

You arm your child self with rational beliefs (rBs)

rB: "I would prefer my mother acting warmly and nurturing, but this is her problem and not mine. I can make close friends, even find myself a substitute mother/father in a teacher at school, at extra curricular events, or the parents of a friend. I can study hard and do well with or without her nurturance."

You counsel your childhood self to replace harmful iBs with helpful rBs.

iBs: My mother was cold and non nurturing, and according to Attachment theory, I will be screwed up and unable to form social or intimate relationships. I am pissed off and would like to go back and blow her brains out.

Substitute rBs: My mother was a young woman with no preparation for marriage, child rearing, or the situation she would find herself in. Her mother might have been distant and not nurturing to her. I would have liked my mother to love and nurture me, but she was a woman with difficult situational problems. I don't need her to have been accepting and nurturing. I will work at mental fitness as much as at physical fitness. I will work at accepting myself and choose not to be constrained by childhood beliefs.

Each time iBs surface, actively challenge and dispute them. At the same time acknowledge life does not have to be free of hassles and mental conflicts.

Of course I never will be free of hassles and mental conflicts, but I can lead an enjoyable life and learn from these past, present, and future hassles and mental conflicts.

In more than 75 books, Ellis offers examples of iBs and how to deal with them in every aspect of life. The REBT method never changes. "A" for Activating Events; "B" for Beliefs, rBs (rational) and iBs (irrational); "C" for Consequences of iBs; "D" for Disputing iBs; and G for Goals that are blocked by iBs.

Stop Musturbating! Don't Should on Yourself!

According to REBT, whenever you think of the present or past and you feel upset or act "self-defeatingly", look for an irrational must (musterbation), should, or ought. "He/she should never had said that behind my back. It was terrible for him/her to do that. He/she must never do it again. He/she should not treat me like that when I am so good to him/her. I must never get upset when he/she treats me poorly."

When you uncover the musts and shoulds, look for the "catastrophizing" that usually accompanies them: "awfulizing, horribleizing, terribleizing, cant stand-it-itis."

If you get upset and miserable because of the anxiety, depression and guilt, these are the second and third level arrows in REBT. Acknowledge you are feeling upset, depressed, anxious, or guilty, etc. You create these feelings by reacting to your reactions to your initial, primary iBs. You create your secondary iBs in the same way as the primary iBs. And since you create them, you have ability to work at changing them. Challenge and dispute the secondary iBs just as you challenge and dispute the original primary iBs.

Look for the musts and shoulds with the secondary beliefs. Stop "musturbating." "I must not be so upset and anxious. It's terrible that I panic like this." As Ellis liked to put it, "Ask where is it writ that you should not be that upset or that anxious. It is uncomfortable and you don't like it, but that is the world we react to."

Feelings: Appropriate/Inappropriate

With REBT, strong feelings of sadness, irritation and concern are considered appropriate and healthy. They help to express displeasure at undesirable happenings and allow you to work at modifying them.

But feelings of depression, anger, and anxiety are usually harmful and inappropriate. They stem from unrealistic commands that unpleasant events absolutely must not exist, and these commands usually interfere with changing or modifying unpleasant events when they do exist.

If you feel disappointment and regret about your boss passing you over for a position, you will be more likely to make an attempt to find out why you have been passed over and perhaps explore alone, or together with a trusted coworker, what you can do that might help you to be considered for a slot in the future.

It is appropriate even to abhor the injustice of being passed over, but at the same time being determined to fight against it. If however, you feel panic, depression, and rage about not being chosen and obsess over it, lose confidence, and not take steps that may help you when a future position comes up, this does not serve you and so is inappropriate. You choose, albeit not easily, between being greatly displeased, but determined to act against unfairness, or being angry, enraged and inactive and feeling helpless.

You "create" both appropriate and inappropriate feelings when your goals and desires are blocked. Inappropriate feelings stem from commanding, dictatorial thoughts, such as, "I absolutely must get this position. It is unfair and I cannot stand injustice. My boss should not behave that way to me. I have to put an end to this and must be treated fairly." The goal of REBT is to work at changing inappropriate harmful feelings to more appropriate desires, wishes, and preferences that overall help you to achieve and not sabotage your goals. As Ellis would say, stop the "musterbation."

Most of us don't have a therapist available at any time of day or night. Ellis is as real in his writing as he is in person and perhaps more so in his audio recordings of his Friday night workshops. It takes time for REBT to sink in and become a functional part of your Narrator. Read a page or so from one of his books as a part of a daily mind-lifting routine.

Unconditional Self-Acceptance

You are the only one who can unconditionally accept yourself. It is irrational to put preconditions on fully accepting who you are when you can choose to accept yourself unconditionally. You can choose not to, but the choice is irrational. It is not rational to choose anything that keeps you from working on a philosophy of self-acceptance and self-actualization.

Unconditional self-acceptance is essential to well-being and peace of mind. Others may or may not accept you, and may put you down. It is essential that you accept yourself, though, without preconditions. When you set conditions for acceptance, you accept yourself when you do well or when others rate you highly, praise you, and seem to accept you. But accepting yourself with preconditions means, for example, unless you do well and others accept you, you do not fully accept yourself. You put up roadblocks blocking growth.

Some of these roadblocks are shoulds, oughts, musts, commands and demands, implicitly or explicitly governing our lives. We want to be competent, accepted, and appreciated. We want praise and good performance ratings. We want to be loved by our families. But turning these wants into preconditions for self-acceptance stacks the deck against us and sets us up for suffering.

Letting go of preconditions for self-acceptance does not mean we no longer want to be competent, accepted and appreciated. We all want all this and most of us want more. We want a great body, success, and an abundance of wealth. Suffering in the form of anxiety, depression, and stress, comes from replacing wants to conditions for self-acceptance.

Choosing to accept yourself and be as happy as you can, warts and all, is philosophically sound. Choosing not to accept yourself, though also philosophically sound, is an irrational choice, since non-acceptance or preconditioned self-acceptance blocks your goal of an enjoyable life.

It is not easy, but you absolutely can do this. You can accept all the parts of your body as a part of a unique you. It is not easy, but it is essential. When you learn to accept yourself unconditionally, legs, butt, chest, breasts, nose lips, face, hair (or lack of), this will be a major step toward a solid foundation of mental health. No one can tell you how to do this. You must find the way.

Others will define you. They will say you should be this and shouldn't be that. They will ask why you are so fat or thin. Why you are so effeminate or macho.

Well, they'll stone you when you walk all alone

They'll stone you when you are walking home

They'll stone you and then say you are brave

They'll stone you when you are set down in your grave

But I would not feel so all alone

Everybody must get stoned

Bob Dylan

It took me seventy years. Then it took an instant. I could have accepted myself unconditionally in any prior instant of my life. Amazing. Or as Albert Ellis phrased it, "Fucked up, fallible human beings."

Unconditionally Accepting Others

It is hard enough to unconditionally accept ourselves. It is a really difficult and maybe impossible to unconditionally accept others. But letting go of hating and blaming is unburdening a load that makes this life easier.

You can sit around all day and blame others for the suffering you have endured and are continuing to endure. It is not a good idea, though, because the more you do this the worse you feel, and the more you will continue feeling lousy. If you want to feel good more of the time, you need to attempt to begin to practice letting go of hate and blame. It takes lots of doing, over and over. It's at least somewhat doable!

Rational Emotive Self-Talk (REST) Script #1

No matter how or when I acquired my irrational beliefs and habits, I now, in the present, choose to maintain them and that is why I am now disturbed. Poor conditions in the past and present affect me, but they don't disturb me. My present philosophy creates my current disturbance.

It is not easy to let go of blaming and damning. It is a pattern of thinking that is easy to fall back on. But if there is comfort, it is short lived. The long-lasting hatred, anger, and mental and physical upset and discomfort puts you on the negative side of the scale of equanimity.

REST Script #2

I accept the fact that though conditions in my life are not as comfortable and free from hassle as I would like them to be, but that's the way things are and will most likely continue to be. It's not awful or horrible and I can stand it and will continue to stand it.

We want things to be comfortable and free of hassle. But the Buddhists got it pretty much right. We are all suffering. Even the people who seem to have it all are suffering. Just when you think you have it made, life beans you with a fast ball. It takes ongoing awareness to maintain our welfare. What is important is to not slip into self-defeating states of mind and stack the deck against you.

REST Script #3

Anything I choose to believe, I can choose not to believe, even though I have been strongly indoctrinated, and now indoctrinate myself.

REST Script #4

I am never an incompetent or rotten person for making myself anxious and making myself anxious about my anxiety. I am merely a person who has some unfortunate philosophies that I can work at changing.

As Ellis liked to say, "No matter how badly I inconvenience and handicap myself with feelings of stress and panic, they are only that, inconvenient. Never awful or horrible! Only, a royal pain in the neck!

If it helps, make your own scripts.

Just Do It!

Early on, Ellis said, "Do it and emotions will follow." This was his advice as to intimacy, when the feeling is gone. When an ultra-orthodox rabbi approaches a Jew in a mall, rather than tell them to come learn about Judaism, he has them put on tefillin right then and there. Tefillin or phylacteries are a small set of leather boxes containing parchment inscribed with verses from the Torah. One box is placed above the elbow of the left arm, with a thin leather strap wound around the forearm and hand. The other box is placed on the forehead. The point is to start with the action, not talking or learning about the meaning of the action. It is not necessary to believe in God; it is necessary to go through the physical motions.

Does REBT Work?

When I was in Japan, a Japanese friend read my book and said REBT doesn't work. Does reading a book about maestros make you a musician? A change in the way you think by changing self-defeating beliefs and indoctrinating yourself with beliefs that bring better results is an ongoing lifetime process. We humans are not rational beings. It takes conscious effort to think even a bit more rationally. Like pure drops of water falling into a bucket of dirty, clouded water, drip by drip the dirty water is replaced by the pure water. But there is always more dirty water to be replaced.

So many self-help books explicitly or implicitly promise major change within a short period of time. I have devoted my life to exploring mental and physical fitness and I have not found a program that comes through on that promise. Mental and physical fitness are lifetime commitments, not a short term fix. If you stop working, you slide. That is not the message most people want to hear and not a message that sells books.

Though Ellis's books are clearly written and easy to understand, you don't digest and make REBT a part of your life in a read through. You digest it in bits and pieces and ingest and digest the same material again and again, applying REBT to life's traumas and every-day hassles and ruminations, through all the slipping and sliding.

If you routinely workout and pick up helpful tips along the way, you gradually will get in shape. The same for mental fitness. It is a commitment to get and stay in good mental shape.

But there is no fitness center for mental fitness. It is not easy to get in good mental shape. We are in the dark ages. I combine Bibliotherapy, Metacognitive Therapy, Attention Training Therapy, Cognitive Therapy, Open-Focus Training, and Ki Meditation Breathing. Sounds like a lot, but it takes little to no extra time off my day.

12 MINDFULNESS

Our 50 bits of attending limits the scope of what each of us perceives. Each of us perceives a version of what is out there. We live in a world of inattention blindness that can be vastly different for each of us, creating a world of people to people, nation to nation, disagreement and conflict.

Daniel Simons, professor in the Department of Psychology and the Beckman Institute for Advanced Science and Technology at the University of Illinois, studies the limits of our minds and the reasons why we often are unaware of our limits. You can experience what it is like to be a subject in his studies by viewing a couple of his short videos that are available for purchase on his website. A few can be viewed on Youtube (http://www.dansimons.com/videos.html).

In perhaps the most well known of his experiments, the Invisible Gorilla, instructions are to count the number of passes of a basketball made by players in the white tops and ignore the passes made by players in the black tops. In the midst of these players passing the basketball, a person in a gorilla suit enters, stands among the players, and beats on her/his chest before walking off. Although the gorilla is there for about nine seconds, fifty percent of those viewing this video fail to notice the creature.

For the most part, we are distracted not by external stimuli, but by an inner cacophony of competing thoughts and feelings. Constantly we interrupt ourselves. Some researchers call this mind wandering. Others call it time travel. Three people in a room listen to three different internal dialogs going at the same time. Three separate dialogues, three spaces, three focal points of attending. It is a kaleidoscope cacophony of images, sounds, and thoughts.

Though we get annoyed at someone drifting away while we are talking, mind wandering or time travel allows us to contemplate parallel thoughts and goals, reaching forward and back well beyond the limits of the immediate content of the conversation. We all do this. We need to remind ourselves of this when someone fails to hear or respond to what we are saying.

Track Your Suffering

In a 2010 study, with an iPhone app, "Track Your Happiness," Harvard psychologists Matthew A. Killingsworth and Daniel T. Gilbert found that a wandering mind is an unhappy mind. The "Track Your Happiness" app interrupted 2,250 volunteers at random intervals to ask how happy they were, what they were currently doing, and whether they were thinking about their current activity or about something else that was pleasant, neutral, or unpleasant.

Subjects could choose from 22 general activities, such as walking, eating, shopping, and watching television. On average, respondents reported thinking of something other than the involved activity 46.9 percent of the time. So 47 percent of the day is spent thinking about something other than immediate surroundings and most of this mental wandering does not make us happy.

Mark Thornton, author of "Meditation in a New York Minute," conducted a seminar for a Fortune 100 company. Participants sat for few minutes, jotting their most common thoughts. What do they think about in the morning when they get up, while commuting to work, while eating lunch? When they completed listing, they grouped the thoughts into common themes like anxious, content, joyous, fearful, etc.

The categories from these sessions were almost entirely negative with themes like stress, anxious, anger and depressed. These were highly successful people in a top company, the same people that respond "just fine," "terrific," "great," when you inquire how they are doing, Most people would not want to share they are suffering. No one wants to share their precious time with whiners; not unless you are a therapist who monetizes suffering.

You may have attempted to focus on breathing and lasted at most two or three breaths before thoughts churned through your mind for the nth plus time. Thousands of thoughts go through our minds each day, mostly the same thoughts as yesterday; the same internal confrontations with the same people. We replay events, actual and imagined, over and over. If someone were to come up and started telling you the stuff you are telling yourself, you would look for the nearest exit. Everyday narrative, discursive thinking wears you down.

Gain Access to Patterns of Thinking

Minds wander. This is what minds do. You can't stop your mind from wandering for long. You can't stop thinking. But you can focus on your breath and attempt to be mindful of whatever takes you away from this focus. Mindfulness is just that. Be mindful of thoughts, sounds, smells, emotions or feelings. Anything taking you away from this mindful state is what you want to be mindful of. You never fully arrive. Mindfulness is always a practice.

We can gain access to patterns of thinking by attending to breathing, exploring the breath as we take it in, feeling the breath moving through and nourishing body and mind. From this refreshed state we can be meta aware of thoughts, sounds, feelings, emotions, aches, pains, and bodily sensations as an observer rather than a critic. When our mind wanders, we settle back into our breathing, stabilizing and quieting our minds. Mindful breathing with Open Focus is a base to return to each time our mind wanders.

The body provides feedback about how we are affected by and how we react to outside and internal events. The body is the container for emotions. We feel and are present for wordless, sensory body experiences instead of experiences dominated by narrative chatter.

We can work at releasing fixed ideas and interpretations about feelings, emotions and urges. We allow sensations to be present, experiencing feelings and sensation in the body, rather than in the mind. We can work at experiencing feelings, thoughts, emotions and urges as an observer, with simple uninvolved noting. "Isn't that thought/feeling/emotion, interesting?"

By controlling focus, we can attend to the tone of our experience in the body. We can tune in to experience of our body instead of a story about our body from the Narrator's subjective and often judgmental spiel.

It is All About Suffering, Stupid

Buddha is reported to have said, I teach one thing and one thing only, suffering and the end of suffering. Buddhism consists of four Noble truths. First, suffering occurs universally in each of us. To live is to suffer. As we move through life we encounter sickness and pain, loss of lives, loss of love, disappointment in others and ourselves, and frustration about not being able to reach our most cherished goals. Suffering is the common bond of humanity. We don't usually see the suffering in others, but accepting it is there in each of us makes it a bit easier to ease up on judging others.

Alfred Adler and Viktor Frankl knew that understanding human nature lies not with psychologists and psychiatrists schooled in theory, but with those who have suffered and survived. Nothing compares with this depth of understanding. Our values are shaped and actualized by the unalterable suffering imposed upon us. Much of our inner achievements and artistic greatness is built upon a scaffolding of suffering.

Suffering guards one from apathy, from psychic rigor mortis. As long as we suffer, we remain psychically alive. We mature in suffering; grow because of it. It makes us richer and stronger.

> Suffering and trouble belong to life as much as fate and
> death. None of these can be subtracted from life without
> destroying its meaning. To subtract trouble, death, fate, and
> suffering from life would mean stripping it of its form and
> shape. Under the hammer blows of fate, in the white heat
> of suffering, does life gain shape and form. Page 111 "The
> Doctor and the Soul," Victor Frankl.

Ending Suffering

The third (not in order) of the four basic truths is that the possibility for ending suffering exists. Not that we can do away with physical and emotional pain, since they are a part of life. We will continue to experience physical pain and discomfort. The third basic truth concerns avoiding optional, not inevitable, pain and suffering.

Unavoidable pain is the first arrow. You are waiting on a cold windy corner for someone who is very late. You are not dressed warmly enough and you feel the cold wind go right through you. Unbearably discomforting and painful, but that is what happens, especially if you are not dressed for the weather. Now you begin to think, he/she doesn't respect me or he/she should not keep me waiting like this. You begin to feel annoyed and angry. This optional pain is the second arrow, the interpretation that may or may not be true.

The second of the four Buddhist truths is that suffering is craving or desire. Not that all craving and desire leads to suffering, just obsessive craving and desire. In addition to craving and desire, aversion to suffering creates suffering. If craving, desire and aversion lead to suffering, that means major parts of our lives, create suffering. How do you deal with suffering?

Vipassana Insight Meditation

Buddhism centers about the seventh of the Noble Eightfold Path—mindfulness. When mindfulness is thorough, the other parts of the path follow in its wake. With Vipassana Insight Meditation, you pay attention to when suffering arises and take an interest in it instead of attempting to avert it. You learn to be comfortable with suffering instead of shooting second, third, and fourth arrows. You may even begin to see the roots of your suffering.

In what may first seem a paradox, Buddhism is intolerable to suffering. Not the suffering that comes with being human, since physical and emotional pain are part of the human condition. Buddhism is intolerable to optional, second, third, and fourth arrows of suffering. We become irritated, angry, and hostile at the inevitable suffering of physical and emotional pain. We cling to a joy that has passed. We are depressed and obsessed with brain messages that remind us persistently we are too fat, too thin, too masculine, too feminine, ugly.

It is possible, though, to experience pain in a straightforward, uncomplicated way that avoids optional suffering by not attaching ourselves to the Narrator's messages. The Narrator can be the major source of suffering. As difficult as mindfulness may be, the alternative is one of extreme pain, not the straightforward uncomplicated pain, but the agony of dealing with the same tortuous unresolvable messages droning on relentlessly inside our skulls, day after day.

Mindfulness takes willpower and a benefit of mindfulness is that it builds willpower in all areas of life. The brain area associated with willpower affected by mindful meditation is the prefrontal cortex, the executive, problem solving area of the cortex just behind the forehead. Many problems in our lives can be helped to some degree by strengthening willpower or self-control. Poor self-control is associated with anger, violence, poor diet, and alcohol and drug abuse.

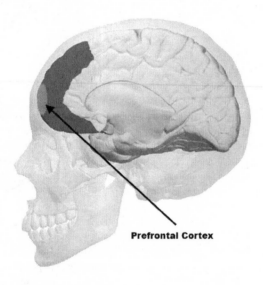

Prefrontal Cortex

Figure 12-1: Prefrontal Cortex

We can use willpower to attend to the quality of the mind without becoming blinded by the things we are concerned about. In a metaphoric sense, we step back and look at the mind. Is it anxious, in a hurried state, relaxed, open, closed? By stepping back and becoming an observer, we take on a wider sense of awareness and perspective. We shift to Open-Focus attention.

There is a time for narrow immersed attention, but we need to balance this with a diffuse focus where we attend to both foreground and background. With a soft focus we attend not only to objects, but the space around them, inside and outside our bodies. We shift from rigidly held narrow focus to lightly held diffuse focus and when needed, back to a narrow focus where we can alertly respond. It is when we hold a narrow focus all of the time that stress builds without release. We need balanced attention, a flexible attention that shifts in and out of narrow and diffuse focus for optimal mental health.

Vipassana insight Meditation diffusely focuses attention and awareness on thoughts, feelings, urges, emotions and sensations without holding and without judging. You look at your thoughts through filters and perspectives instead of getting caught up in the thoughts. You can practice while cooking, washing dishes, cleaning the house, or driving a car. Breathe deeply and easily, allowing thoughts, feelings, urges, sensations and emotions to be.

Any feeling, thought, or emotion, negative, positive, even violent is okay. Allow it "to be." Step back from dialogues, from deliberations and concerns over past and future events, from thoughts, feelings and urges. Move from a narrow straight-jacket perception of self and the world to an open-mode perception with the potential for revaluing and growth.

There is a virtually endless source of mp3s at the nonprofit Insight Meditation Center in Redwood CA. (www.audiodharma.org) You can download sessions on concentration, attention, relaxing, dying, even full-day retreats, then listen while preparing meals, working out, and doing tasks that do not require full focus. Sessions are recorded during actual sitting and walking practice sessions. Mp3s and some of the books on this site and a six week online course are available at no cost. If you feel you have gained from the material, you might consider a donation, but there is no requirement or pressure to do so.

13 FOUR-STEP METHOD

Jeffrey Schwartz's Four-Step Method, very basically, involves mindful awareness of the voice of the Narrator. We can't easily shut this voice out since it is a basic function of the left hemisphere of our brain. The four-step method is a mental string around your finger reminding you not to buy into the Narrator's specious pitch.

Make up a pitch of your own to counteract the Narrator's pitch. Schwartz likes "It is not me, it's my brain." This key phrase is easy to focus on when things get a bit shaky. I sometimes say to myself, "It's not resolvable." This fits with Metacognitive Therapy (MCT) (Chapter 10) and mindful strategies (Chapter 12). It is unproductive to go over and over problems that are unresolvable. Instead, you focus on processes that aid in healing like Ki Breathing Meditation (Chapter 6), Open Focus (Chapter 9)

Acknowledge the Narrator as a nonstop story-spouting machine, an illusion dispenser, not defining who you are. Awareness is the key to freeing yourself from the binding, restricting, limiting illusion of self.

The Four-Step Method with its roots in Buddhist Mindfulness alters consciousness, not by denying the voice of the Narrator, but by separating who we are from the Narrator's convincing account of who we are. We are not this story line spun so intricately into our consciousness.

Buddhist meditators realized thousands of years ago the reality of a non-cohesive self. Neuroscientists conceive of the brain as a collection of neural pathways and circuits, modules interacting with trillions of modules. No central cohesive self, no command central, no thoughts found among the billions of neurons. Our brain is an ant colony of neurons functioning in huge clusters to get different jobs done. Our conscious self is a 50-bit story spun to hold us together. The brain does not consider whether this story is true and whether it helps or hinders.

Jeffrey Schwartz, psychiatrist, researcher, author of "You Are Not Your

Brain," refers to the process of doing almost anything to get rid of uncomfortable thoughts and sensations by automatically responding with detrimental behaviors as "feeding the monster." The monster is the part of the brain generating deceptive brain messages that cause bodily and emotional reactions so uncomfortable you will do anything to make them go away, even things harmful to your mind and body.

These behaviors may be psychologically and physically, as well as legally harmful, yet you respond again and again in a semi-automatic way. You feed the message-making monster, making it stronger, rewarding it with drugs, alcohol, food, obsession, compulsions, rage, sex, and in thankfully extremely rare cases, serial murder. The monster becomes an overlay of your sense of self. You see no way out and resign yourself to believing this is who you are and this is how it must be.

The Four-Step Method is a cognitive, mindful strategy for dealing with brain messages invading our psyche. These repetitive thoughts and feelings make us angry and uncomfortable, causing us to behave in ways unhelpful to setting and reaching goals. If someone were to bring up these thoughts and feelings each time we meet, our meetings might likely be few and far between. Yet they enter uninvited into our own private sanctuary, ad nauseam.

Brain Lock

Becoming familiar with the brain helps me to work more easily with the Four-Step and other methods. For example, it's not me, it is my caudate nucleus locked in gear and unable to shift me out of these obsessive thoughts.

Figure 13-1 Brain Lock

Schwartz calls the obsessive thoughts, feelings, and compulsive behaviors "Brain Lock," the title of one of his books, because the caudate nucleus, a part of the basal ganglia deep inside the center of the brain, gets stuck or locked. He describes the caudate nucleus as an automatic transmission that should allow for the efficient coordination of thought and movement. In a person with OCD, the caudate nucleus is not shifting gears properly and messages from the occipital cortex up front in the brain get stuck and the caudate nucleus can't shift gears and move on to the next thought. Instead, the thought goes round and round relentlessly.

The other part of the basal ganglia, the putamen, Schwartz describes as the part of the automatic transmission controlling body movement.

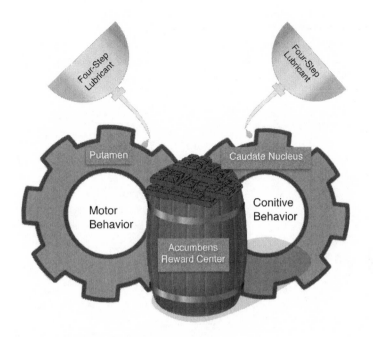

Figure 13-2: Putamen Stuck in Gear

These two parts of the basal ganglia, the caudate nucleus and the putamen, normally function together smoothly, but not in patients with OCD. When they get stuck, you get obsessive thoughts–caudate nucleus– and compulsive acts–putamen. Schwartz's Four-Step Method helps the automatic transmission in the brain shift more smoothly, so that over time the intrusive obsessions and compulsions decrease in intensity.

Step I: Relabel

Separate yourself from automatic maladaptive uncomfortable thoughts, feelings, and emotions. You are not the monster. You are experiencing unhealthy patterns of automatic, destructive, brain messages. Separating your identity, from these messages is what step one is about.

In place of "I've got to go back to see if I've locked the door," you might say "I am having an obsessive thought that I must go back and check the door," or a compulsive urge to wash. You recognize the thoughts and compulsive urges as symptoms of your OCD. You cannot make the thoughts and urges immediately go away, but you can immediately understand the thoughts are false messages from neural pathways firing in the brain. Schwartz quotes one of his patients who coined a phrase, "Don't be polemical, it's just chemical."

It is not enough to create a clever phrase. Schwartz points out that the possible sticking point of his four step method is when the brain starts sending false messages that you cannot readily recognize as false. It is important to observe and be aware of these messages. These are the shoulds, musts, damning and condemning of REBT, the must do well or perform well in order to accept myself.

Step II: Reframe

An easy metaphor is a picture frame. If the girl does not like a part of her face (13-3) and frames it as in the left image, only she sees it as the entire face. An impartial observer views her face as the right image, in full.

Take the POV of the impartial observer who sees the whole person, not defaults. You are not a nose, mouth, eye, or leg. You are not a physical deformity or mental disease. This applies to all irrational patterns of thinking, not just OCD. Practice stepping back from thoughts, feelings, moods, and urges, and viewing the gestalt.

The static image in a photo is not the you others see. They don't see eyes, nose, stomach, neck, hips, legs. They see an animated, moving you. They see a living, breathing embodied soul that not even a holograph can capture.

Figure13-3: Reframe

Recognize and attribute distressful thoughts, urges, and compulsions as spewing from a malfunctioning basal ganglia. Step back mentally and become an independent observer. Observe how your brain is framing these deceptive messages as a basic part of who you are. Reframe. They are not who you are at the core.

Reframing limits the power of these messages to what they are, burnt-in neural loops in your brain. The brain often functions more like a "malprogrammed" chip than in a compassionate, helpful self.

You never know what your next thought will be. Attempting to suppress thoughts and feelings leads to more uncomfortable thoughts, feelings and urges. You can choose not to shine a light on them. You can choose not to focus and hold on to thoughts, feelings, and urges that you may have allowed to define who you are.

Shining a light on deceptive messages, feelings, and urges reinforces the neural networks and makes them return stronger. Shining a light on them leads to overanalyzing and moving deeper and deeper into mazes that are impossible to find your way out of. Be aware, without shining a light.

Psychodynamic therapy can be a death-defying tightrope act without a net. Self-immersion while re-experiencing negative thoughts, feelings, and physiological sensations that accompanied the initial event, entangles the mind in ruminations and obsessions that can spiral out of hand. That is what happened when I went through psychoanalysis. I came close to taking my life. The therapist resorted to a series of electroconvulsive (ECT) treatments, like kicking the TV to get it to work properly, he confessed.

Some people are helped with a simple script or catch phrase for easy recall: "It is a bad brain day." "I'm having a brain storm." "This feels like such a part of me, but I know it is synapses and networks firing away." "I do not have to act on these thoughts, feelings and urges." "I do not have to act in an unhealthy, destructive way." "I do not have to follow deceptive thoughts and feelings with endless loops of analysis."

The brain is acting up. The basal ganglia, the habit forming center of the brain is sending automatic distress signals to the frontal cortex, the executive center, creating a loop between these two brain centers. These two brain centers create an obsessive feedback loop that includes the reward center called the accumbens, the powerful reward center which is part of the basal ganglia. The accumbens is located where the caudate nucleus and putamen —automatic gears — meet.

Basal Ganglia

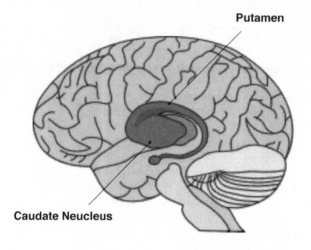

Putamen

Caudate Neucleus

Figure 13-4: Basal Ganglia Habit-Forming Center

Schwartz says the four-step method of self-directed behavior therapy takes weeks or months to change the brain's biochemistry. He encourages an understanding of the role that the structures of the brain play. Understanding the anatomical problem helps to avoid acting on disturbing thoughts, and instead to shift behavior and allow for neurons to fire in new paths.

Overthinking and overanalyzing strengthen maladaptive brain circuits and their associated habitual responses. Schwartz advises to Recognize, Dismiss, and Accept. Recognize the deceptive brain message or uncomfortable sensation. Dismiss the faulty logic or strong pull to act on the sensations. Accept that deceptive thoughts, urges, impulses, and sensations will arise, but that you do not have to act on them.

Basically, you live with paradoxes, unresolvable riddles. It is counterproductive to attempt to solve them. When you focus on paradox and attempt to solve it, it blows up to monstrous proportions.

Live With Paradox

The words of Gary Gilmore, cold blooded killer, likely psychopath, stayed with me since reading the April 1977 Lawrence Schiller death row interview in Playboy Magazine. Schiller asked Gilmore how he could believe he would go to heaven after he was executed. "Philosophical impasse," was his answer that stuck in my mind all these years. He was able to live with paradox; an awareness of the brutal murders he had committed and at the same time believing he would go to heaven. He appeared to be cool, calm, and at peace with himself.

Instead of ruminating on irresolvable problems, living with paradox is key to Meta Cognitive Therapy (MCT) (Chapter 10). Instead of ruminating on irresolvable problems, step back and look at harmful problem-solving methods, like ruminating. Replace narrow perseverative patterns of thinking with flexible patterns of attention. Give up focusing on irresolvable problems. Stop shining the light. Don't feed the monster. Accept paradox.

Do Not Feed!

Figure 13-5: Do Not Feed the Monster

Though Schwartz uses the word deceptive for faulty brain messages, that would be anthropomorphizing. The brain houses no homunculus, no little man behind the curtain pulling the levers like in the Wizard of Oz. No center within the brain that acts to deceive you, rather an estimated eighty-six billion neurons, many firing in parallel and forming linked neural habitual pathways. We create these linked pathways by attending to the same thought patterns over time.

Attending is key. We don't have to react or respond to uncomfortable thoughts, habits, sensations and urges. We do not have to focus on thoughts, feelings, urges, and desires that sabotage our best interests. We can step back, observe, and move on.

In the words of Jon Kabit-Zin, MD, pioneer in applying mindfulness to treatment of chronic medical conditions:

> Every time we are able to know a desire as desire, anger as anger, a habit as habit, an opinion as an opinion, a thought as a thought, a mind spasm as a mind spasm, or an intense sensation in the body as an intense sensation, we are correspondingly liberated. Nothing else has to happen. We don't even have to give up the desire or whatever else it is. To see it and know it as desire, as whatever it is, is enough.

"Coming to Our Senses" Audio Disk

Step III: Refocus

Refocusing involves redirecting focus to an activity of your choosing. Acknowledge and accept that messages and sensations will arise, but that you do not have to act on them. They do not define you. You do not have to get caught up in them other than to recognize them for what they are. Then refocus by shifting behavior.

It might be ideal if you were able to shift focus to an activity immersing you in a state of flow where you are energized and focused. Runners, writers and artists report experiencing flow. You can experience flow in books, movies and video games. But almost any activity that you are able to immerse yourself in will work. Don't get caught up in brain messages other than to recognize them for what they are and shift focus. It does not change anything. The problems are still there. The challenge is to shift focus and live within this paradox. The methods are diverse.

In Viktor Frankl's book, "The Will to Meaning," he describes the effect of a mass shift of focus by a group picketing on the campus of the University of California at Berkeley. When the picketing started, the number of admissions to the psychiatric department of the student hospital suddenly dropped. And it sharply increased once the picketing was over. For some months students had found meaning in the freedom-of-speech movement. But the shift can be to an activity as mundane as washing dishes, preparing food for a meal, cleaning the toilet, and if work, on whatever you are doing. I always have an mp3 readied.

Refocusing does not mean thoughts, impulses, urges, and other unpleasant brain messages will be gone. You refocus despite the fact that they are screaming for attention. By refocusing and changing behavior, you shape new habit pathways in the brain. First become aware the message is calling out from well established, worn and tortuous paths in the brain.

Rather than allowing yourself to indulge and reinforce unhealthy obsessive thoughts, feelings, and urges, make the effort to refocus your attention. You get practice with refocusing on the chapters on Ki Breathing Meditation (6), Open Focus (8), and Attention Training Therapy (ATT) (10).

Refocusing is not a way of ridding unwanted thoughts and feelings. Allow sensations, thoughts, and impulses to be as you engage attention and refocus. Your brain will take you down the same uncomfortable neural pathways until they weaken. That takes refocusing each time you are distracted.

Step IV: Revalue

Revaluing and aligning with deeper values of self gives meaning to life beyond worn repeated brain messages and behaviors. Revaluing and finding a personal why is the fourth step, the long-term part of the Four-Step Method. Schwartz counsels that especially for revaluing, to call upon the Wise Advocate. It is the wise inner Self, an intelligent, loving guide.

The Wise Advocate helps relabel, reframe, refocus, and revalue to make healthier choices in line with goals. The Wise Advocate does not automatically respond to deceptive brain messages in an unhealthy manner. It is mindfully aware of deceptive messages, but shies away from automatically responding to them. The Wise Advocate can help you to refocus and revalue with an activity that can offer a sense of flow.

The Wise Advocate is Self as compared with small self. Small self is the self that is the storied creation of the Narrator, the self you have come to believe defines limits and confines you. Self with a capital "S" is the true present Self. It is the Self that has been buried and takes work to bring to the surface. It is who you are in this moment sans stories and deceptions. It is truth deep within you now.

The goal of Four-Step Method is to live according to your true Self. This means to discover and caringly and lovingly attend to your true emotions and needs. As your mind becomes aware of the destructive, unhealthy, habitual, automatic messages of the Narrator, you can call on the Wise Advocate, your inner true Self, to encourage you to plan and make decisions in a more helpful way based on your best interests, now and in the long run. You call on your inner Self to view the healthy, life-giving forest instead of romping through sweetly pungent, rotting trees. To begin to see Self, you must begin to ignore self. As the balance shifts to Self, your life will become more at peace. Schwartz's book is titled, "You are Not Your Brain," and he is saying you are not your small self.

As you begin to call upon and become the Wise Advocate, it gets stronger. Without a strong inner Self, you are at the mercy of a brain that runs the show uncaringly with unending loops of troubling thoughts, feelings, and urges. As the Wise Advocate strengthens, you are more able to become an observer of, rather than overpowered by distressing neural loops, and to work on living life now. Each time uncomfortable messages and feelings disturb you, rather than attempt to push them away, Relabel, Reframe, Refocus, and work on Revaluing your life.

The Four-Step Method is a form of Metacognitive Therapy (MCT). MTC is about patterns of faulty thinking and coming to terms with life's paradoxes.

14 PLACEBO-MODE HEALING

Relaxation Response

In his two books, Harvard cardiologist and author of "Relaxation Response and "Relaxation Revolution," Herbert Benson discusses how mind-body techniques lower blood pressure, calm brain activity, and balance healthful emissions of nitric oxide in the body's cells.

Next, he wanted to determine whether mind-body techniques might alter gene expression. Which, if any, of the body's 54,000 genes were "turned on" or "turned off" by mind-body techniques. Epigenetics is the turning on or off of genes by life situations.

His team discovered 2,209 genes that are in fact affected by mind-body techniques. These genes affected by mind-body training are associated with stress-related medical problems involving immune response, inflammation, aging, thinning of the brain's cortex, and oxidative stress causing damage to physical tissues by the release of destructive oxygen molecules known as free radicals.

Mind-body practices take a bad gene and make it better. The benefits of mind-body practices include healthful regulation of the immune system, lowered psychosocial stress levels, less destructive oxidative stress, and a reduced tendency toward premature aging. These benefits are associated with healthful gene activity, the opposite of that found in cardiovascular diseases and other medical conditions.

Benson was aware that his relaxation response was due at least in part to the placebo response. But all medication and treatment effects are at least thirty percent due to the placebo effect. The placebo response is the body using its own resources to heal, and healing without medication or surgery is the most natural way of healing.

Rather than discard the placebo response, Benson established the Benson-Henry Institute for Mind Body Medicine (BHI) at Massachusetts

General Hospital in Boston. Ongoing research employs evidence-based techniques to strengthen the natural healing capacities of the body and mind. BHI clinicians serve as a resource in the areas of mind body and integrative medicine available to all departments of the hospital and community.

A part of Benson's program engenders belief, expectation, and faith, by explaining how mind-body healing works. His explanation promotes faith in him and encourages belief and expectancy of a positive outcome. Educating the client regarding the efficacy and value of the program had best be an ongoing part of the program. Of course, the treatment must effectively warrant belief, faith, and expectation.

Benson's relaxation response can be set off while walking or running and paying attention to the cadence of your feet on the ground. Cadence might be left and right and left and right. Swimmers can pay attention to the tempo of their strokes, cyclists to the repetitive sound of pedaling, dancers to the music, or you can pay attention to the rhythm of your breathing. The focusing of the mind in meditation with any repetitive activity causes a decrease in heart rate, breathing rate, blood pressure if elevated, and metabolic rate. This is the opposite effect of an adrenaline stress fight-or-flight response.

Benson and his team ran an eight week mind-body training session and found gene expression of the trainees shifted close to gene expression signatures of a group with more than nine years of mind-body practice. After eight weeks of mind-body training, 433 gene expression signatures are now similar in both groups. It does not take a lifetime or even nine years to make positive changes at the genetic level. Statistically, the probability of these gene signatures of the eight-week trainees and the more than nine-year veteran meditators coming together accidentally is less than one in 10 billion.

Significant positive genetic changes occur in just eight weeks. Mind-body practices such as the relaxation response, breathing meditation, mindfulness, yoga, and prayer have profound effects at the genetic level. The related field is called psychoneuroimmunology. "Psycho" refers to states of the mind including thinking, emotions, and mood states. "Neuro" refers to the neurological and neuroendocrine systems. "Immunology" refers to the immune system.

Benson found mind-body practices affect cancer cells. The gene expression for long-term relaxation response is counter to the gene expression in various cancers including lymphoma, neuro tumors, liver, and leukemia. Even for the eight-week trainees, gene-set expression signatures countered the gene signatures of cancerous neuro tumors, multiple myeloma, and leukemia.

That doesn't necessarily mean you can cure cancer with mind-body relaxation practices. The trainees in this study did not have cancer. Benson compared their genes with cancer databases compiled by the Broad Institute of Massachusetts Institute of Technology, Harvard, and the Weizmann Institute of Science in Israel. With these databases, Benson determined how gene sets in their relaxation-response subjects correlated with cancer-associated gene sets in cancer patients.

According to Benson, the results are "rather startling and highly encouraging for future research and possible medical treatment." Gene-set activity in cancer patients ran in one direction, while the activity of the same group of genes in the relaxation response practitioners ran in the opposite direction. Future investigations are needed to directly compare cancer patients who practiced or did not practice the relaxation response and other forms of mind-body meditation.

Heal Thyself

"The Secret" by Rhonda Byrne sold over nineteen million copies. Want to be driving a Jaguar convertible sports car? According to "The Secret", all you need to do is picture yourself driving it, parking it in your garage, owning it; believe in all of that. You can pretty much get or do anything in life with "the power of attraction."

Byrne was supposedly influenced by Wallace Wattle's 1910 book, "The Science of Getting Rich." His "Certain Way" is to form what you want in your mind, believe it is yours, and it will be created out of "Formless Substance."

Wattle was influenced by Phineas Quimby's mental healing. A medical doctor who lived from 1802 till 1866, Quimby saw patients and traveled about, lecturing. He did not write much, but kept a journal – interesting reading when you get past his ego. He said that he was not religious, but throughout his journal made reference to Christ. He said Christ, the secular man, was the ultimate teacher. Quimby felt that he was a Christ, the ultimate secular teacher in his field of mental healing.

Though a medical doctor himself, he was the anti-medical establishment of his time. He believed disease was an error, and truth or wisdom the cure. Disease is the result of a wrong direction given to the mind, sometimes by doctors. The doctor tells you have a disease and what the disease can do to you. Autosuggestion takes over from there, sometimes instantaneously creating symptoms that match the diagnosis.

His method of healing was sitting with the patient and by discussing their error that binds them to a depleted state of mind and body. He worked with his patient to destroy beliefs that were attached to the disease, replacing these beliefs and opinions with "truths and wisdom." His ideas were, of course, in opposition to the established ideas of the day. His ideas are in opposition to today's medical practitioners who have at most fifteen minutes to spend with each patient. One hundred years later, most doctors write a prescription and move on to the next patient.

After seeing patients daily and corresponding with them for years, he decided he could not spend sufficient time with individual patients and so took his talk on the road to reach large audiences with two-hour talks in hope of persuading others to understand and practice what he labored for, and to reduce his theories to a science.

He said that man's happiness and misery is the effect of his/her belief and that all medical remedies affect the body through the mind. The one who takes the medicine must believe in the medicine and anticipate the desired result. The result is then created by the believer.

Phineas Quimby died in 1866, but it would not be until 1978 when the neurobiology of the placebo effect was born. Up to then, it was known that the placebo sugar pill could block pain (analgesia effect). Now it was shown that the placebo analgesia could be blocked by the opioid antagonist naloxone. This indicated an involvement of opioids produced in the body (endogenous) that were blocking the pain. Expectation of an effect induces the release of endogenous opioids.

That takes a bit of unpacking. What it means is that since the placebo effect of pain relief was blocked by giving an opioid blocker, the placebo effect must be caused by an opioid produced by the body. If it were not an opioid, the opioid blocker would not have blocked it.

Mindlessness

"Wherever you put your mind, your body will follow." Ellen Langer, Harvard psychologist said that, with thirty years of research to back it up. In a 1981 study, she took two groups of men in their seventies and eighties to live in a sprawling monastery in New Hampshire for two weeks. Everything where they stayed, the music, movies, books, magazines, even the black and white TV, vintage radio, was staged back in the 1950s. One group was told to pretend they were young men back in the 1950s. The control group just was told to live in the present.

The results were surprising even to Lang er. For the group that lived back in the 1950s, height, weight, gait, posture, hearing, vision, even performance on IQ tests had improved. She said at the end of the study she was playing touch football with the men, some of whom gave up their canes.

In another study by Langer with hotel maids, half were told the work they do is good exercise and satisfies the Surgeon General's recommendations for an active lifestyle. The maids in the control group were not given this information. After four weeks the informed group perceived themselves as getting significantly more exercise than before. As a result, compared with the control group, they showed a decrease in weight, blood pressure, body fat, waist-to-hip ratio, and body mass index. The results support the hypothesis that exercise affects health in part or in whole via the placebo effect.

Most people Langer says, are in a fixed state of mindlessness. They are not all there. When you are not there, you are more likely to end up where you are being led and where you may not want to be. She defines mindfulness as being aware of everything around you.

She attributes the results of the elderly men and hotel maids to mindfulness. Most of us act mindlessly, including in deference to doctor's opinions, accepting diagnosis and disease, which is pretty much what Phineas Quimby was saying. If you learn to be mindful, you will perceive choices available to you with a better chance of fulfilling your potential and improving your health.

Langer's mindfulness is noticing specific ongoing changes around you. It is comparable with Attention Training Therapy (ATT), where you shift from sound to sound and Open Focus where you shift from space to space. Mindful individuals are less likely to become fixed in an objective reality. They will be open to a completely different point of view. They will be less likely to take a medical diagnosis as the only possible evaluation.

In 1957, when Langer was ten years old, Bruno Kopfler's journal article, "Psychological Variables in Human Cancer" told about a Mr. Wright, a stage four cancer patient who heard about a "miracle drug" Krebiozen, part of a study at the hospital where he was bedridden. Dr. Philip West, his doctor, would not include him in the study because to be eligible the patient must have a life expectancy of at least three months. A prognosis of one week might have been seriously stretching it for Wright, who was immobile with a high fever and gasping for air.

Expectation

Wright begged so hard, though, for what he called this "golden opportunity" that West, against the rules of the drug (Krebiozen) committee, injected him with the drug on a Friday to satisfy the last wish of his dying patient. Monday morning, to his amazement, Dr. West found him moving about the ward without his cane, spreading the good news to anyone who might listen. Upon examining Wright, Dr. West found all of the tumors had melted to half their size.

Wright had received no other medication or treatment besides the one shot of Krebiozen. He had fully expected the drug to make him well. He had read about the miracle drug in the newspaper. He had no doubt whatsoever that Krebiozen was his ticket to recovery and a speedy one at that.

The injections were continued three times weekly for a period of ten days. They were stopped when all symptoms of the disease were completely gone. In ten days he went from a terminally ill patient gasping through an oxygen mask for his last breaths, to a fully active recovery. He was discharged and took off piloting his plane at 12,000 feet with no discomfort.

None of the other patients improved and after two months all of the other clinics reported the discouraging news about the effectiveness of Krebiozen. Newspapers all picked up on this and when Wright read this news, he became discouraged again, began to lose weight, and after two months of practically perfect heath, tumors grew back and he slid back to where he started.

By now Dr. West realized that it was Wright's optimism. His expectation, not Krebiozen was responsible for his amazing recovery. West decided no harm would come in lying to Wright and using his optimism in hope of another recovery. The alternative was Wright dying within a short period of time.

Conditioning

He told Wright not to believe the new reports. The reason for the failure of the trials was the drug had lost potency due to its short shelf life. The clinic would be getting a fresh doubly potent batch the next day, which he expected to produce even more astounding results. Doctors reported Wright was "almost ecstatic and his faith was very strong."

The next day Dr. West administered a shot of fresh water. The results were more astounding than the first time. This time around, it was both expectancy and conditioning. Tumor masses melted and chest fluid vanished. In a short time, in perfect health, he was discharged and took up piloting his plane.

Two months later the AMA came out with their final announcement: "Nationwide tests show Krebiozen to be a worthless drug in treatment of cancer." Wright read the report in the newspaper, was readmitted to the hospital, and in less than two days of his admission he died.

Pure Conditioning

With a conditioned placebo effect, first the active drug is administered. Later, an inactive compound that looks just like the first drug is administered. If conditioning works, the inactive compound produces the effect of the active drug. Wright's second cure was likely due to a mix of expectation and conditioning. It is difficult to know with a human subject whether the cure might have been due to expectancy, conditioning, or some mixture of both.

The way to rule out expectancy is through animal research. In 1975, Dr. Robert Adar, the research psychologist who coined the name psychoimmunology, gave one group of rats saccharine-sweetened water accompanied by an injection of cyclophosphamide, a chemical used to treat malignant diseases that can cause significant suppression of immune responses and stomach pain. A control group got just the sweetened water.

The conditioned group of rats, as expected, would not drink water after the painful association with the cyclophosphamide. Experimenters did not want the rats to die, so they force-fed them water, but they died anyway. The cause was not the cyclophosphamide, because the dose was strong enough to give stomach pain, but was not lethal.

They died from the water, from suppression of immune response and bacterial and viral infections that their immune system could not fight off, just as if they had received a lethal dose of cyclophosphamide. They died from a conditioned placebo response that made the body react as though it had been poisoned.

A more recent conditioned placebo study with dogs was published in October 2014 issue of Applied Animal Behavior Science. The dog is introduced to a new room with its owner. The owner leaves and two minutes later a stranger comes in who attempts to interact with the dog. Then the stranger leaves and the owner returns. This is the "Strange Situation" and rating scale developed by Mary Ainsworth to assess the level of parent-child attachment, this time with owner-dog.

In the next part of the study, before each trial, half the same dogs were given a dose of Sedalin (a tranquilizer) hidden in a piece of liverwurst. The other dogs got a vitamin inside a piece of liverwurst. As expected, the dogs given the tranquilizer were more relaxed.

Both groups were separated from owners in the same room as before. Both groups received a vitamin. The conditioned group (the dogs who had previously been given a tranquilizer) showed less active signs of distress (separation anxiety) and a relaxed passive behavior when the owner left the room. These dogs responded as if they had again been given the sedative.

Meaning

Meaning is an important factor setting us apart from most, if not all other animals. Much of the meaning in our lives originates in the stories we tell ourselves. From an early age we construct stories to make sense of our lives. Though we all have emotional and physical pain and suffering, the stories we create determine the degree and kind of suffering.

The stories we tell ourselves can be a part of our placebos and healing. If we think we are taking aspirin, the placebo effect will be different than if you think you are taking morphine. In most cases, the placebo response is 55 to 60 percent as effective as the treatment. If you "know" you are taking aspirin, the placebo effect will be 54 percent as effective as aspirin. If you "know" you are taking morphine, the placebo effect will be 56 percent as effective as the morphine. Amazing, since morphine is many times stronger and effective as aspirin. Your body puts out a placebo effect geared to the effect of the treatment drug. (even though you are just taking a sugar pill).

The placebo effect is not just in the mind. Its effect mirrors that of the drug. The difference is the drug is a chemical substance manufactured by the drug company, while the placebo response is triggered by natural endogenous chemicals produced by the body including opioids and dopamine.

Drug companies know that different color pills have different effects on our body, so they color the pills according to the desired effect. Taking a red pill or blue pill, once, twice, or three times a day can activate a different placebo response.

Performance

Performance is the "doing" part of the placebo response and can mean a lot of things. For example, the performance of the doctor in making the diagnoses and prognoses can activate a placebo or nocebo response, beyond serving as a nonreactive forecast..

Placebo effects are not limited to pills and injections. Perhaps the most extreme studies of the placebo effect are with sham surgery. Patients do not know whether they are getting the actual or sham surgery. With the sham surgery, the performance involves the complete surgical team, anesthetizing, and making the incision.

In 1939, an Italian surgeon performed a surgical procedure that involved tying off of the mammary artery to treat angina. In America the procedure was tested on dogs and showed that blood flow through the coronary arteries significantly increased when surgery closed off the nearby mammary artery. Tying off the mammary artery that supplies blood to the anterior chest wall and breasts means more blood available to the heart. This surgery was commonly done in America throughout the nineteen forties, fifties, and into the sixties. It effectively relieved pain in three quarters of patients undergoing the procedure.

In 1959 a Leonard Cobb a young cardiologist decided to put this procedure to the "gold standard" test with a double-blind, placebo-controlled study. One group of patients received the surgery where the mammary artery was tied. Another group was put to sleep, opened up, and sewed back up again. Both groups believed they had the same standard surgery for angina. The surgery was equally as effective in the group that had the sham surgery as the mammary artery-tying procedure.

In 2000, sham or placebo therapy was done with patients with Parkinson's Disease. In the actual surgery, holes are bored into the skull so that cells can be injected into the brain as transplants. In the placebo surgery, holes are bored into the skull, also under general anesthesia, but no cell transplant cells injected. Both of the surgeries were equally effective.

The July 2002 issue of the New England Journal of Medicine reported a placebo controlled trial of arthroscopic surgery for osteoarthritis of the knee. In this controlled study, patients who received the arthroscopic treatment surgery were no better off than a placebo sham surgery.

Who is Doing the Healing and Sabotaging?

Wright was seemingly cured of a stage-four cancer because of his expectation and belief in the efficacy of the drug Krebiozen. When he heard the drug was ineffective, the cancer returned. When Dr. West convinced him he would be injected with a twice as potent, fresh batch of Krebiozen, once again he was miraculously cured.

Alas, when he read in the newspaper of the American Medical Society (AMS) final declaration that Krebiozen was worthless, his condition deteriorated rapidly and he died. The placebo had worked miracles until Wright discovered it was a placebo response and not the efficacy of the drug.

Because the placebo response is based upon expectation and conditioning, when Wright learned that he received a medication the AMA called worthless, all the positive effects of the placebo based on expectation and conditioning instantly vaporized. The brain has the power to generate effects in response to whatever it believes to be true, positive or negative.

Since studies have shown the brain can heal the body, and it is our brain and our body, why don't we just heal ourselves? Just as in Wright's case, even when a treatment is producing positive results, you nullify these results if you discover the treatment is a placebo. This is called "the placebo paradox." Our brain has miraculous healing powers, but we have the power to sabotage the brain's powers. Who is curing and who is sabotaging? No controller located anywhere in the brain, just billions of neurons firing with more than one quadrillion interconnections.

You would think knowing the possibilities of the placebo response, more studies would combine treatment with a placebo to enhance the overall effect of the treatment. The placebo is being used, but primarily as the gold standard of research studies where one group receives the experimental treatment and a control group does not receive the treatment. To prove the treatment is effective, results must be better than a placebo or inert treatment. If the treatment is not better than the placebo, it fails the test and is considered ineffective.

Few studies have been done to explore possibilities of combining the placebo to enhance the overall effect of the treatment or to use the placebo to reduce the amount of drug to get an effect equal to the full dose of the drug alone.

Hypothalamic Pituitary Adrenal Axis (HPA)

Perhaps a good place to explore the placebo might be the hypothalamic–pituitary–adrenal axis (HPA). Because the HPA is the system associated with stress, this might be the last place you might look. But the stress system is the same system that effects healing. A system that affects stress and healing is like the nocebo versus placebo.

I find it helpful to know the parts of the brain and adrenal system in understanding and dealing with stress.It basically involves two structures in the brain and one in the body. The hypothalamus and pituitary gland are part of the brain. The two adrenal glands are atop each kidney.The hypothalamus, pituitary and adrenal glands function as the HPA Axis.

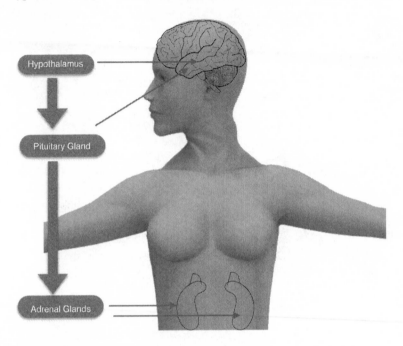

Figure 14-1: Alyson's HPA System

The hypothalamus activates the pituitary gland, which in turn activates the adrenal glands, increasing their secretion of cortisol.

The hypothalamus, level with the bridge of the nose, targets the anterior (forward) pituitary, a pea-shaped gland beneath the hypothalamus, with corticotropin releasing hormone (CRH).

Messenger Molecules

The anterior pituitary targets the adrenal cortex, atop the kidneys, with adrenocorticotropic hormone (ACTH). The adrenal cortex sends cortisol, the stress hormone, back up to both the hypothalamus and anterior pituitary.

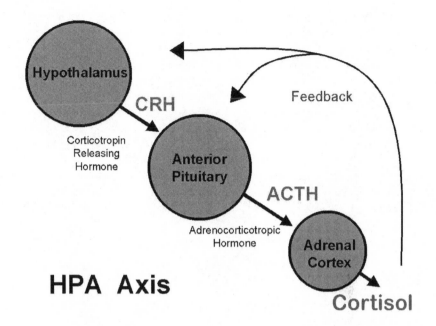

Figure 14-2:(4-1) HPA Feedback

In the first seconds of stress, the hypothalamus activates the fight or flight sympathetic nervous system with glucose to provide energy to respond to perceived dangers and within minutes the adrenal glands secrete cortisol, the steroid stress hormone that activates adaptive emergency responses in organs, tissues, and cells throughout the body.

Oral corticosteriods identical to cortisol are prescribed to treat inflammatory bowel diseases such as Crohn's disease and ulcerative colitis, autoimmune diseases such as hepatitis, joint and muscle diseases, allergies, and asthma. They are also used as replacement treatment for people whose bodies have stopped making their own steroids—Addison's disease.

In the short term when the body produces cortisol there is no problem. Trouble comes when the stress goes on for hours, days, months, years; for a lifetime as it does for so many of us. With prolonged stress comes a buildup of adrenaline and cortisol hormones that function as messenger molecules carrying information from one part of the body to another.

Messenger Molecules Remember Trauma

In "The Psychology of Mind-Body Healing," Ernest Rossi describes how these messenger molecules carry information that is state dependent, meaning you are affected in a way related to your emotional state at the time of the original trauma. The messenger molecules encode state-dependent memory, learning, and behavior that can take you back to childhood trauma you relive in a heightened state of alarm, and when prolonged this is devastating emotionally and physically.

When you come back down you are left in a state of depletion, fatigued, depressed, and withdrawn. For some people this leads to addiction in attempt to get back to a higher energy state.

Clinical studies indicate prolonged stress causes death of neurons in the hippocampus, a small stretch of neurons in a fold of the temporal lobe about level with the ear. The hippocampus ordinarily tells the adrenal glands to stop secreting the stress hormone cortisol. But now with the death of neurons in the hippocampus, the adrenal glands continue to secrete cortisol, spiraling the HPA axis into a higher and higher state of stress. This excessive cycle of stress is associated with Parkinson, Alzheimer's, and aging.

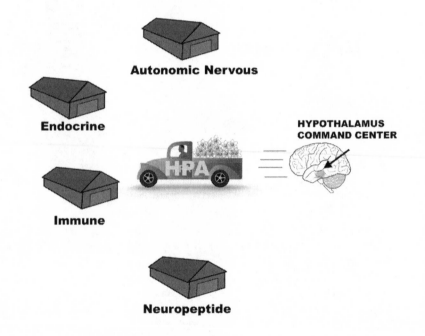

Figure14-3: HPA Messenger Molecule Delivery System

Mind-Body Connection

The endocrine system runs on autopilot years on end before it runs amuck, makes us sick, and kills us.

The hypothalamus signals the pituitary gland which sends out messenger molecules to regulate hormone-producing organs of the endocrine system.

Neural messages of the mind are converted into neurohormonal messenger molecules that regulate the hormone-producing organs of the endocrine system.

The messenger molecules —neurotransmitters of the autonomic nervous system and hormones of the endocrine system — direct the endocrine system to produce steroid hormones that reach into the nucleus of the cells of the body, helping to control metabolism, inflammation, and immune functions. Think of these messenger modules as keys that open the receptor locks on the surface of cells.

It all starts with a thought, feeling, or perception in the brain that filters through a lifetime of state-dependent memories and behaviors through the limbic-hypothalamic system via messenger molecules sent by the pituitary gland into the endocrine glands, down into to cells and genes. You trigger this mind-endocrine pathway into healing or disease.

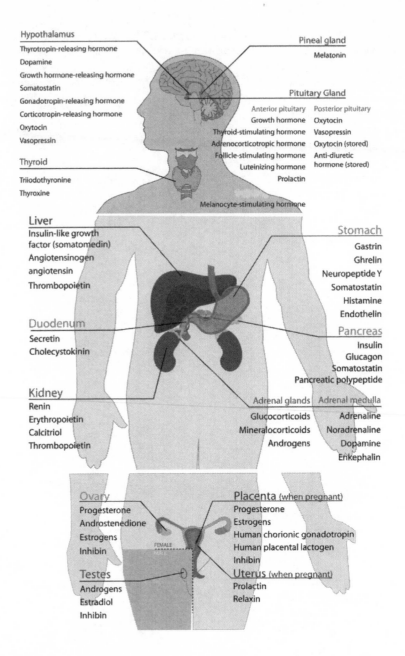

Figure 14-4: Endocrine System

The pituitary links the central nervous system with the endocrine system into one integrated neuroendocrine system, keeping stress in check by allowing the stressful event to subside.

Some people, like those with OCD, take an excessively long time to come down from a stressful event. Once the stress is generated, the event plays over and over, gaining strength with replays. Even a small amount of stress builds into a monstrous reaction, making it disastrous to allow the system to run autopilot. By midlife I knew I had to deal with stress constructively or I would land in prison.

Stress is ubiquitous – emotional, family, friends, enemies, financial, work, and personal factors. You spend much of your time at work and many workers are stressed by their manager, lack of recognition, being asked to take on more and more responsibility for insufficient remuneration, and difficult coworkers.

Cortisol, the stress hormone, rises and peaks in the morning. As soon as I wake in the morning, I get right up and Ki Breathe Meditate as I stretch, brush my teeth, get dressed, and make breakfast. (At least that is what I shoot for.) When stress hits, I am (hopefully) reminded to begin to Ki Breathe if I have stopped.

Mind-body systems that heal communicate via the same messenger molecules that regulate the stress system. The HPA axis promotes optimal functioning of hormones of the endocrine system, healing mind and body. Messenger molecules (neurotransmitters and hormones) communicate information including state-dependent memory, learning, and behavior throughout the body directing the endocrine system to produce steroid hormones that reach into the nucleus of the cells of the body.

As opposed to stress, the positive healing of the HPA axis is set off by creative work, flow, and images of health and well-being. When the HPA axis functions smoothly, it modulates the biochemical processes within the cell and optimizes the functioning of the autonomic nervous system, endocrine, immune, and neuropeptide systems.

The autonomic nervous system, the endocrine, immune, and neuropeptide systems communicate via the messenger molecules encoded with state-dependent memory, learning, and behavior. Awareness of this interconnectedness helps facilitate healing through mindfulness down to the molecular language of the body.

15 SOMATIC PSYCHOTHERAPIES

Body First

In a 1894 article "What is an Emotion," William James said that in terms of emotion, the body comes first. From the physical experience of the nervous system, we "discover" the emotion or how we are feeling. The sequence starts with the sympathetic or parasympathetic nervous system and morphs into feeling or emotional experience. James argued that emotional experience or feeling results from the experience of bodily changes. Everyone else argued that it was the other way around, that bodily changes result from the emotional experience.

James posed a now famous thought experiment. You take a nice relaxing walk in the woods when suddenly you encounter a bear. The question is whether you run because you are afraid or are you afraid because of a bodily response that includes running away.

The common sense answer is that you see the bear, are afraid, and run away. But James said what happens is you see the bear and your body reacts physically. A couple of seconds later as you are running away fear sets in. You don't know you are afraid just by seeing the bear. Instead you nonverbally tell yourself my heart is beating in my throat. Adrenaline is coursing through my blood. My breath has been taken away. I am running like hell. I am afraid of the bear.

Everyone thought James went off the deep end on this one. His theory was in contrast to the current thinking of his time that bodily changes follow from the perception of seeing the bear and a feeling of fear. You would see the bear; you would cringe with fear, your heart would pound, and adrenaline would flow.

Not so said James. If you take away the heartbeat, the adrenaline coursing through your blood, the out-of-breathiness, if you take all this away, you would see the bear and you would not get scared. Psychologists could not believe this. William James had to be wrong.

If what William James was saying were true, then someone who is paralyzed from the neck down would not get scared if they came across a bear in the woods, because the message of what was occurring in the body would not be relayed up to the brain. That did not make sense. Or did it?

Antonio Damasio says this is exactly right. The message is not relayed up to the brain, so a paralyzed person from the neck down would not get as scared as able-bodied people. He said studies were done in this area by a paraplegic psychologist who thought that he felt less emotion than he did before he became paralyzed. He talked to other paralyzed victims and they reported the same. These studies report that people who had once been able-bodied and then became paralyzed were less happy and less sad than able-bodied people.

Leaving the body out of the attention equation is like severing the head from the body. Yet in all of my long dealings with therapists that is precisely what they do. And I have taken more than one hundred psychology credits and not one of these undergraduate or graduate classes spent significant time on the body in terms of therapy.

If I were to design a psychology curriculum now there would be classes in Character Analysis, Feldenkrais and Alexander Method, Somatics, Hakomi Therapy, Self-Body Image, BDD, Gender Dysphoria, various forms of meditation, and medications, for starters.

Stand up Straight

The simple act of adjusting your posture works as an instant shift of focus. You may not notice the difference in how you feel, but research indicates a shift in affect after adjusting posture. Initial studies were not how posture affects affect, but how the body reacts to emotional and feeling states.

Darwin studied the physical expression of affect, practically everything from screaming infants causing the contraction of muscles around the eyes, to the bodily expressions of grief, suffering, joy, love, meditation, determination, shyness, shame, and devotion. He covered just about every way the body displays feelings and emotion. Some of this was documented in his 1872 book, "The Expression of the Emotions in Man and Animals." That publication began an era concerned with how affect effects the person.

It took another hundred years before researchers turned this paradigm around and began studying the effect posture has on affect and behavior. In 1982, the first study on the effect of posture on motivation, emotion, and behavior appeared in the journal Motivation and Emotion. The study (actually four studies) examined the effects of stooped relative to upright physical posture on depressed mood and helplessness. It asked the question, is a slumped-over relative to an upright physical posture a nonverbal depreciating of oneself?

They found no significant difference in self-reporting of self-confidence between the slumped and the upright posture groups. But that does not mean that posture does not affect affect. It means the subjects were unaware of the effect the posing had on them.

When each subject was given a series of puzzles to solve, some of which were actually unsolvable, there was much lower persistence in working on the insolvable puzzles in the stooped-posture group. And after this puzzle-solving session, subjects who were in the slumped-posture group rated themselves as having significantly stronger feelings of helplessness and external control. This group also reported being more stressed. Posing had a definite effect on affect. Posture is more than a passive refection of emotional states.

Affect of Posture on Neuroendocrine System

A study published in September 2010 in "Psychological Science" looked at power poses. Humans and other animals express power through open, expansive, postures, and they express powerlessness through closed contractive postures. This study asked if these power postures cause a person to become more powerful. It asked if power postures cause neuroendocrine and behavioral changes in male and female participants.

Other studies have shown the neuroendocrine profiles of the powerful differentiate them from the powerless. In humans and other animals, testosterone levels reflects and reinforces dispositional and situational status and dominance. The powerful and dominant have more of this hormone than the powerless. Testosterone rises in anticipation of a competition and as a result of a win, but drops following a defeat.

The other hormone that separates the dominant from the meek is cortisol, the stress hormone. Power holders show lower basal cortisol levels and lower cortisol reactivity to stressors than powerless people, and cortisol drops as power is achieved. The chronically elevated cortisol levels of low-power individuals are associated with impaired immune functioning, hypertension, and memory loss. When you have chronically high cortisol levels, you are chronically stressed out.

So wouldn't it be great if you could increase testosterone levels, become more dominant, and decrease cortisol levels and become less stressed simply by adjusting your posture? The results of a study with 26 females and 16 males shows you can. Subjects were randomly assigned to the high-power pose or low-power pose. A high-power pose is an expansive, open posture in contrast with a constrictive, closed, minimum space, collapsing inward, low-posture pose.

The goal of the research was to test whether high-power poses produce power in terms of not only feeling powerful, but with elevation of the dominance hormone testosterone and the lowering of cortisol, the stress hormone. Participants were randomly assigned to the high or low-power pose and held two poses in their assigned category for one minute each. The experimenter placed an ECG lead on the back of each calf and the underside of the left arm. Saliva samples were taken before and approximately seventeen minutes after the power posing. The subjects had no idea of what the poses signified. They were told the study was about the physiological recordings of how electrodes were placed on their bodies. They were told the research was about the most effective positions to record the ECGs. They had no idea the study was about power posing.

High-power poses caused a significant increase in testosterone compared with low-power poses. Low-power poses caused a significant increase in cortisol. The authors conclude that by simply changing physical posture, an individual prepares mentally and physiologically to endure difficult and stressful situations and perhaps to actually improve confidence and performance in situations such as interviewing for jobs, speaking in public, disagreeing with a boss, or taking potentially profitable risks.

Power Poses

Figure 15-1 Power Posing

Fake it Till You Make It

A part of the study involved a gambling task to see how willing subjects were to take a risky, but rational bet. The subjects indicated how "powerful" and "in charge" they felt on a scale of 1 (not at all) to 4 (a lot). Powerful-feeling subjects were more likely to take the bet.

The findings of this study suggest that in some situations requiring power, people have the ability to "fake it until they make it." Over time and in aggregate, minimal postural changes can improve a person's general health and well-being. It only takes about two minutes for a beneficial effect from an expansive, open-limb power pose.

This potential benefit is particularly important when considering people who are or who feel chronically powerless because of lack of resources, low hierarchical rank in an organization, or membership in a low-power social group.

Drowned in Words

In all the psychotherapy I received over the years, the body was left out of the equation. I was never asked how I felt about my body and I never thought of bringing it up, even though body image was an issue from early on.

The body is the container of feelings and emotions, source of security and self-confidence, insecurity, and lack of self-confidence. Mind/body, somatic/psychic dimensions are inseparable. It is essential to come to terms with a somatic body and a body image, that can sometimes be unrecognizably apart.

The Alexander Technique, Feldenkrais Method, Rolfing, Somatics, and Orgone or Vegetotherapy are a few of the body therapies of the early to mid 1900s. Wilhelm Reich who developed the last two was considered father of body psychotherapy. Reich knew Freud and Freud referred patients to him. Reich went through psychoanalysis himself for fourteen years.

Initially, Reich was a Freudian psychotherapist. He sat behind his patient who lay on a couch. The patient free associated saying just about anything that came to mind. Dreams were analyzed fragment by fragment. But Freud shared little in his lectures or writing as to exactly how to do psychoanalysis. When Reich questioned associates, they all said just do it and you'll understand.

The therapist looks for neurotic symptoms of repressed instinctual impulses. The "cure" was brought about by making the repressed drive conscious. So when Freud admitted later in his career that this did not necessarily lead to a cure, Reich gave up on psychoanalysis.

Reich developed what he called at times Orgone Therapy, Vegetotherapy, and Character Analysis. He came to believe that in many cases words obscure the expressive language of the biological core. He felt that psychoanalysis of years' duration was a victim of a pathological kind of language. Rather than disclose vital questions of life, psychoanalysis drowned them in verbiage.

Reich said that people do not think rationalistically. They do not do things "in order to." People function at the level of biological tensions and needs. You cannot understand a person's consciousness from the world of language. We have traded the language of words for the understanding of "the basically different language of the living function."

We cannot express our deep biological nature through language. What we hear when others speak is an impression, an interpretation in terms of what we can experience. But all living things have an identical "functional identity" enabling us to be "impressed" and understand even the functioning of a worm. We perceive the emotional expression of pain, for example, which is the same ours would be in the same painful situation. In this way we comprehend the biological emotions of all other living organisms in terms of a universal living function.

I think Antonio Damasio, Professor of Neuroscience at the University of California was getting at the same crucial insight in his discussion on what may be going on in the brain in deep states of meditation. He talked about a screen, and behind the screen is a deep state of primordial being that expresses the experience of the cells and tissues and systems that make up the body. He said that this is a place deep in the brain where there is a fusion of mind and body where extremely important realities reside, that can enlighten and have therapeutic effects.

Character Analysis

Orgone Therapy or Character Analysis takes place outside the realm of word language. Instead of the focus on words, the focus is on the total expression of the person, or the total impression the person makes. Rather than words, the therapist observes the emotional expression or the lack of or inhibited emotional expression. Inhibited emotional expression, Reich said, is exhibited by lack of facial expression, retracted pelvis, pulled back shoulders, shallow respiration.

Character Analysis attempts to break through muscular rigidity or armoring. The goal of therapy is to release the muscular and character armoring, to allow the person to give up holding back and participate in any experience, be it work or pleasure. Knowledge, work, and natural love, Reich says, are the sources of our life.

Figure 15-2 Body Builder

Hard to be loving suited up in knightly armor. Body armoring built up over the years blocks orgastic pleasure. Sexuality is pleasurable and healthy, and the blocking of sexuality causes anxiety, neurosis and disease. By releasing the rigidity or body restrictions, emotional memories return and dissolve the corresponding pattern of psychological restraint.

Since muscular and character armor function to prevent the person from experiencing, during the course of therapy, muscular armor is dissolved segment by segment, starting with the face and moving down to the pelvis. This is not done physically, but rather by working with expressive and nonverbal language and determining the difference between emotions expressed and those held back. The therapist must feel the expressive language, rather than try and understand it through words.

The top segment of this armor is ocular. This is expressed by contraction and immobilization of the eyeball muscles, the lids, the forehead, and tear glands, etc. It is not difficult for the trained therapist to observe the immobility of the forehead and eyelids, empty expression of eyes, and a general mask like expression or immobility. All the organs and muscles of the ocular segment work together. The next segment down called the oral armor has its own set of organs that work together, including the mouth, chin, and throat.

Reich believed the overwhelming majority of people suffer from orgastic impotence. This damming-up of biological energy is the source of irrational thought and action. The cure is brought about by the reestablishment of the natural capacity to love. He attributed the psychic illness of a society that thrives on violence and war to this damming up of energy.

Reich linked mental illness with an authoritarian society that espouses a negative attitude toward life, sex, and pleasure. He said that when society represses life itself, people develop pleasure anxiety, that later becomes physiologically anchored in chronic muscular spasms. His book, "The Sexual Revolution," published in 1945, was a major influence on the sexual revolution that was to come about some fifteen years later.

Part of the process of releasing body memories is through posture, movement, and breathing. Though Reichian body psychotherapists may occasionally use deep pressure to force the release of muscle tension and break up restrictions in connective tissues, I don't recall anything about deep pressure or other physical therapy in any of Reich's own books.

He discusses physical muscular armoring paralleling character armor and resistance, but his Character Analysis or Orgone Therapy is a psychic approach as opposed to hands-on body work. Character resistance, he said, expresses itself in the manner of talking, gait, facial expression, etc. What is important is not so much what the patient says or does, but how he talks and acts. Reich's psychotherapy is a whole-person approach that includes body symptoms, sensations, feelings, thoughts, and emotions. It uses all of these as clues to inaccessible, armored parts of the client.

Today psychiatrists routinely go through the basic check list for depression as a part of a med check. Are you able to enjoy things? Are you still interested in the things that mean a lot to you? Are you able to sleep at night? But an absence of questions about body image: Do you dislike your body? How often do you compare your body with others? How often do you check any part of or your entire body in a mirror or reflection?

There is a functional unity between mind and body that needs to be addressed as part of any therapy. Much of this functional relationship must be observed and understood without words. Emotion plays a role as a bridge between soma and body.

You hear little of Reich today. He spent the last two years of his life in prison. He invented what he called the orgone energy accumulator. You enter what looks like a wooden outhouse he claimed generated orgone, a kind of universal life force energy. It supposedly offered improved ejaculations. The Food and Drug Administration (FDA) obtained an injunction barring interstate distribution of all orgone-related materials. The FBI led by J Edgar Hoover built a case on Reich over the course of fourteen years that led to his arrest and imprisonment. Documents signed by J Edgar Hoover are a part of his case file. He happened to live in the wrong place and wrong time.

Hakomi Therapy

Hakomi Therapy is a body-centered mindfulness therapy based on the idea that mindfulness is not about words. Founder Ron Kurtz, influenced by the work of Wilhelm Reich, admonished therapists to be present for the client and not focus on asking questions and gathering information. Instead of a focus on what the client is saying, the focus is on what the client is doing, what she/he is expressing nonverbally in the moment. Hakomi therapists say it is about what cannot be seen in an email message or text.

Kurtz was influenced by Wilhelm Reich in that Reich paid attention to the way a person walked, shook hands, facial expression, way of holding oneself, and to the person's verbal productions rather than content. In this way, Reich was able to deal more effectively with the person's defensive structure.

In Hakomi Therapy, the therapist guides the client to a state of mindfulness, watching for both habitual and moment to moment behaviors. Momentary behaviors give clues of present experience. Habitual behaviors offer clues to underlying memories, emotions, and implicit beliefs that organize what the client can and cannot experience. Behaviors can be virtually anything, for example, shrugging shoulders, breathing patterns, pace of speech, hand movements, eye contact, facial expressions, and posture.

During an initial "tracking" phase, the therapist looks for clues to the client's unconscious core beliefs. These beliefs lie beneath the surface of the client's words. Some of the more common beliefs include: "I'm not lovable." "The world is not safe." "I'm a bad person." "My feelings are bad or dangerous." The therapist watches behaviors and listens for key words that stand out as clues to unconscious beliefs.

Kurtz says a person's behaviors can tell a skilled and experienced practitioner what kind of world the person is imagining they are living in. The goal of Hakomi therapy is to enhance well being by reducing suffering that results from these over-generalized core beliefs. This is done by evoking the original experience and associated emotions and bringing the client's core beliefs into consciousness.

Once the core beliefs along with uncomfortable memories surface, the therapist reacts in an unexpected way in order to break through the habitual way the client views the world. For example, if someone constantly shrugs their shoulders as if to say it's not my fault, the therapist might say, "It wan't your fault." Since they were expected to be blamed, this would run counter to what they are expecting and should evoke a reaction, sometimes a disbelief that the therapist means what they say. At this point the therapist offers quiet support and even a comforting touch, perhaps a hand on the client's shoulder.

Hakomi therapy begins by observing the way the patient walks into the office. Posture plays a huge role in understanding a person's character.

Kurtz says a person with a puffed-up chest is saying,"I have to be tough." "I can't let people in." "I can't be honest with people."

Clinicians are trained in Buddhist practices of being present, loving, and compassion. For example, when meeting and looking at someone, look for something to like. This will reflect back from the other person. And to be present in order to be constantly aware of the client's present experience. Being in the present moment allows the therapist to learn about the client's implicit beliefs, beliefs that are beneath the surface of the client's conscious thinking. It enables the therapist to see beneath the surface and experience the client's suffering.

The concepts in Hakomi are useful in dealing with others. When dealing with a difficult person and confronting them face to face, focus on something about them you like. Focusing on something about them that you like and staying in the present moment for them rather than an unpleasant past is a tool for connecting with others. You reflect subtle feelings that reflect back.

Hakomi Therapy involves a self-awareness as well as an understanding of others. The training of a therapist involves developing an attitude of loving presence and a nonjudgemental, gentle acceptance. Hakomi therapy is practiced with mindfulness. It is a union between client and therapist, where the client, rather than therapist solves problems.

The therapy is not about past memories or experiences, but about the structure of experiences in the present moment. The beliefs and experiences of the past are present in patterns of behavior, perception, and limitations experienced in the present moment. The client is helped to see how these limiting beliefs no longer apply in the present moment. Transformation happens naturally.

Ron Kurtz died in 2011. Hakomi Therapy is a work in progress.

Feldenkrais and Alexander Methods

F.M. Alexander was in his early twenties and performing in amateur theater when he developed a hoarseness. It got worse and after performances he could not speak. When he began gasping for air during performances, advice from his doctors led nowhere, so he began a process of self-examination.

Instead of trying to speak correctly, he found success inhibiting wrong movements. He broke everything down and eliminated any unnecessary movement. He learned not to focus on the end goal, but rather on the process. His respiratory problems completely disappeared and the foundation of the Alexander Method was established. The answer came from within, not from a therapist.

Feldenkrais was six years old and still living in Russia when F. Matthias Alexander first published "Man's Supreme Inheritance." In 1910, after World War II, Feldenkrais came to London and studied with F.M.

Alexander's assistant.

The Feldenkrais and Alexander methods are programs of slow, small movements to regain a body awareness apart from the image we hold of our bodies. Both methods evolved from men motivated by a need to overcome or compensate for a physical impediment.

Israeli Moshe Pinchas Feldenkrais injured his knee and could barely get around. A judo expert, he studied and broke down movement, discovering that life and movement are practically one. He realized his inability to walk was not just due to structural damage, but that learned habits of movement contributed to the problem. He understood our movements flow from a self-image made up of sensation and feelings formed during the first fourteen years of our lives. The nervous system has no direct perception of the outside world.

Feldenkrais believed the best way of changing a person's behavior is through the body, since it is easier to make a person aware of what is happening in the body. A body approach yields faster and more direct results for both mind and body. Feldenkrais approached unity of mind and body through retraining the muscular and skeletal system, thus affecting the body, feelings, and awareness of oneself and the environment.

A good presentation of Feldenkrais Method comes from Ruthy Alon who studied with Feldenkrais in Israel from 1959 until 1967, during the time that Feldenkrais was well known in Israel as the personal tutor of Prime Minister Ben-Gurion. When Feldenkrais decided to come to America in 1972, he suggested Alon start teaching classes there and she did, at Esalen Institute in California where she gradually evolved her own way of presenting the Feldenkrais method.

Alon presents Feldenkrais awareness through movement in her book "Mindful Spontaneity: Lessons in the Feldenkrais Method." Her movements flow seamlessly from one movement to the next over time. This is illustrated in her book in a series of small drawings that slowly change position across the page. Her videos on Youtube show the same movements and are beautiful and informative to watch. Here is the first of her series, "Movement Nature Meant." https://www.youtube.com/watch?v=igpJeOkgfzw

Somatics

Thomas Hanna became acquainted with Feldenkrais in 1973. In 1975, then director of the Humanistic Psychology Institute (now Saybrook University), Hanna arranged the first Feldenkrais training program in the United States. Continuing his studies with Feldenkrais, he and his wife Eleanor founded the Novato Institute for Somatic Research and Training where he worked with thousands of clients using the Feldenkrais Method. Whereas Feldenkrais went deeply into the philosophy behind his method, Hanna who coined the term Somatics, wrote in a straight forward, practical way in his 1988 book "Somatics: Reawakening the Mind's Control of Movement, Flexibility, and Health."

You will not come away with an ability to practice the Feldenkrais method after reading Feldenkrais's own books, but Hanna's "Somatics" offers detailed description with images to put the method into practice. Both men's books are well worth reading. I don't think I would have looked into Somatics if I had not read at least one book by Feldenkrais and been smitten by his genius.

Hanna believed seventy-five percent of chronic pain suffered by American adults is caused by sensory-motor amnesia (SMA). Sensory nerves are on the dorsal root (branch), the back of the spinal cord. Motor nerves are on the ventral root (branch), the belly side of the spinal cord. Inside the brain, the two systems merge and branch.

Everything we sense travels up the sensory nerves on the dorsal-back root of the spinal cord, controlling our perception of the world and of ourselves. All movement, everything we do, travels from the brain down the belly side or ventral root of the spinal cord. The nerves of both paths weave in and out of the spinal cord. Though the spinal cord ends at the base of the thoracic part of the spine, nerves of both pathways extend on downward.

These two nerve paths reach upward into the brain. The brain integrates incoming sensory information with outgoing commands to the motor system in a feedback loop of movement and perception, perception and movement.

With sensory-motor amnesia (SMA), the cerebral cortex looses part of its ability to voluntarily control all or some of the muscles of the body. Instead of the frontal cortex of the brain voluntarily controlling muscles, control is taken over by the subcortical (beneath the cortex) subconscious areas. Reflexes taken over by the subcortical brain cause muscles to automatically contract. We, or our cerebral cortex, have lost voluntary control.

Muscles held in chronic partial contraction become weak and painful and cause a constant energy drain. Structurally, the symptoms are evident in postural distortions and eventually what is mistaken for arthritis, bursitis, or other misdiagnosis. Doctors often have no idea of what to do other than to prescribe medications serving to mask the symptoms.

Involuntary contraction of the muscles in the body's center of gravity affects the contraction of muscles in the periphery of the body. The contraction of these periphery muscles then causes a compensating contraction in muscles at the center of gravity. You experience these powerful muscles contracting at the center of gravity. That is why so many of us experience back pain.

Somatic Education

Somatic education involves integrated, sensory-motor feedback. The problem is mainly functional; the brain has lost voluntary control of the bodily functions. Problems of lost control due to memory loss are not irreversible structural deterioration of body parts. Rather than treatment by a medical doctor, Somatics involves education.

We have lost the memory of what it feels like to move certain muscles and are in a state of constant contraction. We need to learn how to start moving the muscles voluntarily. Many so called disorders of aging can be prevented and reversed through educating and retraining sensory awareness and movement. These are disorders that can be solved by us, not by a doctor.

In a sense, Somatics involves body psychotherapy, since the cause of the body problem is the result of everything that has happened to us during our lives. Our brain reacts and adapts to all of the anxiety, fear, and despair, to the shocks to our system, to serious illnesses and accidents, to surgery. The brain compensates automatically and unconsciously in an attempt to rebalance the system. Education is needed to help the brain become aware of lost memories in order to change and adapt in a positive way of healing an inefficient body system that we easily mistake for "old age."

To develop this awareness, Somatic exercises cause gentle contraction a bit more than the already involuntary contractions. Once you sense the muscles and have an awareness what the contracted state feels like, you take back voluntary control and are able to relax the muscles. Somatics is about an awareness of muscles and their involuntary state of contraction in order to take back voluntary control and get a sense of well being.

Somatic therapists manipulate the body to help the client sense and have an awareness of contracted muscles. It is a short-term therapy. Hanna worked with most clients for only days and weeks. Once the client experiences an awareness, they can practice the basic exercises on their own.

It makes life harder to manage when we are in contracted in pain. We have forgotten how to take voluntary control after moments of stress and so the stress continues on, spreading to other body systems. By regaining voluntary control, instead of expending most of our energy fighting our stressed physical bodies, we more easily continue to move ahead throughout our lives.

In my early twenties, I worked in the post office and sprained my back one night loading heavy sacks of mail onto the boxcar of a train. X-rays showed a collapsed vertebrae in the lower lumbar of the spine. Other than surgery, not much can be done other than medication to relieve the pain. I sometimes barely could get up out of my futon during the night to go to the bathroom. I struggled to get the covers off my body, then inched my legs to the edge of the futon. Trying to stand, the shock of pain was so intense, sometimes I crawled to the bathroom. I now do a simple exercise that takes only a few minutes and I get up out of bed with no pain. This sold me on Somatics.

Though X-rays show a picture that cannot easily be disputed, X-rays don't necessarily show the complete cause of the problem and, of course, do not prescribe relief. X-rays too often are viewed in terms of a brainless mechanical structure demanding surgery or some other reengineering. But Somatics treats at least a part of the problem as hyper-tensed muscles caused by sensory-motor amnesia (SMA). Somatics are a set of eight exercises to relearn, sense, and control hyper-tense muscles. The exercises retrain the brain to regain voluntary control of movement and posture and relieve the brain of its habitual mode of automatic involuntary response.

Figure 15-3: Pandiculating Cat

Pandiculation Exercises

Somatic body movements involve pandiculation to reset control of the brain back to the voluntary cerebral cortex. Hanna describes pandiculating as a strong voluntary muscular contraction that feeds back to an equally strong sensory stimulation of the brain, resetting the system from a subcortical involuntary pattern of response to a voluntary cortical one.

Pandiculation is the stretch a dog or cat does when they awaken; what an infant does in the womb. It is the basic resetting mechanism of vertebrates. When a cat or dog wakes up, it pandiculates by contracting the large extensor muscles of the back that are essential for running. Then it may pandiculate in reverse by contracting the anterior muscles into a flexed posture.

The pandicular response is a voluntary muscular contraction that "wakes up" the sensory-motor cortex of the brain. It awakens the feedback connection between the sensory and motor areas of the brain, improving voluntary muscular control. This ancient sensory-motor cortical arousal is linked with awakening in all vertebrates. Somatic exercises or movements are rooted in this concept of pandicular contraction.

Since the back is an issue for so many people, I'll include the basic one here. Lie on your back and pull your feet in towards your body, both feet flat on the floor so your knees are an inverted "V" pointing up at the ceiling.

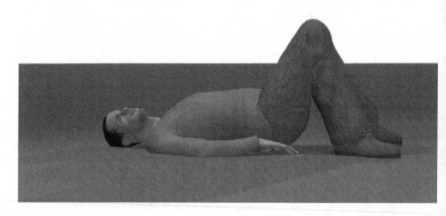

Figure 15-4: Back Exercise

Press your back gently down flat against the floor. Inhale as you press down on the base of your spine, on your tailbone, so that your back arches just a bit at the belt from the floor. Feel the contraction through your lower back.

Exhale as you ease your back down flat against the floor, flat and (not contracted) relaxed. Inhale as you press down on the tailbone and arch the belt line and contract. Exhale as you lower your back, flatten and relax.

When you feel comfortable with this contract and relax movement, try pressing your tailbone down firmer to arch the back a just a bit higher. And when you bring your back down flat, push the opposite way, slightly lifting the tailbone. The concept is a wave-like contraction. Do this exercise slowly and gently. It may not feel like much is happening, but you will notice a difference in pain relief.

I do this before I go to bed and in the morning before breakfast. Hanna recommends doing this exercise for about 20 reps per session, but I get pretty much relief from back pain with five to seven reps.

But I also do my own stretches each time I wake up during the night. I get up three or four times. I relax and bend further and further down toward my toes until I touch my toes. Then I stretch up and back, reaching up and back with both arms outstretched.

Somatic exercises change your muscular system by changing your central nervous system. Unlike calisthenics, it is better to do slow, minimal movements giving your brain the chance to notice all that is happening in your body as you move. You don't want to jump ahead to another movement until you internally experience the one you are working on. The exercises are progressive, so successful learning depends on learning the movements at the previous levels. The goal is to make this awareness a part of your regular pattern of movements.

We constantly seek out the latest innovations and in this incessant quest, the basics get buried. Feldenkrais's work has managed to survive the years, perhaps because it is the basic foundation of many other systems.

Unconditional Body Self-Acceptance

If it is to be effective, unconditional self-acceptance had best be a basic part of any form of somatic therapy. As difficult as it may be, any alternative to unconditional self-acceptance will likely lead to failure.

Stress builds when you reject and become detached from your body. You may find it hard to feel physical pleasure. You likely compare yourself with other people or to some ideal of what the body should be. It may make you unhappy to think of or feel your body. You may dislike being touched. All these are signs of Body Dysmorphic Disorder (BDD).

Unless you find a way to accept and attune to your body, your body reacts to this disconnection with stress, pain, and disease. When you are attuned, your body has an amazing ability to correct discomfort and disease. This is an incentive to learn to accept and feel comfortable in your body. The process begins with awareness.

The more aware, the more sensitive you are to your body. But this is a sensitivity without the unresolvable dead-end problem solving. It is bodily awareness with minimal body image. It is the process of stepping back from the worry and rumination of perceived body image problems.

Ki Breathe into your body, breathing in awareness and acceptance throughout your entire body and into individual problematic parts. You are the decider. You choose to accept yourself or not. Choose to accept, not punish yourself with stress, pain, and disease. Make the decision to unconditionally accept yourself and it will make a noticeable change.

You can seldom shut out the bothersome thinking and the existential gnawing. But you can practice letting thoughts and feelings come and go with a detached third-person POV. You get better at this with practice.

16 WHO IS PLANTING SEEDS OF ACTION IN OUR 50 BITS OF ATTENTION

We don't need no education

We don't need no thought control

No dark sarcasm in the classroom

Teachers leave them kids alone

Hey! Teachers! Leave them kids alone!

I am one of the teachers my students might think back on hearing that song. I was resentful ending up a classroom teacher. After a couple of years I left teaching to pursue my career as a school psychologist, and it was a fluke landing back in the classroom; a tragic fluke.

I was interviewed in Kauai, Hawaii, where I was school psychologist for the island's seven schools. At the time I was interviewed, I was not married and had no intention of marrying. But before I left that tiny island, I was in a kind of shot-gun wedding. Her father threatened to hunt me down if I did not send for her when I settled in Korea.

When I got settled, I came to my senses. She was an island beauty, but marginally mentally retarded. I felt sick, but knew I could not bring her over. I found that I was eligible for a family separation allowance that I accepted. That was my downfall. It was years later when I was teaching at a middle school and friends with the principal, that he decided to check out what was going on. He went to the superintendent and found that when I accepted the allowance, I messed up the budget for the school year. Admin thought I was single, so the allowance blew their budget for the year. I was never to be promoted to the position of school psychologist I had been promised.

The principal told me this with a promise I would never tell anyone what he had told me. He strongly suggested I put in for a transfer to Europe DoDDS (Department of Defense Dependent Overseas Schools) (now DODEA) and he would be sure I got the position of school psychologist since I was highly credentialed for the position.

I was in love with Japan. I loved the people, the culture. I loved the food and travel around the country. I had never experienced anything like this and could not consider giving it up. With OCD, though, a classroom teacher was the worst possible job and I had spent three years in graduate school at one of the best programs in the country to get out of the classroom. But because of OCD, I kept at it for twenty-four more years at a cost of giving up a position of school psychologist that I loved and was really good at.

The start of each school year was rough. The high school students reacted to me with baggage they carried in with them. It was apparent to them I was different and they tested that in every way possible. But I came equipped with graduate training in behavioral psychology. In order to gain control, I developed systems for everything, and after several weeks the kids — like lab rats — were operating within these systems. I put checkmarks next to their name each time they added something, anything, to our class discussion. At first they worked for the checks. Some of the jocks humored me along, "Did you mark a check for me, Mr. Dames?"

They soon discovered they could direct the discussions in ways that applied to their lives. After a few weeks, no one seemed aware of the checks. No one except for me. In the manner of a true obsessive compulsive, I micromanaged everything with seven or eight colored pens; checks in class participation, homework, tests, exams, etc. In two months the group completely changed from the start of the school year.

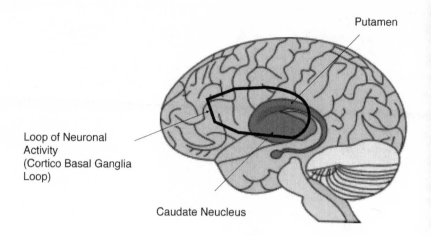

Putamen

Loop of Neuronal
Activity
(Cortico Basal Ganglia
Loop)

Caudate Neucleus

**The striatum is the caudate
nucleus plus the putamen. It
is a snail-like structure.**

Figure 16-1: Cortico-Basal Ganglia Loop

My method of teaching was a mix of OCD and operant conditioning; operant conditioning that had been drilled into me in graduate school: "Animals don't think." These kids did. I questioned the class about the assigned readings. They responded to the readings in terms of their own backgrounds and lives at the time.

Each time they responded, they were rewarded with a pencil check, and following the laws of operant conditioning they connected their response and checkmark to my verbal response. I added up the class-discussion checks—fifty percent of their grade. I created cortico-basal ganglia loops in my "subjects." I wanted them totally focused on classroom discussions the entire period and behavioral reinforcement achieved that goal. For my own survival, I was totally into mind control.

The striatum, a part of the basal ganglia, is where habits are made. (Actually, the habit is made in both the frontal cortex and the striatum, kind of a redundant parallel processing.) Once the habit is formed and the dopamine reward locks it in place, the image in the frontal cortex fades away. The dopamine comes from the substantia nigra, below the striatum, close to the brain stem. (Figures 16-1 and 13-2)

Once a habit is locked in, it is locked in for life. You can't get rid of it, but with disuse it will weaken. An alcoholic or drug addict is never really cured. But if they do not drink or smoke and reignite the habit, they can live an alcohol or drug-free life.

Brainwashing Masses

Had I been familiar with public opinion guru Frank Luntz, I surely would have added his style of brainwashing to my routine. Luntz's book, "Words That Work: It's Not What You Say It's What People Hear You Say," is about brainwashing, essentially scripting the minds of others to think as you want them to. Unfortunately for me, fortunately for my students, his book was published in 2007. I burnt out of the classroom in 1992.

Luntz encouraged the Republican Party to substitute "death tax" for "estate tax." He found in polling that if you call it an estate tax, about 50% of Americans want to eliminate it. When you think of an estate, you tend to think of someone with considerable wealth. If you call it the death tax, about 70% of Americans want to eliminate it. Americans perceived it wrong to incur a tax upon the family of the deceased. In 2017 though, only individuals with an estate worth more than $5,490,000 would have been taxed. But facts mean little once the script of unfairness gets imbedded in our minds. And it took just two "magic" words.

When Luntz polled Americans and asked them whether they would be willing to pay higher taxes for additional law enforcement, 51 percent said they would. When he asked if they would pay higher taxes to halt rising crime rate, 68 percent said they would. Luntz says the secret is to focus on results, reducing crime, rather than the process of law enforcement.

In the later half of the 1990s, while Newt Gingrich was Republican Speaker of the House of Representatives, he made tapes and videos instructing lawmakers on how to communicate. Many of Gingrich's ideas were developed together with Luntz. In 1996 Gingrich wrote a memo to the House GOP listing words they should memorize. Words like common sense, family, and freedom would give power to their message. When talking about their opponents the list included sick, welfare, failure, and trader. And from basic neuroscience, Frank Luntz knew the power of a message or script repeated many times.

The words he shared with Gingrich were tested in focus groups and dial sessions. What sets a dial session apart from a focus group is that everyone holds a small wireless remote control dial with a numerical display from 0 to 100. When they hear something they like, they dial up toward 100, when they dislike something they dial down toward "0."

Figure 16-2: Like or Dislike

On the other side of a one-way mirror, a second-by-second digital line graph plots gut reactions to speeches, commercials, clips from a television show, movie, live presentations of a conversation, etc. Colored line graphs instantly plot for each of the subgroups within the main responding group. Luntz says this is the research equivalent of an EKG measuring a combination of emotional and intellectual responses, getting inside each participant's psyche, isolating his or her reaction to every word, phrase, and visual.

Implicit, Explicit Memory

Dial sessions pinpoint words and phrases with positive or negative emotive impact. Luntz advises clients to use these words over and over on their target audience, implanting implicit memories. An explicit memory is conscious and cognitive, but an implicit, unconscious memory involves affect, feeling, and emotion over cognition. An irretrievable implicit memory is processed in a very close, but different part of the brain than a conscious, retrievable, explicit memory.

Planting an Action With a Word

You want to know all you can about priming, because planting, implicit, unconscious memories alters our thinking and perception, causing us to respond like automatons. Once the implicit memory is planted, we see and judge a person, situation, or product through the primed frame with no awareness of the prime being planted and no awareness of it after it is stored in our brain. We are bombarded with political and commercial primes to favor parties, people, products, services, and values, and to disfavor others.

Just Because

A word as common as "because" can become a cue, a magic word setting off a social behavior. If you want to skip to the front of a queue, start out by saying, "Excuse me," then make sure the clause that follows begins with "because." Excuse me, but would you mind if I step in here, because I'm nine months pregnant and I'm starting to feel labor pains."

It doesn't have to be nearly as dramatic. In 1978 Ellen Langer, Arther Blank and Benzion Chanowitz carried out a now classic study where researchers attempted to cut in at the front of a queue to a copy machine. They compared three approaches:

"Excuse me, I have five pages. May I use the Xerox machine, because I am in a rush?"

"Excuse me, I have five pages. May I use the Xerox machine?"

"Excuse me, I have five pages. May I use the Xerox machine, because I have to make copies?"

More than ninety percent of the people let the researchers cut in front of them in the first situation, when they added "because I am in a rush." When in the second situation they offered no excuse at all only sixty percent of the people let them cut in line. So you might expect the same in the third situation, because they offered no excuse other than they wanted to make a copy. But this was not so. In the third situation about the same percentage of people let them cut in line as they did in the first situation; more than ninety percent.

The word "because" is the cue or prime that gets others to allow them to cut in line. "Because" sets off an automatic and mindless neurological response of compliance. But it does not work all of the time. If the number of copies are high, the frontal cortex steps in and overrides a mindless response. When they see someone with a stack of papers attempting to cut into line, they do not get sucked in by the prime.

Since people often respond to the structure of the message rather than the actual message, if you set up the right cue, you increase the chance you get the person to mindlessly comply. And by becoming aware of the different forms of cues that set off mindless routines of behavior, you can avoid being primed into mindless compliance.

Warm it Up for Success

Words are only one of many forms of primes. In the classic study by University of Michigan professor John Bargh, "Experiencing Physical Warmth Promotes Interpersonal Warmth" (2008), a confederate who is blind to the study's hypothesis meets volunteers in the lobby of the psychology building. The confederate carries a cup of coffee, a clipboard, and two textbooks. During the elevator ride to the fourth-floor laboratory, the confederate casually asks participants if they will hold the coffee cup for a second while he/she records their name and the time of their participation. After the confederate writes down the information, he/she takes back the coffee. The temperature of the coffee, hot versus cold, is the only factor being manipulated.

Figure 16-3: For some reason, I feel he's kinda nice.

When participants arrive at the experimental room, they receive a packet containing a personality impression questionnaire describing the target person they are to evaluate. They rate the target person on five bipolar, warm-cold personality traits and five traits unrelated to warm-cold.

The subjects who held the hot coffee rate the person significantly warmer on the five "warm-cold" traits than those who had held the cold coffee. There is no difference in ratings for the five traits unrelated to warm and cold. This demonstrates the brain's association between sensations of physical warmth and judgements of interpersonal warmth.

Carry a hand warmer or use biofeedback to warm your hands before shaking hands with someone important to you.

The prime was the physical experience of holding a warm or cold cup of coffee. As with other primes, it operates on an implicit, unconscious level. Holding the warm or cold cup of coffee influenced feelings of interpersonal warmth or coldness without the subject being consciously aware they were being primed.

The processing of physical temperature and interpersonal warmth/trust both take place in a pyramid-shaped part of the brain tucked under parts of the temporal and frontal lobes called the insula. The insula plays a role in both the sensation of skin temperature and the detection of trustworthiness of others. It is a mind-body coordinator.

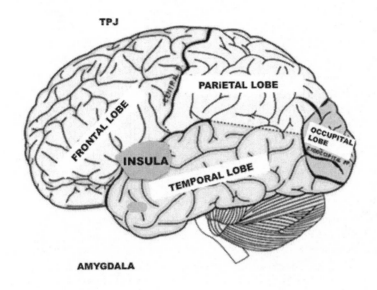

Figure 16-4: Insula

This study illustrates what is called the social perceiver's "first pass" in determining whether or not someone can be trusted as a friend or at least a "non-foe," or is someone who will interfere rather than help with one's ongoing goal pursuits. The assessment, judgement, or evaluation does not take place in the conscious mind. It is an automatic and obligatory evaluation by the brain, not requiring the perceiver's intent.

Bargh relates this to Harry Harlow and John Bowlby. In Harlow's experiments, monkeys formed an attachment to the warm cloth mother over the wire mothers that fed them. Bowlby demonstrated the need for direct physical contact with the caretaker over and above the caretaker's satisfaction of the infant's primary needs of hunger and thirst.

Because of early life experiences with a warm and caring caregiver, a close mental association develops between the concepts of physical warmth and psychological warmth. Bargh discusses research on the neurobiology of attachment, adding support for the link between tactile temperature and feelings of psychological warmth and trust.

Warmth is considered the most powerful personality trait in social judgement. In an instant, people decide whether or not to do business with you or have anything at all to do with you from that time on, and it can hinge on a warm or cold coffee or handshake.

Planting a Sensation That Drives Behavior

Haptic sensations are another prime. The Oxford English Dictionary defines haptic as "Of pertaining to, or relating to the sense of touch or tactile sensations" and as "having a greater dependence on sense of touch than on sight, especially as a means of psychological orientation." Haptic is a form of social communication often used by non-human animals, but some people, maybe the ones who formed a close attachment in infancy and childhood, are haptic.

People like me with a poor childhood attachment may be extremely uncomfortable with haptic communicators. I have to keep myself from physically withdrawing from people who touch in communicating.

"Incidental Haptic Sensations Influence Social Judgements and Decisions," published in 2010 in the journal Science, describes the study where Joshua Ackerman and John Bargh had subjects evaluate job resumes of applicants. The only difference between the resumes was the weight of the clipboard holding the resumes. One clipboard was heavier than the other. Subjects holding the heavier clipboard evaluated the job candidate as more serious.

The brain processes literal and metaphorical versions of touch in the same brain region as warm and cold, the insula. Our neural circuitry does not differentiate between real and symbolic. The heavier weight of the clipboard unconsciously triggers the metaphor of heaviness for seriousness in the subject's brain and the applicant is rated as more serious.

Rude Words = Rude Behavior

In another Bargh study, participants made sentences as quickly as they could from five scrambled words. Three versions of the scrambled-sentence test were constructed. One was intended to prime the construct "rude," another to prime the construct "polite," and a third consisted of neutral words.

When participants complete the task, they are told to take the test paper to the confederate who is standing and talking with someone. The confederate ignores the subject, so the only way she/he can hand in her/his paper is to interrupt the conversation by saying something like "Excuse me," or "Sorry, but." The moment the participant butts in, the confederate who is timing to see how long it takes for the subject to interrupt, stops his/her stopwatch. The maximum period timing can go on is set at ten minutes.

Within this ten minute period, subjects primed with polite words interrupted the confederate about eighteen percent of the time, while subjects primed on rude words interrupted about sixty-five percent of the time. Subjects primed on neutral words interrupted about thirty-eight percent of the time.

Healthy Words Lose Weight

Primes get you to purchase unhealthy foods. So researchers in the Netherlands wanted to see whether overweight and obese people could be primed to purchase healthy snacks. The prime is a flyer handed to them when they enter the supermarket, primed with healthy words within a recipe.

Overweight and obese participants who received the flyer with health and diet-related words bought almost 75% fewer unhealthy snacks than overweight and obese participants who received the same flyer without the health and diet-related words. The priming effects were independent of whether or not participants thought about the flyer while shopping.

"Using Health Primes to Reduce Unhealthy Snack Purchases Among Overweight Consumers in a Grocery Store"

Much of our decision-making goes on inside the neural networks of our brains, outside of the conscious mind. Priming affects a wide swath of psychological systems of evaluation, perception, motivation, and behavior. You can be primed to judge a person with kindness or hostility. Companies sell products with primes. Candidates get elected with the help of primes.

Primes can be used as a health-intervention tool to fight obesity. More likely they will continue to be used to get people to buy high-calorie, sugar-laden snacks. Once primed you have no conscious awareness the priming has on your decision-making process. As my father admonished when I borrowed the keys to his car, "Keep your wits about you."

Good Stereotype, Bad Stereotype

Stereotypes are solid, deep, implicit memories operating at the unconscious level. Like priming, stereotypes can have a negative or positive influence. Claude Steele, then professor and dean of the school of education and social psychology at Stanford University, demonstrated how just the threat of a group stereotype affects performance on an aptitude test.

In his classic 1995 study published in "Journal of Personality and Social Psychology," Black and White students with similar SAT scores were given a test of difficult items from the verbal Graduate Record Exam (GRE). One group was told the test diagnosed intellectual ability and the other group was told the test was a problem-solving situation.

Black students scored lower then Whites when the test was perceived as an ability test, but scored as well as Whites when told it was a problem solving situation. Black students were threatened by the stereotype of Blacks being less intelligent than Whites.

In 1999, as a PhD candidate at Harvard University, Margaret Shih, Associate Professor at UCLA Anderson School of Management, published a research report, "Stereotype Susceptibility" in Psychological Science. Before taking a test, each of the Asian, female undergraduate students in the study filled out a questionnaire. One questionnaire primed them as female, the other as Asian.

Be Careful of Questionnaires

Questions on the "female-identity-salient conditions" included whether their floors were coed or single-sex, which they preferred and why. Questions on the "Asian-identity-salient condition" included whether their parents or grandparents spoke any languages other than English, what languages they knew, what languages they spoke at home, and what opportunities they had to speak other languages on campus.

Participants in the Asian-identity group answered an average of 54% of the questions correctly. Participants in the female-identity group answered an average of 43% correctly. Participants in a neutral control group answered an average of 49% correctly. Both positive and negative performances were activated by subtle, implicit priming of their identity. Asians were purportedly smarter, and at the time, females not so smart. The next time you are asked to participate in a survey or to fill out a questionnaire, be on guard as to who is footing the bill and the purpose of the study.

Stigmatized Behavior

A 2009 study published in Experimental Aging Research demonstrated the influence of stereotyping on older people. When older subjects were told that older people perform poorly on a particular memory test, they performed poorly. The study demonstrated that memory suffers when senior citizens believe they are being "stigmatized," meaning others look down on them because of their age.

The negative effects of age-stereotyping are strongest for adults with the highest levels of education. Adults who value their ability to remember things are the most likely to be sensitive to the negative implications of this stereotyping and most likely to exhibit the problems associated with the stereotype.

Adults who do not feel stigmatized exhibited significantly higher levels of memory performance. If you are confident that aging will not ravage your memory, you are more likely to perform well on memory-related tasks.

I will be eighty on my next birthday and cannot help feeling stigmatized. Some of it is subtle, some blatant, but there is rampant ageism out there. It is virtually undetectable until you get up in age. I constantly remind myself not to let it get to me. Though I dislike being called "Sweetie" and being asked if I would like help carrying out one very small bag of groceries, I'm letting it all slide and allow people to rush ahead of me to hold open doors.

What I find difficult to let slide is the stigma of mental illness. But I should not be so harsh. People don't know the reason for the behavior of someone with a mental illness. They cannot see inside their head. Most conclude the person is different. Very different. The Other.

Wired for Prejudice

Stereotype frames show up in brain scans. The amygdala, activated by fear, anxiety, and aggression is metabolically active when viewing faces of "other" racial groups. In one brain scan study, faces were presented rapidly, much faster than can be consciously perceived. The amygdala especially reacted when white subjects view non familiar black faces. The amygdala even reacted when white male subjects looked at faded unfamiliar black images in old yearbooks. (See Figure 16-4)

This activation of the amygdala is a non conscious stereotype response to racial groups and the impact can be literally deadly. Stanford psychologist Jennifer Eberhardt had subjects rate how "stereotypically Black" a group convicted of murder appeared. Some of the men had been sentenced to death and some were given less severe sentences, but the subjects did not know about the sentencing. The results showed that the men rated "stereotypically Black" were more than twice as likely to be sentenced to death if their victim was white. They did not get any stricter sentences if their victims were Black, though.

On a hopeful note, studies by Princeton University social psychologist Susan Fiske show that if you make the subject think about the person as an individual beforehand, the amygdala no longer lights up. In one study, White subjects who viewed the Black faces were asked a simple question like what kind of vegetable might he like to eat. This changed the social frame. When White participants had to place Blacks into a different social category, they reacted to the Black face the same as with a White face.

Are We THAT Irrational?!

Anchoring illustrates just how irrational our implicit thought process gets. Anchoring refers to the presentation of a value or attribute that is used as a reference point to influence a decision. In a German study of judges with an average of more than fifteen years of experience on the bench, each of them read the case of a woman who had been caught shoplifting. They were then asked to give her a prison sentence (a mock, but serious sentence) for the crime. Before announcing the sentence, each judge rolled a loaded dice that came up with either a three or a nine.

These numbers served as anchors. The average sentence given by judges who rolled a three was five months and the average sentence for judges who rolled a nine was eight months. The effect of these random numbers serving as anchors amounted to a 50% influence on the time the woman would have spent in prison.

People anchor their responses to any random number.

Figure 16-5 Roll again please, your honor!

An Israeli study compared paroles granted by real-life judges handing down sentences at different times of day. A prisoner appearing before the judge early in the morning received parole over sixty-five percent of the time. If the convict appeared before the judge later in the day, he received parole only ten percent of the time. If the judge took a break, the parole rate shot back up again when he returned refreshed. Paroles by robots would be more equitable.

Globalizing

A huge form of stereotyping we do across all sectors of the population is globalizing. Globalizing, not in the dictionary sense of international influence or operation, but in Albert Ellis's sense of letting one part of a person define the person as a whole.

We globalize students, labeling and stereotyping at the negative side of the spectrum as discipline problems. Certainly penalties had better be given for infractions of rules. But the student's bad behavior is different from "the student is bad." We don't want to impose our negative globalizations on students, making it that much harder for them to unconditionally accept themselves.

Throughout most of my elementary school years, I was the class behavior problem. Cooperation, Dependability, Citizenship: F's in bright red ink down the left side of my report card. Throughout each day, my name was screamed at me as a pejorative. I was a "Discipline Problem" and ironically, perhaps because I was branded as such, I never changed my behavior until I got away from elementary school..

Principals with Department of Defense Overseas Dependent Schools

(DoDDS) where I taught for twenty-five years, rotate from district to district, rarely staying at one school for more than a few years. They come into the classroom once a year, usually unannounced for their "observation." From the back of the room they sit taking notes.

It made no difference year to year who the principal was or if they ever came into my classroom at all. I was "Average," "C," a reminder of the red Fs down the left side of my report card. My principal told me "C" was an adequate rating and I asked how he might like a "C" rating from his wife for his performance in bed. Education was a major part of my life. I was putting too much into it to be labeled Average.

You've Got It, Or Not

Most people make up their minds about a person in seconds and it never changes. Our intuitive system operates automatically. I have been told again and again there is something different about me. As far as job performance evaluation, not a good thing. You don't want to be different, not in that way. You want to be outgoing, positive, fun to go out with for a beer.

A study by Harvard psychologists Nalidy Ambady and Robert Rosenthal set out to determine what makes an "effective" high school teacher. They set up a video camera in the classroom and taped the 50 minute class. Eight judges who did not know the teacher, rated him/her on a number of personality traits after watching the video, without sound. Their ratings correlated highly with the school-year principal ratings.

Then they tried something radical. A teaching assistant randomly selected portions of the 50 minute videos, splicing them together to create 5 second and 2 second video clips. When judges now rated the teachers based on these brief silent clips, the correlation was just a bit lower, but still highly significantly correlated with the principals' annual ratings. When they compared these short video ratings with ratings students gave to teachers at the end of the semester, the correlation between the student ratings and the judges ratings from even a 2 second silent clip was significantly high. People make snap emotional judgements instantly even without hearing someone speak.

In another study, two interviewers trained for six weeks in employment interviewing techniques, conducted one-hundred-fifteen, twenty minute videotaped interviews. After each interview they rated applicants. The tapes were edited down to fifteen-seconds showing the job applicant entering the room, shaking hands with the interviewer, and sitting down.

When an independent group rated the fifteen-second video clips, their ratings correlated strongly with the trained interviewers. Then the tapes were edited down to just the handshake. On nine out of the eleven traits the applicants were judged on, observers viewing the tape just up through the initial handshake significantly predicted the outcome of the interview.

We globalize others, limiting focus to one or a small cluster of traits. We globally rate them on their physical appearance, skin color, ethnic background, warm or cold handshake. Kids learn to globalize about themselves by saying things like, "I'm a 'C' student." "I'm a loser." "I'm lousy at sports."

Making 'C's in every subject is different from being a 'C' student. Behavioral changes affect a change in grades. Take a front-row seat. Volunteer. Take text notes before class and fill in with class notes. Ask questions. Follow rules. If you continue to get 'C' s, you are never a 'C' student. You are a student who continues to get 'C's. You can continue to work at changing that.

When I was in my first year of graduate school I was getting all 'A's, but one teacher gave me a C on a paper I had written that I thought deserved an 'A'. I went up to the teacher pointing out where I thought it was 'A' work. And I explained that I needed all A's to get into the psychology program. The professor took the paper and handed it back the next day with the grade change to 'A'. Never knew you could do that.

Controlling the Script

In athletics some kids get an early start, but everyone improves with practice. We perform at some level of proficiency and choose or choose not to work hard at improving our performance. A mental change is as important in athletics as it is in academics. It is essential to learn how to control the script and not let it get programmed for you.

If our behavior can be changed without our knowing, shouldn't we be able to make willful changes? How are we priming ourselves that may be holding us back? What are conscious and unconscious scripts through which we interact with the world?

We need to be aware of how irrational we are, more irrational than any creature on this planet. We have much of the irrational behaviors of other animals, but we go further. As Albert Ellis pointed out, unlike any of the other animals, we talk to ourselves and tell ourselves sane and insane things. What makes this world inconceivably irrational is we all have our ongoing self-talk, beliefs, attitudes, opinions, and philosophies, impenetrable to others.

It takes knowledge, skill sets, and patience some of us spend our lives attempting to acquire, to live, work, love, and function with others. This awareness helps to stop blaming and condemning ourselves and others. We can let go of thinking that people and things should be this way or that. We plod along, to a large degree incomprehensibly irrational and that is the way we are. As you make changes in yourself, you will see this even more clearly in others. It might be nice if you could make changes in them. But you have enough to work on.

17 BELIEFS R US

Belief drives science to the next level and beyond. There is no progress in science without belief. Reason is a fundamental part of science, but the parent of reason is belief.

Heliocentrism, the astronomical model setting the sun at the center of our solar system, was first proposed in 9th or 8th century BC Sanskrit texts in India. Heliocentrism was again proposed in the 3rd century BC by a mathematician and astronomer from Ionia, a part of present-day Turkey. He added that the stars were distant suns. His beliefs were discarded as preposterous non science.

Heliocentrism came up a few more times, but in 1593, Nicolaus Copernicus published "On the Revolution of the Celestial Spheres," the first scientific treatise to provide detailed scientific support for heliocentrism. It was received with lots of skepticism during his lifetime.

The next heliocentric believer was Johannas Kepler, who added that the orbit of the planets around the sun is elliptical. Then in 1633, Galileo Galilei was sentenced to prison by the Inquisition on a charge of heresy for advancing the Copernican model of planetary motion in his book, "Dialogue Concerning the Two Chief World Systems."

Moving closer to acceptance, Sir Isaac Newton published "Principia Mathematica" describing the physical laws governing the motion of the planets. But it was not until 1757 that Pope Benedict XIV suspended the Catholic Church ban on works that support the heliocentric model.

A few years before that in 1738, Daniel Bernoulli published a book called "Hydrodynamical" with the idea that air flowing past the top surface of an aircraft wing is moving faster than the bottom side, and voila, you've got lift. At the time, who would have believed this? The first glider flight would not come until the 1890s by Otto Lilienthal, a German engineer. The world suspended its skepticism ("If God wanted us to fly, he would have given us wings.") on December 17, 1903 with the first successful flight in history of a self-propelled, heavier-than-air aircraft by the Wright brothers near Kitty Hawk, North Carolina.

Religiosity

Belief is the foundation of AA's Twelve-Step method. Five of the twelve steps directly mention God. One step refers to a spiritual awakening and another to a Power with a capital "P" that is greater than ourselves.

Charles Duhigg in his book "The Power of Habit," mentions a National Institute of Mental Health (NIMH) study that found alcoholics who practiced habit replacement could stay sober until there was a stressful event in their lives. But alcoholics who believed in some higher power could ride out those stressful times.

Song writer Howard Tate had a string of hits in the 1960s, along with an abundance of fame and fortune. At this early peak of his career, instead of feeling like a king, he was bitter about his financial standing in the music industry and sank into a depression. He felt that he was not receiving all the royalties he deserved. He saw himself as a victim, so he walked out from stardom into a life of working for the next fix of cocaine.

At first he sold insurance, but got depressed whenever he thought about his past successes. He thought drugs would alleviate his depression. Drugs led to homelessness and a subculture he believed he was trapped in for good. He was begging people and would walk miles to clean out their garage or wash a car so he could have twenty dollars for the next fix to satisfy an urge he could not walk away from. It took him decades before he found the courage to pull himself together and make another recording.

He prayed and admitted that he was hooked on crack and saw no way out of this subculture he was trapped in but death. After he made this open confession, the urge lifted. By the mid-1990s he had overcome his addictions and became a minister. He returned to the music world with his 2003 come back album "Rediscovered," an album nominated for a Grammy. At 64 he was back on the road touring, releasing four more CDs before he died. He said what saved him was his confession to God.

Fresh Air Remembers Soul Singer Howard Tate   December 9, 2011 Interview originally broadcast on October 27, 2003   Singer Howard Tate and Producer Jerry Ragovoy

Albert Ellis might have said this worked for him, but it is an ineloquent, irrational belief. From what we know from brain imaging studies, though it may not be rational and eloquent, belief in something larger than ourselves can be an effective therapy, precisely because it targets the non rational part of the brain that needs to be rewired.

Isolated and small, living with a lack of control in a world of unfairness and injustice, we need to know how to deal with and cope with our suffering. We need guidance, kindness, structure, and appreciation. Starting at an early age we need to learn about navigating this life. When we come face to face with mortality, we need something to lift us, to sooth our agitated soul and calm it down.

Besides the comforting belief in something larger than ourselves, religion offers a sense of structure, with reminders from morning to night and throughout the calendar year for life events large and small. Religion ties learning to the calendar year, so we learn and are reminded to remember specific things at different times of the week, season, and year. This occurs year after year, so there is ongoing relearning throughout our lifetimes.

In school we learn in a class lecture at 9 a.m. and by 3 p.m. we have forgotten ninety percent of the material we may never encounter again. Religion takes into account that we are forgetful creatures in need of constant relearning and reminders.

The Buddhist, the Christian, the Muslim, and the Jew may all get answers to their prayers in spite of the enormous differences among their stated beliefs. There is some evidence that a higher level of spirituality and belief correlate with greater well being, physical and mental health, less substance abuse, more stable marriages, even better military performance. It is not because of the particular creed, religion, affiliation, ritual, ceremony, formula, liturgy, incantation, sacrifices, or offerings, but rather because of belief or mental acceptance and receptivity about that for which they pray.

Alain de Botton, author of "Religion for Atheists: A Nonbelievers Guide to the Uses of Religion," feels you can engage with religion without having to subscribe to its supernatural content. The focus instead can be on soul-related needs of community, festivity, renewal, even rituals. Nonbelievers can cherry-pick from Buddhism, Christianity, Islam, Judaism, and the tens of other major (and minor) belief systems. You can be an atheist and be a spiritual person believing in something bigger than yourself.

We have the need for community offering us a sense of belonging. We may join a religious organization for companionship or for credentials of membership in a club or community organization. It may have nothing to do with rites and ceremonies, but more to do with an existential search for purpose in life.

In his introduction to "Religions, Values, and Peak-Experiences," Abraham Maslow divides organized religion into two extreme camps, the mystical versus the organizational. Most partake in the organizational and organized religion is largely a set of habits, dogmas, and forms, at times even the anti religious antagonist of spiritual experience.

Spirituality & the Brain

Very few university professors in the science fields dedicate their research to spirituality and survive. Andrew Newberg, Director of Research at the Myrna Brind Center for Integrative Medicine at Thomas Jefferson

University Hospital and Medical College is board-certified in internal medicine and nuclear medicine. He put his reputation on the line, devoting his research to the interface of neuroscience, religion, and meditation. He uses the methodology of scientific research to delve into what happens to us when we are religious and spiritual. He is author of several books including "God and the Brain: The Physiology of Spiritual Experience."

Newberg explores religious, spiritual, and meditative practices with a goal of finding contemplative exercises to strengthen neurological circuits involved with consciousness, empathy and social awareness. He looks for ways of optimizing spiritual, religious, and meditative practices to lead us into a more compassionate approach to our lives.

Newberg found the longer we engage in spiritual practice, the more control we gain over mind and body. And not unexpectedly, he found that brain responses of religious experiences lie along a continuum just as with secular experiences. A specific experience for some will be intense. The same experience for others barely elicits a neuropsychological response.

In order for meditation or prayer to change the brain's circuitry, it must be longer than just a few minutes. The longer the period of meditation or prayer, the greater the change in the brain. When meditation is practiced within the context of regular religious activity, health benefits accrue, even extending length of life. Different parts of the brain are affected at different points of the meditative session. Toward the end of a twelve minute session, there is decreased activity of the parietal lobe.

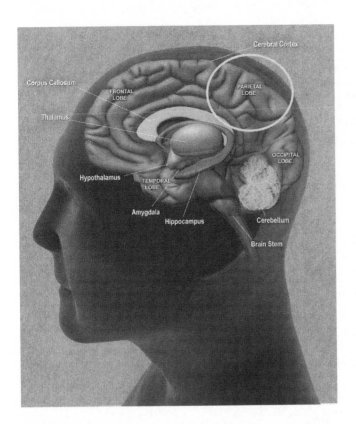

Figure 17-1 Parietal Lobe

The parietal lobe is the cortical part of the brain associated with constructing a sense of self. One of the goals of meditating is to move from a sense of self to a unified state of oneness. The nuns in Newberg's study reported coming closer to God toward the end of a session.

After eight weeks of twelve-minute basic daily meditation, brain scans showed decreased activity in parietal lobe and significant increase of neural activity in the prefrontal cortex behind the forehead, the cognitive and executive part of the brain. The prefrontal cortex strengthens selective attention and the ability to focus on goals and involves some memory functions.

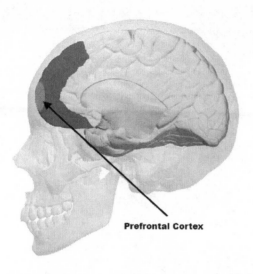

Prefrontal Cortex

17-2 Prefrontal Cortex (Figure 12-1)

Eight weeks of meditating produced significant increase of neural activity in the anterior cingulate cortex (ACC), the small structure sitting at the center of the communication junction between the frontal lobe which initiates thoughts and behaviors and the limbic system which processes a wide range of feelings and emotions. The ACC integrates messages from the limbic system below and from the cortex above. It monitors attention. The neurological heart of compassion appears to be in the ACC.

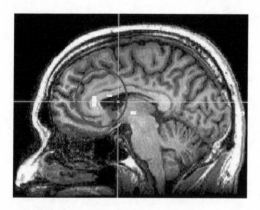

Figure 17-3: ACC Anterior Cingulate Cortex (MRI Image)

Activation in the prefrontal cortex and ACC can improve memory and cognition and counter the effects of depression. Parkinson's and Alzheimer patients show reduced metabolic activity in the ACC and Newberg concludes that meditation should slow down the deterioration caused by these diseases.

The ACC integrates messages from the limbic system below and from the cortex above.

It monitors attention.

The ACC is more activated with novice than advanced meditators, apparently because beginners have more conflict with distracting events and thoughts and feelings. When the ACC activates and strengthens, this gives beginners more power to resolve conflict by focusing attention away from emotional and external distractions.

Mystical Experience

Newberg and others have found that people who have had mystical experiences often report them as more real than reality. They perceive the experience to represent a more fundamental reality than the every day material reality we inhabit. One of the descriptions people give to the experience is a reality existing prior to subjective even objective sense of reality, meaning it existed before we as human beings apply our mental processes to it, if ever we perceive it. It is boundless, even of time.

During mystic experiences, people report the material world is no longer there. Newberg questions whether it is possible that through spiritual experiences we gain access to some level of reality that we normally don't have access to. We really don't know what is actually out there, what is outside of our brains. The eyes send ten million bits/second to the brain every second versus the 40 bits/second we consciously perceive. In order to know reality, we would need to find some way to get outside of our brains to see what is actually out there.

> For several moments I experience a happiness that is
> impossible under ordinary circumstances, and of which
> most people have no comprehension. I feel a complete
> harmony within myself and in the whole world, and this
> feeling is so strong and affords so much pleasure that one
> could give up ten years of one's life for several seconds of
> that ecstasy, perhaps one's whole life.
>
> Dostoevsky and the Dynamics of Religious Experience, by
> Malcolm Jones (Page 75-6)

Who can say that beyond this world a super-world does not exist? Just as the animal can scarcely reach out of his environment to understand the superior world of man, so perhaps man can scarcely ever grasp the super-world, though he can reach out toward it in religion, or perhaps encounter it in revelation. A domestic animal does not understand the purposes for which man employs it. How then could man know what "final" purpose his life has; what "super-meaning" the universe has.

Victor Frankl's "The Doctor and the Soul: From Psychotherapy to Logo Therapy"

Dostoevsky and Frankl describe an experience I had. It was like stepping from the third dimension out into the bright clarity of a higher dimension. What I was seeing was out there, what had already been out there before I perceived it, not something in my head.

My brain stopped filtering, allowing me to perceive a suddenly revealed external reality. This happened more than forty years ago and I have never shared it, because it is like describing being abducted by aliens. Had I heard it from anyone else, I would doubt their credibility. Yet it was the most significant event of my life. And now I learn it is not so uncommon.

During the school year of 1967-1968, I was a high school dormitory counselor on an army post in Pusan, Korea. employed with U.S. Department of Defense Dependents Overseas Schools (DoDDS). My job was virtually stress-free since I could relate to the kids as a counselor rather than as a teacher or parent. And since I was dorm counselor, I had my days free while they were in class.

Most days were spent wandering about the local village snapping photos and developing and printing black and white blow ups in the photo lab back on the army post. An ideal life for me. One day I wandered out the back instead of front gate and in a matter of minutes I was out in open countryside. After a short walk, a curtain opened and closed in my mind and I found myself on the other side. It was unlike anything I had known. No words to describe it. The Narrator was absent without a trace.

I had never known the world from this perspective. It was clear, vivid, pellucid. This was the true world that had been hidden from view. Truth existed everywhere on this side of the curtain. How could this truth exist so clearly and yet be hidden. All around in the hills, rocks and trees, fields, everywhere, there was what I can only put into words as a spiritual presence. I saw this with crystalline lucidity. No doubt of what I was seeing. Not to be able to see this world is blindness. I remember thinking I could give up all my possessions. I needed nothing.

How could truth be all around and I could not get a glimpse of it before this? And how can I be like a blind man now back on this side of the curtain? How could I return to a material life where everything is a noisy story; thoughts and thoughts about thoughts. Devoid of reality; devoid of truth.

> Do not keep saying to yourself if you can possibly avoid it, but how can it be like that? Because you will get down the drain into a blind alley from which nobody has escaped. Nobody knows how it can be like that. (Richard Feynman, Nobel Prize-winning physicist)

> A human being is part of a whole, called by us the Universe, a part limited in time and space. He experiences himself, his thoughts, and feelings, as something separated from the rest, a kind of optical delusion of his consciousness. This delusion is a kind of prison for us restricting us to our personal desires and to affection for a few persons nearest us. Our task must be to free ourselves from this prison by widening our circles of compassion to embrace all living creatures and the whole of nature in its beauty. (Albert Einstein)

For centuries, mystics and philosophers have speculated about other worlds in higher dimensions. An ant has no cognizance of the world all about and we may not be aware of higher dimensions existing around us. This is not farfetched mysticism or science fiction. Superstring theory predicts the number of dimensions to be ten. There is a growing acknowledgment among physicists worldwide that dimensions exist beyond the commonly accepted space and time. Thousands of research papers relating to hyperspace have been published in scientific journals by modern physicists. Michio Kaku attempts to make this knowledge base of theoretical physics accessible to the lay audience in his books, including his 1995 book "Hyperspace."

Out of the millions of bits of information our brains process each second, 45 bits give or take are devoted to conscious thought. We can give our total conscious attention to around of one millionth or 0.000001 of the sensory input available to our brain.

Objective reality is the reality we all agree upon that enables us to communicate with each other. Apart from this subjective and objective reality, there is a third reality with a capital R. This is the Reality that is out there whether or not it is perceived.

Most of the reports by those who have had mystical experiences say it is as if the brain opens up and the other ninety-nine percent suddenly comes on line. It is like stepping out from a two-dimensional picture book into the world of three dimensions.

Stroke of Insight

In "My Stroke of Insight," Jill Bolte Taylor, a Harvard-trained neuroscientist describes what she experienced when she suffered a stroke caused by a severe hemorrhage in the left hemisphere of her brain. She describes it as an awakening to a space outside of her conscious mind and body. Her cognitive mind had shifted away from her normal perception of reality to this altered higher level state of consciousness.

She describes the experience of floating in one moment from space A to space B with no connection between; of being in the clarity of the present moment and at one with all that is. Everything including herself radiated energy and all was connected. She spoke of being entranced by the feelings of tranquility, safety, blessedness, euphoria, and omniscience. Nirvana.

The Marsh Chapel Experiment

The Marsh Chapel Experiment took place in 1962 on Good Friday at Boston University's Marsh Chapel. Walter N. Pahnke, a graduate student at Harvard Divinity School designed an experiment under the supervision of Timothy Leary. He wanted to see if psilocybin mushrooms could induce a religious or peak experience. He felt that "to use your head you had to go out of your mind."

He gave 10 students psilocybin and 10 students niacin. Niacin is called an active placebo since it has the immediate affect of flushing, so some of these students thought they had ingested the magic mushroom.

Reverend Mike Young was one of the grad students who was given the mushroom. Fifty years after the experiment, he said this was one of the most significant experiences of his life. Before this, he had doubts that he wanted to go into the ministry. He said he is a Unitarian Universalist minister at least in part due to that experience. All but one of the ten graduate students who took psilocybin became ministers. None of the graduate students who took the placebo became ministers.

Roland Griffiths, psychopharmacologist at Johns Hopkins, repeated this psilocybin experiment with with double blind controls. The results were published in Journal of Psychopharmacology in 2008. Fourteen months after the experiment, over half of the participants rated the experience one of the most meaningful of their entire lives.

Griffiths went back to Pahnke's study and other studies to find the basic ingredients common to each person's experience. He came up with a list of 6 key factors:

1. A feeling of awe and wonder.

2. Transcendence of time and space.

3. Feelings of peace and joy.

4. Unity - A sense of cosmic oneness; a connection to everything that is, every blade of grass and grain of sand.

5. Ineffability - Can't be described in words; nonverbal; indescribable.

6. An intuitive belief that the experience is a source of objective truth about the nature of reality.

Unseen World

William James (1842-1910), psychologist and philosopher, was trained as a medical doctor. He gained widespread attention and recognition with the publication of his two volume, twelve hundred page "Principles of Psychology."

James collected first-hand reports of mystical experiences and although he never had a mystical experience himself, he experimented with nitrous oxide and reported that when sufficiently diluted with air, nitrous oxide stimulates a mystical consciousness. In this state he experienced what he called a "depth upon depth of truth," a truth he said had never been shaken. He said that our normal, rational consciousness is but one type of consciousness while all about it and separated with a filmy screen lie potential forms of consciousness that are entirely different.

In "The Will to Believe," (copyright 1896, available online at no cost as a Project Gutenberg EBook), James writes:

Our science is a drop, our ignorance a sea. Whatever else be certain, this at least is certain—that the world of our present natural knowledge is enveloped in a larger world of some sort of whose residual properties we at present can frame no positive idea.

He illustrates this with an anecdote of his terrier who bites a teasing boy. The father of the boy demands damages. Though the dog may be present at every step of the negotiations, and sees the money paid, he has no awareness of what this all means and without a suspicion that it has anything to do with him.

Just as we encompass our world and the dog's world within it, encompassing both these worlds may be a still wider world as unseen by us as our world is unseen by the dog, and to believe in that world may be the most essential function that our lives in this world have to perform.

By belief in that world, James does not imply religion, not religion as many think of it. He distinguishes between personal religion and institutional religion. The institutional religion of churches, he said, is second hand and experienced through rituals, deities and ideas. In contrast, the founders of the religion experienced a deep experience with the primordial source.

James believed the men who do not go to church or have any religious convictions are the best. Praying, singing of hymns, and sermonizing are pernicious. They teach us to rely on some supernatural power, when we ought to rely on ourselves.

Antonio Damasio, Professor of Neuroscience at the University of Southern California, where he heads USC's Brain and Creativity Institute, often credits the work of William James when dealing with the conscious mind, emotion, and feeling. He considers James' thinking as a precursor to current studies of cognitive neuroscience.

In an interview at the NYC Public Library in 2010, Damasio discussed what may be going on in deep states of meditation and what may be blocking us from this sought-after state. In deep meditation it is possible to go behind the screen and enter into a deep state of primordial being and experience the cells and tissues and systems that make up our body.

In this state there is a representation of a presence of life itself without the narrative. This presence gets to be represented in the structures of the brain stem that has been with us in evolution for a very long time. This is the place in the brain where you have a fusion of mind and body. Deep inside, you find extremely important realities that can enlighten and have therapeutic effects.

But our complex brains store huge banks of memories about ourselves, of others we have interacted with, of books we have read, movies we have seen, and the world around us. Memories built upon memories and verbiage to describe them, serve to set up an opaque screen, blocking us from the great world of biology and reality within us. All we are aware of is the discursive brain chatter defining the world and who we are.

If someone were to ask me, is this all there is, I would answer this is a but a shallow facade. And because of this truth, I keep on working to open up more and more of my mind. I may never get back to where I was for that short space of time in Korea, but I know there is infinitely more to work toward, and each step rewards with new joy.

18 SHIFT THE CURVE TOWARDS OPTIMISM

System One versus System Two

Daniel Kahneman, winner of a Nobel Prize in 2002 for his work on decision making, says that our emotions dictate our beliefs to an extent of which we are not aware. In his book "Thinking Fast & Slow," Kahneman divides thinking into system one, the fast, intuitive system, and system two, the much slower reasoning system. System two, Kahneman says, mostly endorses what system one whispers. Our intuitions determine our judgements. Intuition and emotion affect our belief system. Fast, intuitive, and easy takes precedent over slow and rational. The brain alters the circuit board so that faster system one, the intuitive emotional belief system, overrides system two, rational, but much slower.

For poultry farmers, male chickens are mostly useless. The female eggs are the economic driver, so it is critical to determine the sex as early as possible. Chicken sexers determine gender with day-old chicks by checking their rear ends. Nothing obvious to be seen, yet chicken sexers have almost perfect accuracy, though most cannot explain how they do it.

They are trained by an expert who tells them if they are right or wrong when they guess at the sex. On-the-job decisions must be split second with no time to consciously think. It becomes a subconscious process where the brain is making the instant decision.

Other examples of the brain changing the circuit board and subconsciously taking over controls include chess players, wine tasters, bird and airplane spotters, and experts at medical diagnosis, all who routinely make instant evaluations. Once the brain learns the bits and pieces over time, the process goes on with split second accuracy below conscious awareness.

Learned Helplessness

The brain does not care, though, whether the subconscious processes it creates are helpful or harmful. Learned helplessness is a subconscious process whereby a person or animal learns to behave helplessly. Understanding how learned helplessness comes about began with a series of experiments by American psychologist Martin Seligman, then a graduate student at the University of Pennsylvania.

Seligman, together with fellow graduate student Steven Maier, conducted a series of experiments on three groups of dogs. These experiments challenged the basic concept of behaviorism, that behavior is entirely and directly shaped by rewards and punishments.

The first group of dogs received a shock. By pushing a panel with its nose, a dog in this first group could turn off the shock. This group of dogs would have control because one of its responses mattered.

The second group of dogs received the shock at the same time as the first group. But they had no control, because no matter what they did the shock would be turned off when a dog from the first group pushed his nose against the panel and shut off the shock for both groups. A third group received no shock at all.

Once the dogs went through this first part of the experiment, they were taken to an enclosure where they could easily jump over a low barrier and escape. When they were shocked now, the first group leapt right over the barrier. When the third group of dogs were shocked they also leapt easily over the barrier. But the second group lay there as they continued receiving shocks. Though they could have easily escaped, they had learned to be helpless. These dogs learned that nothing they could do would matter. Seligman coined the term "learned helplessness."

Donald Hiroto, a graduate student at Oregon State University, duplicated Seligman's three-group study with humans. In place of the shock, he used a loud uncomfortable noise. All three groups were subjected to the loud noise. The subjects in the first group could learn to turn off the noise by trying out combinations of buttons to press. The second group of subjects were yoked to the first just like the second group of dogs.

The first group were in control of the situation. As soon as they got the correct combination, the sound turned off. It turned off at the same moment for the second group. But the second group had no control to stop the noise themselves. The third group were not subjected to noise at all.

Just like the yoked dogs, the yoked human group that had no control just sat there when placed in a condition where they could easily have shut off the noise. The other two groups took action and shut off the noise.

Instead of shocks, we are awash in unpleasant messages, feelings, and urges generated from our own brains. We take learned helplessness even further than the hapless dogs. We blame ourselves for not taking action. We blame ourselves for uninvited, unwanted messages in our heads, and urges and feelings in our bodies.

If people can learn to be helpless in so short a span of time in an experimental situation with a relatively trivial irritation, what about people who grow up in homes where their lives are intolerable for years on end? But not only children growing up; adults live in uncomfortable family and job situations that stress them nonstop.

Tragically, the CIA employed Learned Helplessness in their torture program.

Genes Load the Gun, Environment Pulls the Trigger

Not all adults who had poor attachment, abuse, or partook in war combat missions will have PTSD or be adversely affected in later years. Though poor attachment and maltreatment in very early years increase the chance of impulsive, aggressive crimes in men, most maltreated children do not become delinquents or adult criminals. Even soldiers with the same genetic make up who experience virtually the same combat trauma will not all end up with PTSD.

Genes load the gun, but environment pulls the trigger. Whether obesity, heart failure, or violence, genes tell only the nature part of the story. The extent to which a gene is turned on and expressed is strongly affected by environment or nurture. Just because you have a gene for obesity, heart failure, or violence does not mean that gene will be expressed.

The MAOA the Better

A key genetic component of bad behavior is a gene on the X chromosome that produces an enzyme called MAOA, monoamine oxidase A. MAOA metabolizes neurotransmitters including serotonin, norepinephrine, and dopamine. The more MAOA enzyme, the more efficiently these neurotransmitters are broken down. The long form of the gene produces lots of MAOA to metabolize the neurotransmitters and so keep them in balance.

There is a short form of this gene, though, that produces low levels of the MAOA enzyme, so the neurotransmitters that are between the synapses of nerves in the brain do not get broken down. This is associated with antisocial personality, aggressive behavior, and violent criminality. If you have the short form of the MAOA producing gene, you are more likely to act aggressively and get into trouble with the law.

At least that was believed until a 2002 New Zealand study went through criminal records of hundreds of men to determine who had exhibited antisocial or criminal behavior by age twenty-six. They found no significant statistical association between low MAOA gene status and antisocial behavior.

What they found is if a man with a low-activity MAOA gene had been abused as a child, he was extremely likely to exhibit antisocial behavior. But the men with the low-activity MAOA gene that had a secure attachment as a child had no greater risk of antisocial or criminal behavior than those men with the high-activity MAOA gene. By turning genes on or off, different environments change identical genomes into different people.

Who Gives Up? Who Rarely Feels Defeated?

One subgroup of the subjects, both human and dogs, did not succumb to this lack of self control from the start. Another group, about one in ten of both humans and dogs, were helpless from the start. The helpless dogs took the shocks, and the helpless humans took the loud music, resigned to suffer without attempting to escape their suffering.

Seligman became interested in both of these subgroups. He began a seven-year journey carrying out studies to find out who readily gives up and who rarely feels defeated. What he found is encouraging. The attribute of resilience in the face of defeat is not necessarily an inborn trait. It can be learned.

Resiliency

The U.S. army called upon Seligman to develop a test that would serve as an assessment of resiliency. Aware of Seligman's success with the insurance industry where resiliency is required by insurance agents in cold calling new clients, the military wanted to develop a resiliency in combat situations.

On the average, insurance agents get turned down ninety percent of the time. In the first year on the job, fifty percent of these agents quit. The ones that stay on get more and more discouraged and produce less and less each year. Seligman focused on resiliency, a critical ingredient needed to successfully navigate through each of our lives, and turned the Met Life Insurance company around.

For the military, Seligman developed the Global Assessment Tool (GAT), an emotional assessment tool taken by U.S. Army soldiers of all ranks at regular intervals to assess their psycho-social well being in four basic areas: emotional, family, social, and spiritual. The army merged the results of this emotional assessment with their own military physical assessment data base, creating one of the largest data bases in history.

Performance on the GAT provides a way of strength-based training where training is individualized and personal strengths are leveraged. This led to the U.S. Army's official 5-pillar Comprehensive Soldier & Fitness program, CSF2. The five pillars or training modules to build resilience are: social, emotional, family, spiritual, and physical resilience.

Based on a number of replicated studies, the program proved to be a success, but The Military Religious Freedom Foundation threatened the army with a lawsuit. The computerized GAT asks soldiers to rank themselves on statements like, "I am a spiritual person. In difficult times, I pray or meditate. I often find comfort in my religion or spiritual belief. I attended religious services." The first amendment of the Constitution forbids the government from establishing religion.

Seligman says the spiritual module is not theological but human, supporting and encouraging soldiers to search for truth, self-knowledge, right action, and purpose in life. This module helps soldiers to accept their imperfections and to realize they are the primary authors of their lives.

From Helpless to Flourish

Learned Optimism was a huge shift of focus for Seligman. His previous book titles included, "Helplessness: On Depression, Development and Death" (1975), "Human Helplessness: Theory and Applications "(1980), and "Abnormal Psychology" (1984 & 1985). A few years after that last publication, he concluded that focusing on the down side of life caused psychologists and psychiatrists to become depressive, while focusing on optimism caused mental health care workers to become more positive. He said he never met a more positive group of people than his co-workers in the field of positive psychology.

His books reflect the turnaround: "The Optimistic Child "(1995), "Authentic Happiness: Using the New Positive Psychology to Realize Your Potential for Lasting Fulfillment" (2002), and "Flourish" (2011). These last two books and especially Flourish reflect the change from the emotion of happiness to a more broadly defined sense of well being. Well being as Seligman defines it is comprised of positive emotion, engagement, meaning positive relationships, and accomplishment.

The first book of his series on positive psychology, "Learned Optimism, How to Change Your Mind and Your Life," was published in 1990 and for several years positive psychology got hyped by Readers Digest, Redbook, Family Circle, and other consumer magazines, placing it into the category of pop psychology. Behind this media hype, positive psychology is a science backed by rigorous research. It moves the focus from disease and what is wrong with us, which most of us are too aware, to maximizing potential.

Don't Worry, Be Happy

Seligman offers seven compelling reasons to work against pessimism.

1. Pessimism leads to depression.

2. Pessimism results in inertia rather than activity in the face of setbacks.

3. Pessimism results in more subjective feelings of blueness, worry, and anxiety.

4. Pessimism is self-fulfilling. Pessimists don't persist in the face of challenges, and therefore fail more frequently even when success is attainable.

5. Pessimism is associated with poor physical health.

6. Pessimists are defeated when they try for high office.

7. Even when pessimists are right and things turn out badly, they still feel worse. Their explanatory style converts the predicted setback into a disaster, and the disaster into a catastrophe.

Seligman claims pessimists can learn to be optimists by learning a new set of cognitive skills that basically involve changing the way we explain things to ourselves. We need a set of skills, so we can talk to ourselves when we suffer a personal setback or defeat. The way we talk to ourselves determines whether we give up like the yoked dogs and humans or get up and make a positive plan and move on it.

Medicines too, work better with a boost from an optimistic belief system. Placebos are effective in part because of an optimistic outlook. Nocebos contribute to a host of ills in part because of a pessimistic belief system.

Optimism is a belief system affecting most everything in our lives. The Four-Step Method, REBT, and all of the other cognitive therapies require a shift in the scale from pessimism to optimism for them to be effective. You can read about the Four-Step Method and REBT, commit the systems to memory, but if you are a pessimist and doubt that it will work for you, it likely will not work.

Seligman employs REBT to shift the curve toward optimism. With REBT and other cognitive strategies, you learn to recognize the automatic thoughts and pessimistic beliefs that come between an event and the emotional and behavioral consequences.

Even with aptitude and motivation, we are unlikely to succeed with a pessimistic belief system. If we believe we can't do something we will soon give up. If we want to change our thinking and behavior, we need to work on developing a positive, optimistic explanatory style. We need to talk to ourselves in a different style.

Three Life-Changing Ways to Explain Events

Seligman defines three crucial dimensions of explanatory styles: permanence, pervasiveness, and personalization.

1. Permanence

Permanence is about time. Pessimists believe that bad events will last a long time and will undermine everything they do. They believe that bad events are permanent. When optimists are confronted with the same bad events, they believe the events are a temporary setback.

Howard Tate could have benefited from this this when he zeroed in on his perception that he was being taken for a ride financially. He may have been taken for a ride, but he was a rising star. He was making lots of money. He had a future that need not have included people he did not trust. The situation was not permanent. He cut off a life of opportunity by walking away from a highly successful performing career.

When Floyd Mayweather, Jr., five-divisions boxing world champion was sentenced to jail time for domestic violence, rather than let it negatively influence his upcoming fight or public image, he said, "The only thing it can do is make me grow mentally strong as a person. It's all part of life. You have good days. You have bad days. But the main thing is to grow mentally."

I certainly do not condone domestic violence. I am in awe, though, of his explanatory style. Nothing negative in his life is pervasive or permanent. That is part of what made him a multi-weight champion.

2.Pervasiveness

Pervasiveness is about space. Pessimists globalize failures and other bad things that happen to them. By globalizing negative events pessimists tend to give up on a host of other things when failure strikes one area of their lives. Optimists will take these same negative events and put them in a box, so they continue to function in other aspects of their lives. If they are in the throes of a divorce, they will continue to perform in their jobs. Their personal misfortune does not pervade their lives.

A friend of mine has diabetes and injects himself with insulin throughout the day, carefully monitoring the timing and content of each meal in relation to blood glucose. He was experiencing sudden and unexpected low blood sugar and fatigue while seeing clients, so gave up his psychotherapy practice. His wife died of breast cancer. Soon after he developed a throat disease, could not swallow, and had to blend all foods to a pulp in a food processor for more than six months. And, he gets around at a snail's pace because of wear and tear on his knees and hips.

During all of this, he continued his writing and publishing professional books, journal articles, and works of fiction. He continued to travel across the country visiting and advising staff at colleges throughout the U.S. and Canada on the topic of student misconduct. Unbelievably, for each of these trips he packed two large suitcases of his published books.

Through all of this he met and is now married to a charming and intelligent woman. He is an indefatigable optimist, able to keep the different areas of his life apart. When bad things happen, he compartmentalizes them and continues on with all other aspects of his life.

3. Personalization

Personalization is about internalizing or externalizing good and bad events. A pessimist internalizes bad events and externalizes the good things that happen. If a pessimist loses his job, he might say I goof things up. I can't hold a job. I don't fit the corporate image. If he were to land a good job, he would say he was lucky he got picked.

Learn to Pick the Winning Team

Seligman gave the Attributional Style Questionnaire (ASQ) to fifteen thousand Met Life Insurance Company applicants nationwide in an attempt to identify totally optimistic people. The questionnaire was successful in predicting the success of new agents and Met Life used the questionnaire as part of their hiring strategy. They hired agents who scored in the top half of the optimism questionnaire. Agents scoring in the top half are persistent; they don't give up because of rejection. Met Life increased its share of the personal-insurance market by an amazing fifty percent.

CAVE, content analysis of verbatim explanations, is a method of determining the explanatory style of famous people without meeting them or having them fill out an explanatory-style questionnaire. If a professional football team kicker is quoted in the news as saying he missed the goal because the wind was against him, that quote would be rated as high on the optimistic side of the scale. Nothing is as impermanent as the wind. It is not pervasive, since the wind being against you does nothing to affect other areas of your life. And the statement is not personal, because the wind is not the kicker's fault.

With his obsession for sports, Seligman's research team conducted a study to explore how different explanatory styles might predict which team would have a higher batting average under late-inning pressure. They went through thousands of pages of newspapers, analyzing quotes of players for explanatory style. They attached CAVE numbers to each quote. For example, when a pitcher said the reason he walked a player was that "some moisture must have gotten on the ball," this would be rated very temporary, specific, and external, so very optimistic.

Seligman chose two teams, the Mets and the Cardinals, who were evenly matched and battling for the Eastern Division pennant in 1985. The Mets had an overall optimistic explanatory style and the Cardinals had a pessimistic style. So in the next year, 1986, the Mets should have excelled and the Cardinals deteriorated compared with their performance in 1985. That is what happened. The Cardinals fell apart in 1986. In spite of massive talent, they batted only .236 overall and deteriorated to a miserable .231 average under pressure.

Seligman compared the 1985 explanatory style for all twelve National League teams and got the same results. Teams with an optimistic explanatory style in 1985 bettered their win-loss record in 1986, while pessimistic teams did worse in 1986 than they did in 1985. Optimistic teams hit better under pressure in 1986 and pessimistic teams fell apart under pressure in the 1986 season.

Basketball is easy to apply the CAVE system to because for each game there is a handicap, a point spread that tells how many points the stronger team will win by. If the stronger team wins by that amount of points, they have covered the point spread. To determine how optimism affects this,

Seligman and his crew read more than ten thousand sports pages, picking out explanatory remarks by NBA Atlantic Division players and coaches for all of 1982-83. They assembled about a hundred event-explanation quotes for each team.

Both the Boston Celtics and the New Jersey Nets were strong teams with explanatory styles at opposite ends of the spectrum. The Celtics were at the positive, optimistic end and the Nets at the negative, pessimistic end. The Celtics explained bad events as temporary, specific, and not their fault. Explaining a loss, "The fans (at the opponents' home court) are by far the noisiest and most outrageous crowd in the NBA." They put the blame on the fans, and so are saying the loss was not their fault.

The Nets, on the other hand, explained losses as permanent, pervasive, and their own fault. "We are missing everything." And from the coach, "This is one of the physically weakest teams I've ever coached." "Our intelligence was at an all-time low." The Nets had a pessimistic explanatory style.

In 1983-84, the more pessimistic Nets covered or beat the handicap point spread only 37.8 percent of the time in games following losses. The optimistic Celtics beat the point spread 68.4 percent of the time in games after losses. A team's explanatory style for bad events strongly predicts how they will do against the point spread after a loss. The optimistic teams cover or beat the spread more often than the pessimistic teams do. Explanatory style predicts how teams will do above and beyond how good a team is. Success is predicted by optimism and failure is predicted by pessimism.

SAT scores are used to predict success in college, but the correlation between these scores and college success is not all that high. If you look at this correlation by examining scores supplied by The College Board, more than sixty percent variance can not be accounted for by these scores. Seligman suspected that at least some of this variance may be accounted for by explanatory style or the level of student's optimism.

Three hundred students of the class of 1987 at the University of Pennsylvania took the Attributional Style Questionnaire. Seligman waited until they took midterms and final exams to see who would do better than predicted by the SAT and who would do worse.

At the end of the first semester, fully one-third of these students did much worse or much better than their SATs, high-school grades, and achievement tests had predicted. The students who scored high on the ASQ for optimism did far better in their first semester of college, and those who scored high on the ASQ for pessimism did far worse. Optimism accounted for at least part of the sixty percent that could not be accounted for by the SAT plus high school grade averages.

There are many good reasons to be an optimist rather than a pessimist. Pessimists blame themselves and this usually does not help to work towards a solution. Optimists focus on the situation rather than on themselves. They perceive setbacks as a challenge to try harder and work toward a solution. Pessimism promotes depression and inertia in the face of setbacks. Pessimists tend to give up if it will take a long time. They fail more frequently, even when success is attainable. If all that is not sufficient reason to work toward a goal of optimism, pessimistic explanatory style is a risk factor for physical illness.

Good Pessimist, Bad Pessimist

There is something to say, though, on behalf of pessimists– but in saying this, I am reminded of the time I was teaching fifth grade in a low socioeconomic area. The teacher across the hall taught sixth grade. I think he worked as a fireman nights, so he had little time to prepare. We both had our doors open, so I could hear him loud and clear. He was telling his students about a rule that could never be broken. Never. He repeated this over and over and then had the class repeat in military cadence. "How often?". The class responded, "Never." "Louder." he commanded. "How often?" "Never!!!!" they shouted back. "Louder! Let me hear it!!!" "Never!!!!" Then silence as he turned the page. "The only exception is when . . . . ."

You should always be an optimist. Always! No exceptions! None!!!

Except for people who are skeptical and do not accept anything without documented facts to back it up. They use defensive pessimism to constructively evaluate a situation before coming to a conclusion. They hope for the best, but prepare for and expect the worst. You don't pay a lawyer who expects the best and does not take precautions. You expect her/him to anticipate what might go wrong and protect you. You don't pay your stock broker commissions to be optimistic and cheerful. You want her/him to be on the lookout for disaster and tell you when to cut your losses as well as, of course, when to buy.

Defensive pessimists come up with all kinds of reasons why things might go wrong. They are not easy targets for sales people or commercials. They focus on the potential downside when someone pitches a seemingly fantastic deal or venture. Their lack of enthusiasm for new and exciting projects might drive a staunch optimist up a wall, but they are a blessing in disguise.

Defensive pessimism is different than dispositional pessimism, though it may be hard to perceive the difference. Pitch a defensive pessimist a great idea and they react in silence. They digest all of the parts and steps before putting it back together to evaluate a strategy. They are like athletes who prepare for upcoming performances by going through routines with vivid imagery and detail, including every possible mistake and how to recover, if recovery is possible.

Feeling good is not their target. They work through negative feelings and emotions and learn to tolerate them, to live with them. They delay gratification, learn from bad experiences, take time to listen to what others have to say, and carefully assess opportunities and inherent risks. Defensive pessimism can be empowering.

Dispositional pessimism can lead to hopelessness, helplessness, withdrawal and depression if it is chronic. Dispositional pessimists believe bad outcomes are personal, pervasive, and permanent. They blame themselves when things go south and let one situation bleed into others and become all encompassing.

There are times for optimism and times to weigh things carefully and shift to a defensive mode of pessimism. If a situation is risky or the future uncertain, this is the time for defensive pessimism. What will be the cost of failure? Consider all angles and possibilities and be prepared for the worse. If you are tempted in having an affair, it is the time for defensive pessimism. Weigh the costs. Might it break up my marriage? Is the pleasure worth the risk? What is the worst that could happen? Am I really ready for this?

Shift the Curve Towards Optimism

Some of us are more pessimistic when we wake and move progressively toward optimism during the day. We hit highs late mornings and early evenings. Many hit lows around four in the afternoon and very early in the morning. If you tend to wake up at four in the morning and worry about everything in your life, you know this well. Women sometimes experience regular cycles from optimism to pessimism and back during the course of each month that coincides with their menstrual cycle. We all have cycles of optimistic highs and pessimistic lows.

If you want to move from pessimistic to optimistic thinking, you need to recognize automatic thoughts that hold you back:

1. Bad events are permanent.

2. Bad events are pervasive. When one area goes south, most everything else takes a hit.

3. Personalize bad events and blame them on yourself.

Self-Therapy Might Include:

Don't personalize. Instead of thinking you are to blame, attempt to place at least some of the blame on external forces beyond your control. Bad things happen. Your boss or coworker is a jerk. You are okay. (Not to blame your spouse or partner, though.)

Keep it in perspective. Keep the bad things contained in the area of your life they most affect, even if it means putting up a front. Another good friend of mine had serious family problems for the past twenty years. But he told me when he arrived at his office, he put on a smile and was cheerful, so no one had an inkling of what he was going through. This included his personal secretary. He said he always greeted her with a warm smile. He is a pleasure to be with and an extremely successful businessman.

When things go bad, try to see it as a transient state. Perhaps you can think of the times in your life when things were a mess and you pulled it together into a different point of view.

It takes mindfulness to move along the continuum from pessimism to optimism. When you use cognitive awareness and self-talk to deal with automatic pessimist thoughts and shift toward optimism, it can feel like you are going through the motions. But there are reasons to keep at it. Even a small shift toward optimism leverages a difference.

You can work on shifting your curve toward optimism by becoming actively aware of three categories of evaluating events: permanent, pervasive, and personal. An optimistic outlook considers positive events permanent, pervasive and personal. An optimistic outlook considers negative events transient, isolated, and external, not personal. Don't blame yourself. It may be hard at first to note progress, but in time you will see the shift, maybe not as much from your own progress as from observing the unchanged outlook of pessimists you leave behind.

Find your base-level score on Selligman's optimism/pessimism questionnaire. (https://www.authentichappiness.sas.upenn.edu/testcenter)

Seems like a lot of extra work and time to make this change from pessimism to optimism. You have 45 bits of attention and think of the garbage you are filling it with at least a good percentage of your time. It is the proverbial garbage in garbage out. You don't need extra time. You need to fill your 45 bits with more good stuff that will help rather than make you crazy. Nudging your explanatory style toward optimism is good stuff. Ki Breathing Meditation is good stuff. Keep an arsenal of good stuff at hand. You will change your life.

19 YIP YIP YIP YIP YIP YIP YIP YIP BOOM BOOM BOOM BOOM BOOM BOOM
GET A JOB

Our complex internal lives cause sufficient suffering, yet most of us have to work, and work can be major source of suffering. It forces us to function with and interact with other irrational people. For most of us a fulfilling job is an oxymoron. The Japanese coined the term karoshi, literally "death from overwork," to describe the situation where seemingly heathy people in their prime are suddenly dying.

From Gallup's 2013 State of the American Workplace:
Of the approximately 100 million people in America who hold full-time jobs, 30 million (30%)are engaged and inspired at work, so we can assume they have a great boss. At the other end of the spectrum are roughly 20 million (20%) employees who are actively disengaged. These employees, who have bosses from hell that make them miserable, roam the halls spreading discontent. The other50 million (50%) American workers are not engaged. They are kind of present, uninspired by their work or their managers.

A part of Victor Frankl's existential search for meaning within his Logo Therapy involves work. It does not depend on what kind of work. If a person's occupation does not lead to a sense of fulfillment, Frankl says—and this is a bit hard to take—the fault is with the person and not in the work. Frankl explains that work is a framework for serving people. It is what the individual brings to his work as a human being that gives work meaning.

The nurse who sterilizes syringes, carries and changes bedpans, can find reward from work. The nurse is doing far more than regimented duties by offering these services to the ill. Frankl says many occupations allow for bringing meaning to a job, so long as the work is seen in the proper light.

Einstein said, "In the middle of difficulty lies opportunity." That has become a cliche, but it contains meaning. I had ongoing problems with administrators during most of my years of teaching. And since a whisper, the tapping of a pencil, anything at all distracted me, I took medication to be on stage six periods each day in front of classrooms of teenagers. But the kids got me out of my shell and forced me to be outgoing and positive. And the job offered me the time I needed to exercise, research and write.

On the other hand, I was crazy to remain in a job for 30 years that sickened me from the start and forced me to medicate myself into a stupor during the day and to knock me unconscious with even more addictive medications nights. And until the shattering end I never considered myself an addict. I had a respectable job and my candymen were board-certified specialists who also had respectable jobs.

Parnassa

The Lubavitcher orthodox Jews' definition of work is that it is something you do to have the money to be an observant Jew, i.e., to study Torah, and donate to the cause. Amazingly, this attitude seemingly helps them adjust to almost any job condition. I never met a Chabadnic complain about their job. They believe work is not an end, but a part of a process they call parnassa.

Most of them have amazing stamina. They show up for a very early service before work every day; some fit in an afternoon service at work, then an evening service, as well as services on both days of the weekend. And there are 24-hour fast days scattered throughout the year that include abstinence from any liquid including water; and there are several all-night gatherings.

The prayer for parnassa sums up their philosophy of earning a living:

Prayer for Parnassa (livelihood)

G-d, who prepares sustenance and clothing for every creature

and sends each their livelihood,

please grant me a proper livelihood.

Please sustain me,

all the members of my household,

and all of Israel

with a good and respectable livelihood,

calmly and without pain,

in legitimate and permissible, not prohibited ways,

with honor and not with disgrace.

It should be a livelihood without shame or disgrace,

a livelihood where I will not need the gift of flesh and blood,

but only Your full and wide Hand.

It should be a livelihood where I can be involved in

Your Holy, Pure, and Perfect Torah.

Prepare my food and that of my family and all of our needs

before we need them

so that my heart should be free without any bother

to be involved in the words of your Torah,

to keep Your commandments, and

to sit in peace on my table with dignity

with all of the members of my household.

I should not need to look to anyone else's table.

I should not need to become indebted to any man.

The yoke of no man should be upon me,

only the yoke of Your Kingdom,

in order to serve You with a complete heart.

Our garments should be worn with dignity and not with shame.

Save us from poverty, destitution, and lowliness.

Allow us to merit inviting guests,

to do acts of kindness to every man.

Give me the wherewithal to give charity to those that deserve it

and not stumble upon improper recipients. Amen

from the Otzar Hatefillot prayer book

Another version with transliteration at:

https://artscroll.files.wordpress.com/2009/01/the-chapter-of-manna.pdf

Their philosophy concerning work is encapsulated in this prayer. If you ask a Lubovitcher orthodox Jew about their job, they may likely respond, "Parnassa." Work serves a purpose. They don't seem to bring it home with them. They don't seem to over-identify with their job, so when they come home, the office doesn't come with them. They don't take Steve Jobs to heart:

> You've got to find what you love and that is as true for work as it is for your lovers. Your work is going to fill a large part of your life and the only way to be truly satisfied is to do what you believe is great work. And the only way to do great work is to love what you do. If you haven't found it, yet, keep looking, and don't settle. As with all matters of the heart, you'll know when you find it. And like any great relationship, it just gets better and better as the years roll on. So keep looking until you find it. Don't settle.

Steve Jobs was living in the iCloud. What about the slave workers in

China that make the Apple products; and the retail big box workers, the sanitation department workers, dishwashers, construction day labor, truck drivers, on and on. When you are a citizen of the lower socioeconomic culture, it may take two or three jobs to pay the rent and feed the family each month.

The paradox of having a job you identify with is that the line gets blurred between work and play. You check emails and phone messages every waking hour. In a real sense, you are constantly at work. When problems come up, they, along with the anxiety and frustration come home with you so you never can truly leave the office.

Teaching is the job that got me into graduate school to get out of teaching to become a school psychologist. but the classroom is where I ended back up. It was the last place I wanted to be, so each day after work, I would go from one coffee shop to another with my yellow pad, and flow into writing the "great American novel." That fantasy, along with aikido, kept me going many years. Actually way too many years, but teaching for DoDDS allowed me to stay in Japan and offered the time to exercise, write, and travel. I made it a point to avoid job-related discussion once I left it behind 3 p.m. each day. Most teachers I knew put up a fire wall.

A belief in an infiniteness beyond the self gives the 12-step program much of its success. Belief is an integral part of parnassa. It taps into a part of the brain that may otherwise be inaccessible. A belief in something greater than self affects lives in all aspects. It is unfortunate that only a small fraction of us can tap into this.

The belief of something greater need not be spiritual. Fresh out of college, I was hired by Food Fair Stores as a Junior Locations Analyst. I would be trained to take over the metropolitan New Jersey, New York, and Connecticut area. One day as we were driving from the airport in Connecticut, my boss said, "The engagement is over. When I go to bed at night, I am thinking about what I plan to do the next day." I thought he was crazy. I would never become like that.

I recently came across a passage from Freud's Civilization and Its Discontents" (page 10) that I did not understand when I read it in college. Now when I read it again so much later in life I understand what my boss was communicating to me.

> Laying stress upon the importance of work has a greater
> effect than any other technique of living in the direction
> of binding the individual more closely to reality; in his
> work he is at least securely attached to a part of reality, the
> human community. Work is no less valuable for the
> opportunity it and the human relations connected with it
> provide for a very considerable discharge of libidinal

component impulses, narcissistic, aggressive, and even erotic, than because it is indispensable for subsistence and justifies existence in a society.

And yet as a path to happiness work is not valued very highly by men. They do not run after it as they do after other opportunities for gratification. The great majority work only when forced by necessity, and this natural human aversion to work gives rise the the most difficult social problems.

Out From the Killing Fields

In Andrew Solomon's "The Noonday Demon: An Atlas of Depression," he tells about Phaly Nuon, one of the survivors of Pol Pot's killing fields in Cambodia in the 1970s. She was tied to a tree and forced to watch as a battalion of soldiers raped and then murdered her twelve-year-old daughter. She escaped into the jungle with her six-year-old son, nursing her infant. She and her son survived on roots of trees, constantly on the run for two years, but her milk dried up and her infant died.

When she returned after the downfall of Khmer Rouge, she lived in a border camp near Thailand. She was one of the only educated people there, because almost of the educated people had been executed. Knowing several languages, she could communicate with the aid workers. She made a request to set up her hut as a counseling center.

The PTSD in the camp was palpable. The women lay motionless in their huts, staring vacantly, not talking, not caring about their kids or even bothering to feed them. Nuon was like a psychiatrist, dispensing whatever antidepressants the aide workers could bring in. She first listened to each of them tell their story. When they reached the point where they could think about other things, she went on to help them learn to work, even if it was only to keep their own place clean and take care of their children. They had to have something they knew they had to do and then start doing it in order to have a purpose, a direction and focus.

Telling the story of their traumatic experience was a part of Phaly Nuon's counseling with killing field women survivors. The first thing she did was to sit down with them and listen to their story. Then she would help them to replace memories with new things to think about.

Nuon set up an orphanage, so as soon as a woman was able to function and take care of her home and children, they could help to take care of lost children in the orphanage. Work gave purpose to their lives. Her program was an amazing success. Noon was nominated for the Nobel Prize several times, but died before she received it.

Beyond the Limits

One day as I boarded a bus, the trim, black, middle-aged driver greeted me and all the other riders as he might welcome guests stopping by for a visit at his home. The tone of his voice reflected his positive professional attitude as he announced businesses, hospitals, and special attractions before each of the stops. No other bus driver did that. Most of his riders departed the bus happy campers.

That was Frankl's message in his Logo therapy. Only by going beyond the limits of purely professional service is it possible to find fulfillment in a job. This bus driver went way beyond these limits and influenced a great number of people along the way. Driving in heavy traffic, getting cut off, having people pull in front of you and slow down, he is dealing with the gamut of humanity on a minute by minute basis. People get on drunk, they throw up, they try to avoid paying their fare or cheat on what they pay. Most bus drivers are not happy campers who call out businesses and attractions to their riders.

When I interviewed Albert Ellis, I asked him if he ever planned to retire. He was 76 years old at the time and working seven days a week, basically every minute of every waking day. His answer was "What would I do, lay in the sun on a beach in Hawaii? I would go out of my fucking mind." He was not a psychiatrist half heartedly going through routine med checks. He took on people's most stressing problems, head on, morning till late at night, one after another. Ellis was diabetic and no one catered to his needs. He made a pile of peanut butter sandwiches and stacked them in the bathroom adjoining his office. He got to eat them in the minutes between patients.

He wrote over fifty books and many more journal articles and all profits went to the institute. He lived in an apartment on the third floor of the institute. He told me he needed eight hours of sleep each night, "the bane of my life", so all he had time to do each day after work was get ready for bed, sleep, and get up and make his daily supply of peanut butter sandwiches. To each of his clients throughout the day, he gave his all. Sundays was time for writing his books and journals and personally responding to mail and years later email.

His life was not free from hassle. The nonprofit he built from the ground was run by a board of directors. In his late years, he needed money for severe medical problems associated with his diabetes. He could not get the board to approve of this. Of course, it was far more complicated than this. He likely needed more money than the institute could provide and survive. But the end of his life was cluttered with law suits and bad feelings on both sides.

My boss at Food Fair Stores had a belief in something beyond himself. I

192

think it was on that same ride from the airport that we passed one of those gigantic Food Fair trucks and he asked me something I thought was absurd. He asked if when I saw the Food Fair truck, did I get the same goose pimples as when standing for the Stars Spangled Banner. Now I see he was as fortunate as the Lubavitcher orthodox Jews and the 12-Step believers. He did not have the conflict with work that I would never resolve.

20 MORITA THERAPY

Karoshi - Death From Overwork

The Gallup State of the American Workplace concludes that most of us can't put ourselves into our work and lead a satisfying life. We have a disaffected if not hostile relationship with our jobs. During the time I was in Japan from 1968 until 1992, Japanese salarymen–office workers–worked from morning till late at night. Many of the mid and upper managerial class put in eighty to a hundred unpaid overtime hours each month. For many these days, it is the same in the U.S..

Perhaps Americans would not call going out to bars and drinking work, but salarymen are forced to go out with their associates after work and they are expected to drink whenever someone orders drinks or pours for them. They cannot say I have to leave now, my wife is expecting me home for supper. Rarely do they get home in time to share a meal with their family or in time to see their kids awake.

After years of returning home late at night and getting up for work the next morning, hangover and all, this work ethic takes its toll. These workers are disengaged from their families. A large percentage of Japanese males smoke and this contributes to their health problems. It is not unexpected to hear of men in their forties and fifties dying of heart or brain conditions, of acute cardiac insufficiency, and subarachnoid hemorrhage. By the late 1980's this became a virtual epidemic in Japan, and newspapers and other media coined a word for it, karoshi (kah roh she) "death from overwork."

Morita Therapy

Sometime in the early 1980s I first heard of Morita Therapy and went to visit the chief psychiatrist at Daisan Hospital in Tokyo where Morita started his program. Morita Therapy centers in large part on adjusting to the world of work. The Zen-based therapy developed by Japanese psychiatrist Shoma

Morita in the early 1920s, in ways similar to Metacognitive Therapy (MCT) and Insight Meditation, makes no direct attempt at reasoning with, changing, or fixing disturbing thoughts and feelings.

The core of Morita Therapy involves a shift of focus from disturbing thoughts and feelings to actively working, writing, painting, gardening and engagement in projects. And in this way it is similar with the Four-Step Method (Chapter 13). The in-hospital patients I observed were dressed in casual civilian attire and engaged in various activities. They calmly and actively engaged with what they were doing and you might have thought they were hospital staff rather than in-treatment patients with debilitating mental illnesses.

Rooted in Zen, the focus is on living in the present moment. Rather than focusing on one's emotional state or feelings, the emphasis is on living a full and engaging life and not being ruled by one's emotional state.

Four Stages of Classic Morita Therapy
Stage One - Agony
The first stage lasting four days to a week is isolation and rest. Even family and friends are not permitted to visit during this initial stage of treatment. Morita expected patients to suffer in agony during this phase because they would be left alone to focus on their disturbing thoughts and feelings. He called this stage "the agony period." This isolation stage is absent in Morita Therapy in the U.S.

One reason for the isolation is so the client may come to realize that others cannot be relied upon for sympathy or assistance. It is not possible to instruct someone to become independent and self-reliant. The client must come to this conclusion on his/her own.

Morita would tell his patients to let themselves experience the pain. Even if the anxiety and pain were unbearable, he would tell them to let themselves experience it. During this phase of the treatment, he allowed patients to obsess about their personal affairs, discomforts, and pessimistic views of their past and future.

Morita reported that when a patient reached a climax of anguish and pain, within a relatively short period of time, even within hours, the pain would dissipate and disappear. By fully confronting and experiencing the symptoms and pain with nothing to distract them, the patient would gradually enter the state of what he called natural consciousness.

Stage Two - No Whistling
In the second stage of treatment, though patients are still isolated and restricted from conversation and amusement, they take part in light work such as raking leaves, weeding the garden, or wood carving. During this stage they are not allowed to do anything to divert their minds, not even going for a walk or whistling. They maintain a serious attitude and continue

to ride out their physical and mental distress and take obsessive thoughts calmly and with patience just as they are, without trying to change anything.

In Morita Therapy there are two ways of freeing oneself of disturbing thoughts. The first, especially in Stage One and continuing to a lesser extent in Stage Two, is to completely become the pain and suffering without attempting to fight or change it. Morita calls this "obedience to nature." This is similar to Open-Focus dissolving pain.

Morita explains this with a metaphor of a donkey tied to the post with a rope. The donkey attempts to escape by walking round and round the post, but the rope gets shorter and shorter until the donkey is immobilized. When you try to think your way out of obsessive thoughts, you go round and round and become immobilized like the donkey. This is like Metacognitive Therapy.

If you persevere through the pain and treat it as something inevitable like the donkey that no longer attempts to escape, you will not become entrapped and can graze freely within the limitations of the rope and post. You are freeing yourself by obedience to nature.

As the patient leaves Stage Two, he/she still focuses on the pain, but rather than becoming the pain, he/she observes, describes, and evaluates it without attempting to eliminate the discomfort or distract him/herself. The pain and suffering become objective entities projected onto the external world. Morita says this is like observing a mountain by stepping away and keeping a distance from it. As much as may be possible, you step away from yourself and see more of the total picture, much the same as viewing your problems from a third person POV.

Following the fourth day of Stage Two, the work becomes more diversified and patients are encouraged to learn new work they have never before done. There is no classifying of work in terms of social status, gender, or lifestyle. As their mental and physical health improves, and when clients seek more difficult work, treatment moves on to Stage Three. The second stage can last one or two weeks, but there are no borders between stages.

Therapists deal with a client's complaints by ignoring them. By the end of the second stage, clients complain with less frequency. And if the clients then report that their headache or heaviness of the head or chest has lessened, therapists ignore this as well. This is because comfortable feelings are always accompanied by an opposite uncomfortable feeling. Morita Therapy breaks down clients' self-evaluating attitudes and constant focus on feelings of comfort and discomfort.

Stage Three - Victim to Survivor

Clients engage in more labor-intensive work, often work they feel is beneath their sense of dignity, such as chopping wood or cleaning toilets. The goal is to acquire patience and endure work of any kind assigned.

Clients acquire the self-confidence that they can do anything others can do. The work is often hard and long hours and presents a challenge in the beginning. But it moves the client from being the treated victim to being the recovering survivor.

During this third stage, clients are encouraged to spend time creating art, writing, painting, anything that puts them in contact with the flow of creative activity. It is through creativity that the client learns to experience a sense of joy, a joy not dependent on practical value or a product, but rather on achieving something beyond expectation and through great effort. This can be considered a stage of spiritual enlightenment that accompanies a knowledge and confidence that much is possible in life.

Stage Four - Break Attachments

Stage Four prepares the client for re-entry into the external world. Training in the fourth stage aims to break all attachments, including fixations on one's own interests. Clients are trained to adjust to changes in external circumstances. This is a phase where the client learns to integrate a new lifestyle of meditation, physical activity, and clearer thinking. They are now equipped to function in a world where they will not always like what they are doing and their lives will not be trouble free. They will no longer be wasting so much of their lives attempting to avoid feelings of displeasure and boredom. They will become more genuinely themselves.

Morita said, "One becomes conflicted when he/she projects his/her experiences and subjective facts onto the external world as an objective model."

This gets us in trouble because just as we can never view ourselves, only a mirror image, photograph, or video, we cannot project our thoughts and experiences onto the external world. Morita of course, did not know of the concept of Narrator, but perhaps he may be referencing the same concept. It all is rooted in Buddhism. The Narrator is the world of subjective "facts." When we take our story and project it onto the external world as reality, this gets us into trouble. Many of us live our lives as prescribed by the Narrator.

Live With Paradox

According to Morita Therapy, you can never rid yourself of the subjective ongoing story of what is happening. When you fight against it, you get in trouble. Morita describes this as trying all kinds of ways of falling asleep resulting in insomnia, or like trying to forget about pain and becoming attached to it; or like forcefully attempting to push away or suppress obsessive thoughts and becoming agonized by them.

In essence, these experiences result from the clients' preoccupation with the contradiction between ideas and reality. You have to accept and at first even embrace the unpleasant thoughts, feelings, and emotional pain as a part of your subjective universe.

As with MCT, you learn to live with the paradox. If you attempt to manipulate and push away unpleasant thoughts, feelings, and emotions, Morita said it is like attempting to willfully control the dice you throw or willfully causing water in a river to flow upstream.

He illustrates this with a Zen story of a monk who questions Dosan, a Zen master. He asks the master how he can avoid the discomfort of the extreme hot of the summer and cold of the winter. Dosan answers: "When it is cold, lose yourself in the cold. When it is hot, lose yourself in the heat."

You immerse yourself in a state of hotness or coldness. Morita Therapy helps the client attain obedience to nature. It assists the client to accept feelings of coldness, hotness, pain, fear, and agony as they are and not try to eliminate these feelings. Only by acceptance of emotional and physical pain and fear can a person be liberated from suffering.

In Zen, the ideal state is one of conducting business in a state of nearsightedness without observing or assessing. The ideal state is also one in which everything remains nameless. Morita quotes Lao-tzu who stated that:

> The principle of universal truth should be called
> 'nothingness' or 'namelessness.' However, once it is named
> nameless, it loses its original nameless identity.

"Principles of Morita Therapy"(page 25)

Focus on Goals and Objectives

Acting with nearsightedness does not mean a lack of focus. It means focus on the objective, not the component parts. Morita explains that focusing on holding a cup and drinking a cup of coffee is different than focusing on the way you hold the cup and drink the coffee. A focus on holding the cup and drinking coffee is directed toward the objective and includes a natural peripheral vision (Open Focus). But focusing on the way you are holding the cup is a self-awareness that eliminates peripheral vision.

The same is true of a pitcher or batter, performing well when they go with the flow. They focus on the objective of hitting the ball or getting the pitch over the plate. If the focus shifts from this objective to the specifics of form, motion, and timing, athletes will likely choke. It is the same for a concert pianist who suddenly shifts in a performance from playing the piece with feeling to a focus on each individual note and placement of fingers corresponding to each note.

Morita would say with a focus on specifics or mechanics you lose a wide peripheral vision (Open Focus). You lose a vision of the forest when you try to figure out where you are from a focus on a plant or tree. In Zen, the state of mushoju-shin is when the mind is alert in all directions rather than single, one-point focus. This is extending ki in all directions.

It all starts to sound repetitious. Mindful therapies are based on schools of Buddhism that have been around for more than two thousand years. Morita therapy began in the 1930s, Fehmi's Open Focus in the 1960s. Both encourage development of a diffuse focus. I'm sure Morita would have adopted Fehmi's phrase, "Do it in Alpha.," had he lived on into the era of access to EEGs.

A restricted, narrow, objective focus lifts brain wave frequency out of the alpha range, affecting our perception, emotion, and behavior in a sometimes unpleasant way. Everything is affected including muscle tension, heart, respiration, neurotransmitters, and hormones. Morita Therapy directs attention away from a narrow focus on symptoms. The work stages are designed to guide clients to spontaneous activity, to concentrate on the goals of the work, and to expand peripheral consciousness away from narrow, repetitive, self-observations.

Morita Therapy is behavior therapy, but not the stimulus-response (SR) or operant conditioning we know in the West. It is a focus on behavior over feelings or thoughts. Key concepts are to do, to act, and not to focus on worries and symptoms. Morita therapy is not about controlling or trying to understand your thoughts, feelings, and impulses. Our minds are fluid and changing; focusing on symptoms is static and unchanging.

Like Albert Ellis, Morita favored "to do" action verbs. He made an effort to minimize use of the verb "to be." When you use the verb "to be" to describe someone, you put them in a box. I taught school for more than twenty-five years, but I would not say I'm a teacher. I taught school and did many other things that were equally as important to my life. I tried to get my students to see people and life in this way.

Do It in Alpha

Morita Therapy is about keeping an Open Focus. If you keep up a prolonged tight focus in teaching, you feel a buildup of stress and tension. You respond to a fearful situation by narrowing your attention and separating yourself from the world. Teachers fear losing control. Students reflect this uptightness back in disorderly behavior.

When I first started teaching, lunchtimes I would sit in my classroom and pour vodka into my tea, so right after lunch I embodied Zen. The kids were focused and communication flowed wordlessly. I would sit at my desk smiling beatifically and they sat smiling beatifically back. I spoke quietly and they got every word. These were low-income, inner-city kids. We entered an Open-Focus state of flow of mind-blowing oneness.

I used alcohol back then, but it is how we balance attention between the world around us and our inner world of thoughts, feelings, and emotions. It is about maintaining an Open Focus where we shift from narrow to all-encompassing diffuse focus. I was able to shift my focus out with the kids, releasing a tense, narrow, inner focus, dissolving I-versus-thou boundaries.

Pain, tension, negative emotions and feelings accompany inflexible, rigid attention, or what Fehmi calls rigid attention syndrome, RAS. The simple basic thing we can do to for our physical and emotional pain and confusion is developing the ability to shift from rigid, narrow, objective attention to a wide, peripheral focus that takes it all in as I did spaced out on vodka. It is a skill you practice over and over like a close-up slight-of-hand routine. Once you get it, it can be performed relatively effortlessly and instantly in most any situation. Without vodka.

Again, it is about attention, 45 bits of it. Therapies come and go, constantly rediscovered and repackaged. Morita Therapy incorporates many facets of Buddhism and so does MTC, Open-Focus, ATT, and of course Insight Meditation. The new is in with the old. And the old focuses on attention.

21 ACT NOW

Harnessing Your 45 Bits

If you choose to start with only one of the therapies in this book, I might choose Ki Breathing Meditation because it affects mind and body. It should be the easiest thing in the world, because really it is just about relaxed breathing. But attention is the hard part. In order to do Ki Breathing Meditation, you must harness your 45 bits of attention to keep coming back to your breathing. But if your mind is like mine, it can be an unbridled runaway machine.

With Insight Meditation you breathe in and out as you ordinarily do. But almost immediately your mind jumps to a thought, feeling, emotion, urge, or desire, away from a focus on breathing. Keep coming back again, and again, and again. You don't need to stop doing anything other than to stop being judgmental. With only 45 bits available to attend with, coming back to your breath without being judgmental is about all you can do. Once you latch onto a thought or feeling, you forget all about breathing.

With Insight Meditation you diffusely allow into your awareness thoughts, feelings, urges, emotions, sensations, and desires, without entanglement. Just be aware, then return to a focus on your breath, again and again.

It would seem that combining Insight Meditation and Ki Breathing Meditation you are totally involving mind and body. But if you are not familiar with either, you would probably need practice each separately before you could combine the two. Download an Insight Meditation mp3 and give it a try.   http://www.audiodharma.org

You fill your 45 bits of conscious attention with crap in an instant. So KISS (Keep it simple stupid!). All you need to do is let the crap be there. Just don't focus on it directly. Over and over return to focus on your breathing, as deep and relaxed as feels comfortable.

201

Flow

Each of us needs to find our own source of flow. You don't need to justify your life to others. Most people might think I don't have much of a life. I only go out for shopping and exercise. I spend no time on the phone and very little time on social media.

But I have found my source of flow. I have a rich life of literature, research, and writing. Not enough hours in the day. Not enough years left. So much to read and write and discover. So much to share with others.

The best literature on mp3s transports me to other lives, other ways of viewing this life, other ways of living, other worlds. I listen to at least a book a week; most of the time more than one book. When I come across a good book, it is like hitting the jackpot. Listening, researching, and writing for me is a meditative state I can't achieve it any other way. I am as blessed as the bum I told you about in Chapter 9, Healing Power of Reading– he with art and I with my reading.

I recently watched a talk by a Dr. Exekiel Emanuel, Chair of the Department of Medical Ethics and Heath Policy, University of Pennsylvania. His message: He wants to die by 75. He has seen what happens to people by the time they reach 75. They are no longer creative and productive. They are sick afflicted with dementia and physical disease. They can't walk a quarter mile. There are exceptions, but by definition we can't all be exceptions.

We can all continue to be creative, productive, and grow. I am writing this and growing at 80. The person I was five years back is not someone I think of as me. Yet five years back I was proud I had reached a peak, and the same for the previous peak a before that. I started as a violent monster and yet have an infinitely long journey. But along the way I discovered the journey is all and the end of the journey is dying.

Attention Therapies

I began working with attention therapies in the later years of my life. Open Focus and Attention Training Therapy (ATT) are not perpetual sitting meditative practice sessions. Part of the initial learning involves meditative exercises. Then when you grasp the basics you deploy with them as a part of your day-to-day-arsenal.

You learn to use Open Focus and Attention-Training Therapy (ATT) as you learned to ride a bicycle; training wheels at first. Once you balance and take off on your own, these therapies are tools to enrich your everyday life.

If you have a fear of public speaking and are giving a talk, you move from a focus of speaker out among the audience and beyond. Distracting coughing, paper crumpling, cell phones ringing, texting, present opportunities to shift focus of attention. You shift back and forth, open, receptive and communing among everyone and everything.

When you are home Ki Meditation Breathing can be an effective, healing, meditative practice. Out in the world it is an active state of mindfulness. Relax, weight underside, weight down low in your abdomen, ki flowing outward indefinitely as you proceed with whatever you are doing.

You never get there. It is a process, like global warming,but positive. You cannot pinpoint global warming to individual events. Over the years there is an observable warming trend. During the course of any year, though, it may get frigidly cold. Deniers use the frigid cold periods to deny global warming.

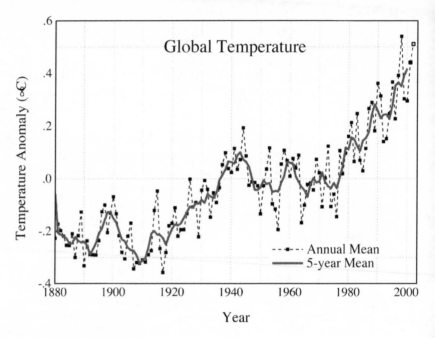

Figure 21-1: Global Warming

We cannot solve many problems yet we can't run away from them. Marriage, family, and work are hotbeds of irresolvable problems. Life is inherently difficult and painful. There are no answers to chronic problems. . There is a process of discovery that is painfully slow, up and down, but there are no limits to our growth. It is all about the journey, whatever point we are at this moment.

In the moment is the only place where we have control. The moment is the place we can practice. We undoubtably forget to employ these therapies and the time and place to get back on track is the present moment.

Albert Ellis would say, "It is fucking hard, but it is never too fucking hard." When we are knocked for a loop, we get up and start again. Over time we hit higher and higher points on the graph and we break through limits that are unimaginable in this present moment of time.

Epigenetics

Researchers are identifying genes, hundreds of genes that are affected by our subjective mental states. Living in a depressed state turns on genes that leave us vulnerable to infection and chronic disease. Feeling relaxed and peaceful turns off those genes and turns on genes that help us heal and fight infections. Researchers have developed a device that is controlled by EEG states to trigger a gene switch that modulates the creation of certain chemical agents. The system uses theNeuroSky MindSet EEG headset.

But you can effect the same EEG state without the MindSet EEG headset. Neurofeedback is just one way to achieve alpha EEG states. But you need the headset on, attached to a computer or mobile device, and you are unlikely to wear this when you go out.

I had been following the work of Herbert Benson from the time of his first best seller "The Relaxation Response," back in 1976. Benson was a Harvard-Professor of Medicine cardiologist who founded the Mind/Body Medical Institute at Massachusetts General Hospital (MGH) in Boston. In his research he discovered that the Relaxation Response reduced metabolic rate, rate of breathing, heart rate, and blood pressure if elevated. This is the opposite effect of an adrenaline-stressed fight or flight.

Benson found as that gene-set activity in cancer patients ran in one direction (either on or off), while the activity of the same group of genes in the Relaxation Response practitioners ran in the opposite direction.

How could simple meditation turn genes on or off?

Research published in the journal Frontiers in Immunology (June 6, 2017), reviewed 18 studies, 846 participants, over 11 years documenting a pattern in the molecular changes which happen to the body as a result of meditation, yoga, and other mind-body practices. They concluded that mind-body practices reverse inflammatory effects of the fight-or-flight stress reaction at a cellular level. The inflammation is useful as a short-lived fight-or-flight reaction, but if persistent, leads to a higher risk of cancer, accelerated aging and psychiatric disorders.

Emotional Contagion

There is evidence that smiling causes people to feel happy. Well, not exactly, but "in a state of emotional neutrality, putting a smile on your face can tip you in the direction of a positive feeling."

Requiring people to smile, no matter how they really feel at first, results in increased positive feelings. Frowning conversely decreases positive feelings. In 1989 Robert Zajanc published a study showing that saying the long vowel e (smile) pushes you in the happy valence; long vowel u pushes you toward sadness.

Make it a real smile in your eyes as well as mouth. "Smile, when you're feeling blue."Maybe not so easy to do, though, when you are down and out.

A study at the University of Cardiff in Wales found our emotions are driven by our facial expressions. People who were not able to frown due to botox injections reported feeling happier and less anxious.

An MRI study at Technical University of Munich in Germany scanned botox recipients who were not able to frown while asking them to mimic angry faces. Their brain scans showed much lower activity in the brain circuits involved in emotional processing and responses as compared with controls who had not received the treatment. This was seen as documenting they felt less anxious than the controls who were able to frown.

In another study researchers applied an uncomfortable intensity of heat to the forearms of participants who were asked to either make unhappy, neutral or relaxed faces. The participants who made unhappy faces perceived the heat as most painful.

Mind on Pain: The Psychology of Pain. Scientific American Mind. September 2009.

Robert Zajanc summarizes the findings of facial feedback studies. http://science.howstuffworks.com/life/smiling-happy1.htm

Hatfield, E., Cacioppo, J. L. & Rapson, R. L. (1993). Emotional contagion. Current Directions in Psychological Sciences, 2, 96-99.

Zajonc, R.B., Murphy, S.T. & Inglehart, M. (1989) Feeling and facial efference: Implications of the vascular theory of emotion. Psychological Review, 96, 395-416.

Other people's emotional expressions affect our mental states triggering neural circuits in our brain. The mirror neuron system (MNS) is an interconnected network of cells in the brain that records the emotional displays of others and signals them as mirror displays in our brain.

If you are with someone who is bright and happy, your MNS records their facial expression, body language, vocal tone, and emotional state, and mirrors the same display in you. But people are not bright and happy all of the time. The MNS records and signals angry and depressed displays from others' facial, vocal, movement, and emotional states deep into the neural core of your brain.

The process of emotional contagion is fast, unconscious, spontaneous, and automatic. When you smile at a baby, the baby smiles back. Stick out your tongue and the baby sticks its tongue back out at you.

It happens continuously during the course of a normal conversation. A rapport is built with an ongoing mirroring of facial expressions, speech patterns and body language. A lack of mirroring results in a lack of rapport.

You have little control over the merciless brain messages and mirror neurons reflecting the fear and anger of others. You need to be aware of the mirroring mechanism reflecting positive and negative feelings and emotions of others. You can choose to avoid people who broadcast negative vibes and hang out with positive people. But you might be minus your family, job, and friends. And it might mean rejecting anyone down and out and needing a little help from a friend.

Recognize that the uncomfortable emotions and feelings are generated by a mirror neuron system (MNS) in your brain in the same way that the Narrator module generates stories. The highly uncomfortable feelings I'm experiencing are caused by the MNS in my brain. When I am around someone projecting negative feelings, my MNS automatically mirrors their negative feelings. These uncomfortable feelings and emotions set off by my MNS reflect the way someone else is feeling or behaving.

You can't change someone else from feeling, or behaving, or believing. Focus on breathing. Accept the reflected feelings without claiming ownership and without blaming the owner of the negative feelings for passing them on. Try not to enter into an irresolvable, reactive loop.

No Time To Ruminate

Mindful meditation shifts the focus from rumination and clinging to irresolvable problems to a focus on breathing or Ki Breathing Meditation.You stop clinging to irresolvable problems. You stop challenging thoughts, feelings, emotions, and urges. The mp3s you download from the Insight Meditation Center offer sessions in focusing and attending in virtually every aspect of life and serve as a rich source of therapeutic insight as you meditate.

There is never time to ruminate when you practice attention therapies. Each time distracting thoughts pull you away, come back to Breathing Meditation. Focus on posture. Don't push thoughts away. When you try not to think of the white elephant, that is what pops into your mind.

A focus on Ki Breathing Meditation, Insight Meditation, Open-Focus, Attention Training Therapy(TT), and Metacognitive Therapy (MTC) leaves no space in your 45 bits of conscious-attending for rumination. Spend your slice of consciousness on healing attention strategies in place of harmful rumination on thoughts, feelings, emotions. and irresolvable problems.

Bibliotherapy

Bibliotherapy is a tool of Self-Renewal. I am constantly plugged into an mp3 or researching award-winning literature. It is a way of getting into the heads of others with different beliefs and ways of seeing the world. And it is a form a meditation. While I listen I am transported into different lives and worlds. Some of this has lasting effect on my outlook. But it is like all of the other attention therapies, the effect is over periods of time, though sometimes–rarely–I am moved to change my thinking by one book.

It is helpful to analyze why you are feeling a certain way in order to learn how to cope. But analyzing often causes an additional layer of problems caused by ruminating. Rumination is often more damaging than the original problem and becomes the core problem. Bibliotherapy offers a way to gain insight into troubling feelings without immersing in rumination. You do this by self-distancing or taking a third person POV, that of the character in the novel.

> Whether people's attempts to understand their negative feelings are adaptive depends on the type of self-perspective they adopt. Research results supported the prediction that analyzing feelings surrounding a negative experience from a self-distanced perspective (from an observer's vantage point) leads people to display lower levels of negative affect and rumination than does analyzing such feelings from a self-immersed perspective (from one's own vantage point). Journal of Abnormal Psychology, 212, Vol. 121, No. 3, 559-569.

Belief

Thirty percent or more of healing is due to the placebo effect, but deniers experience a nocebo effect. Their denial creates the nocebo. Doctors consider the placebo effect in terms of double blind, placebo controlled clinical trials. In a sense, they are deniers. If the placebo is more effective than the treatment, out goes the treatment along with the placebo.

How do you turn on the placebo effect to help heal mind and body. It is as simple as believing, expecting, and having faith. Yet if you try to believe, expect the best, and have faith, the result may be disastrous. It is like trying to fall asleep. You call upon a placebo and you get the nocebo. The placebo paradox.

Actions must be effective to foster belief, expectation, and faith. If action is ineffective, belief, expectation, and faith are degraded. Ki Meditation, Cognitive Therapy (CT), Open-Focus, Metacognitive Therapy (MCT), and Attention Training Therapy (ATT) are therapies proven effective. You can believe and have faith in them by understanding how they work. Find a balance of therapies that work for you. Include the body as a part of the process; jogging, resistance exercises, balancing exercises, somatics, yoga, swimming, whatever works for you.

Whatever your religious beliefs, prayer is an affirmation of and meditation on your beliefs, faith, and expectation. If it is possible for you to include prayer as a part of your daily routine, you are affirming and expressing belief and faith that you expect it to happen; countering the placebo paradox.

Self-Help Books Don't Help

If you do a read-through and put the book away, nothing much will happen. If you read a hundred books in this way, I doubt much will change. I wrote this book, yet each time I read through again I realize something I could be doing. On a minute to minute basis I forget the simple act of posture. I am always amazed at the affect on affect of simply adjusting posture. Stooped over I am an old geezer. The simple act of adjusting posture leverages a significant change in both mood and outlook.

Add Ki Breathing and results are leveraged even more. But this, too, I forget and need to remind myself moment to moment. Our attention is so limited that if I return to these two simple strategies, Metacognitive Therapy (MTC) kicks in on its own. I am aware of "no room to ruminate," to rehash garbage over and over. I see the problem is rumination itself.

Total Self-Renewal

I spent the last fifteen years of my life working on this book in hope I might help a few others. I am sharing everything that took me from violent spouse-abusing Mr. Hyde to peaceful Dr. Jekyll. If you are familiar with the book or movie version, my change was even more dramatic.

Every night comfortably lying in bed, I am thankful I am not in prison. I don't know how I possibly avoided a long prison or death sentence. I am thankful I did not commit murder.

Please let me know if I have helped you or can help in any way. I am 80-years old and will respond as long as I am here and able. If even one person takes what I have shared and runs with it—even sharing with others—what a blessing. A win-win finale, so to speak.

You can reach me at my blog: www.joeldames.com.

I would soooo much appreciate your review on Amazon.

REFERENCES

Aamodt, Sandra (2016) Why Diets Make Us Fat: the unintended consequences of our obsession with weight loss. Penguin Random House.

Abrahms, Spring, Janis. (2004). How Can I Forgive You? : the courage to forgive, the freedom not to. Harper Collins Publishers.

Adler, Alfred (1956) Individual Psychology of Alfred Adler. Basic Books, Inc.

Adler, Alfred (1998) Understanding Human Nature. Hazelden

Adler, Alfred (1998) What Life Could Mean to You. Hazelden

Albright, Carol Rausch & Ashbrook, James B. (2001) Where God Lives in the Human Brain. Sourcebooks.

Amador, Xavier. (2012) I am not Sick, I Don't Need Help. Vida Press.

Ariely, Dan. Predictably Irrational : The Hidden Forces That Shape Our Decisions. (2008) Harper Collins Publishers & Harper Collins e-books.

Ariely, Dan. The Upside of Irrationality : The Unexpected Benefits of Defying Logic at Work and at Home. (2010) Harper Collins Publishers.

Austin, James H. (1999) Zen and the Brain. MIG Press.

Backderf, Derf (2012) My Friend Dahmer. Abrams Comic Arts.

Bandler, Richard (2008) Get the Life You Want. Health Communications, Inc.

Baron-Cohen, Simon. (2011) The Science of Evil : on empathy and the origins of cruelty. Basic Books, Perseus Books Group.

Barton, George A. (1999) Billy Miske's Last Christmas. The Book of Boxing. Total Sports Illustrated Classics.

Baumeister, Roy F. & Tierney, John (2011) Willpower : rediscovering the greatest human strength. The Penguin Press.

Beauregard, Mario & O'Leary Denyse (2007) The Spiritual Brain. Harper Collins.

Begley, Sharon. (2007) Train Your Mind, Change Your Brain : how a new science reveals our extraordinary potential to transform ourselves. Ballantine Books.

Beilock, Sian (2010) Choke : what the secrets of the brain reveal about getting it right when you have to. Free Press, Simon & Schuster.

Bessel van der Kolk (2014) The Body Keeps the Score: Brain, Mind, and Body in the Healing of Traukma. Viking.

Bissinger, Buzz (2005) Three Nights in August : strategy, heartbreak, and joy inside the mind of a manager. Houghton Mifflin Company.

Blass, Steve with Sherman Erik (2012) A Pirate for Life. Triumph Books.

Blum, Deborah (1994) The Monkey Wars. Oxford University Press.

Blum, Deborah (2002) Love at Goon Park : harry harlow and the science of affection. Perseus Publishing.

Bolte Taylor, Jill (2008) My Stroke of Insight. Penguin Group.

Bowlby, John (1973) Separation : Anxiety and Anger. Basic Books, A member of the Perseus Books Group.

Bowlby, John (1980) Attachment and Loss. Basic Books. A Division of Harper Collins Publishers.

Bowlby, John (1988) A Secure Base. Basic Books. A member of the Perseus Books Group.

Broks, Paul. (2003) Into the Silent Land : travels in neuropsychology. Atlantic Monthly Press.

Brooks, David (2011) The Social Animal: The Hidden Sources of Love, Character, and Achievement. Random House.

Burdick, Alan (2017) Why Time Flies: A Mostly Scientific Investigation. Thorndike Press.

Carson, Shelley (2010) Your Creative Brain : seven steps to maximize imagination, productivity, and innovation in your life. Jossey-Bass, A Wiley Imprint.

Casidy, Jude & Shaver, Phillip R (1999) Handbook of Attachment: Theory, Research, and Clinical Applications . The Guilford Press

Chance, Jeremy (2001) The Alexander Technique. Thorsons, Harper Collins

Charney, Dennis S. & Nemeroff, Charles B (2004) Peace of Mind Prescription : an authoritative guide to finding the most effective treatment for anxiety and depression. Houghton Mifflin Company. *

Cialdini, Robert B. (2008) Yes! : 50 scientifically proven ways to be persuasive. Free Press, Simon & Schuster.

Cloud, Henry (2011) The Law of Happiness. Howard Books, A Division of Simon & Schuster, Inc.

Cohen, Jonathan D. Cohen. (2004) The Neural Bases of Cognitive Conflict and Control in Moral Judgment. Neuron, Vol. 44, 389-400, October 14, 2004

Cole, David J. & Ladas-Gaskin, Carol (2007) Mindfulness Centered

Therapies : an integrative approach. Hyperion.

Costa, Rebecca D. (2010) The Watchman's Rattle: thinking our way out of extinction. Vanguard Press.

Cosolino, Louis (2008) The Healthy Aging Brain : sustaining attachment, attaining wisdom. W.W. Norton & Company, Inc.

Cosolino, Louis (2013) The Social Neuroscience of Education: optimizing attachment and learning in the classroom. (W.W. Norton & Company, Inc.

Cosolino, Louis (2014) Attachment-Based Teaching: creating a tribal classroom. W.W. Norton & Company, Inc.

Cosolino, Louis (2016) Why therapy works : using our minds to change our brains. W.W. Norton & Company, Inc.

Crick, Francis (1994) The Astonishing Hypothesis: the scientific search for the soul. Charles Scribner's Sons, Macmillan Publishing Company.

Csikszentmihalyi, Mihaly (1990) Flow : The Psychology of Optimal Experience. Harper Perennial. Csikszentmihalyi, Mihaly (1997) Finding Flow : the psychology of engagement with everyday life. Basic Books, Perseus Books Group.

Damasio, Antonio (1994) *Descartes' Error.* A Grosset/Putnam Book.

Damasio, Antonio (1999) The Feeling of What Happens, Body and Emotion in the Making of Consciousness. Harcourt Brace & Company.

Damasio, Antonio (2003) Looking for Spinoza. Harcourt, Inc.

Damasio, Antonio (2010) Self Comes to Mind, Constructing the Conscious Brain. Read by Fred Stella on CD. Brilliance Audio.

Davidson, Cathy N. (2011) Now You See It ; how the brain science of attention will transform the way we live, work, and learn. Viking, Penguin Group.

Davidson, Richard J. with Begley Sharon (2012) The Emotional Life of Your Brain : How It's Unique Patterns Affect the Way you Think, Feel, and Live – and How You Can Change Them. Hudson Street Press.

de Botton, Alain (1997) How Proust Can Change Your Life. Vintage International.

de Botton, Alain (2012) Religion for Atheists : a non-believe's guide to the uses of religion. Pantheon Books.

de Botton, Alain & Armstrong, John (2013) Art as Therapy. Phaidon Press.

D'Emillio, John (2003) Lost Prophet : the life and times of Bayard Rustin. Free Press, Simon & Schuster, Inc.

Dempsey, Jack (1960) Dempsey. Simon and Schuster

Dempsey, Jack (1977) Dempsey. Harper & Row

Dennis, Wayne (Ed) (1948) Readings in the History of psychology. The Power of the

Mind Over the Body. James Braid. Appleton-Century-Crofts.

de Waal, Frans (2001) Tree of Origin: what primate behavior can tell us about human social evolution. Harvard University Press.

De Waal, Frans (2005) Our Inner Ape, Riverhead Books.

De Waal, Frans (2009) The Age of Empathy: nature's lessons for a kinder society. Harmony Books

Dicky, R.A. with Coffee, Wayne (2012) Wherever I Wind Up : my quest for truth, authenticity and the perfect knuckleball. Blue Rider Press, Penguin Group.

Dillon, Brian (2010) The Hypochondriacs: Nine tormented lives. Faber & Faber, Inc.

Doidge, Norman. (2007) The Brain That Changes Itself : stories of personal triumph from the frontiers of brain science. Penguin Group.

Doidge, Norman (2015) The Brain's Way of Healing : remarkable discoveries and recoveries from the frontiers of neuroplasticity. Viking (Penguin Group)

Duhigg, Charles (2012) The Power of Habit : why we do what we do in life and business. Random House.

Eagleman, David (2011) Incognito : the secret lives of the brain. Pantheon Books, a division of Random House, Inc.

Erickson, Milton, H. , Edited by Rossi, Ernest L. (1980) Innovative Hypnotherapy: the collected papers of Milton H. Erickson on Hypnosis, Vol. IV. Irvington Publishers, Inc.

Esdaile, James. Letter on Hypnotism and Mesmerism, From James Esdaile to James Braid. Excerpt from The discovery of Hypnosis: The Complete Writings of James Braid. Posted on August 19, 2010 by UK College of Hypnosis & Hypnotherapy.
http://ukhypnosis.com/2010/08/19/james-esdaile-writes-to-james-braid-about-mesmerism-and-hypnotism/

Farmelo, Graham. (2009) The Strangest Man : the hidden life of Paul Dirac, mystic of the atom. Basic Books, Perseus Books Group.

Fehmi, Les & Robbins, Jim (2007) The Open-Focus Brain : harnessing the power of attention to heal mind and body. Trumpeter.

Fehmi, Les & Robbins, Jim (2010) Dissolving Pain : simple brsain-training exercises for overcoming pain. Trumpeter.

Feldenkrais, Moshe (1972) Awareness Through Movement : health exercises for personal growth. Harper San Francisco.

Feldenkrais, Moshe (1972) The Potent Self : a study of spontaneity and compulsion. Frog, Ltd.

Feldenkrais, Moshe (2010) Embodied Wisdom : the collected papers of Moshe Feldenkrais. Somatic Resources & North Atlantic Books

Fields, Douglas R. (2009) The Other Brain: From Dementia to Schizophrenia, How New Discoveries about the Brain are Revolutionizing Medicine and Science. Simon & Schuster.

Fields, Douglas R. (2015) Why We Snap : understanding the rage circuit in your brain. Dutton.

Flanigan, Beverly (1992) : overcoming the bitter legacy of intimate wounds. Wiley Publishing, Inc.

Foot, Philippa (1967). "The Problem of Abortion and the Doctrine of Double Effect," *Oxford Review*, 5: 5–15

Foot, Philippa. (1978) Virtues and Vices and Other Essays in Moral Philosophy. University of California Press.

Frank, Lone. (2009) Mindfield. Oneworld Paperback, Oxford Publications.

Frankl, Viktor E. (1988) The Will to Meaning: foundations and applications of logotherapy. Meridian.

Frankl, Viktor E. (1995) Man's Search for Meaning: An introduction to Logotherapy. Blackstone Audiobooks.

Frankl, Viktor E. (2000) Man's Search for Ultimate Meaning. Basic Books.

Frankl, Viktor E. (2006) Man's Search for Meaning. Beacon Press.

Fox, Elaine (2012) Rainy Brain, Sunny Brain. Basic Books, Perseus Books Group

Freud, Sigmund (1952) The Major Works of Sigmund Freud. Encyclopedia Britannica, Inc.

Freud, Sigmund (1966) Introductory Lectures on Psychoanalysis. (259-260) W.W. Norton & Company, Inc.

Freud, Sigmund (1972) Abstracts of the Standard Edition of Freud. National Institute of Mental Health.

Freud Sigmund (1974)The Freud/Jung Letters: The Correspondence Between Sigmund Freud and C. G. Jung. (Paperback Edition)(Princeton University Press.

Freud, Sigmund (1995) The Basic Writings of Sigmund Freud. Modern Library Edition.

Freud, Sigmund (2003) The Schreber Case. Penguin Classics.

Gabor Mate, MD (2010) In the Realm of Hungry Ghosts, Close Encounters with Addiction. North Atlantic Books.

Gallagher, Winifred (2009) Rapt, Attention and the Focused Life. The Penguin Press.

Gardner, John W. (1981) Self-Renewal: The Individual and the Innovative Society. W.W. Norton & Companty.

Gardner, John W. (1995) Self-Renewal: the individual and the innovative society, revised edition. W.W.Norton & Company.

Garner, Thomson (2008) Magic in Practice. Hammersmith Press.

Gazzaniga, Michael (1998) The Mind's Past. University of California Press.

Gazzaniga, Michael (2011) Who's in Charge? : free will and the science of the brain. Harper Collins Publishers.

Gerstner, Louis V. (2002) Who Says Elephants Can't Dance? Harper Collins.

Gill, Holland, J. (2005) The Private Journals of Edvard Munch : we are flames which pour out of the earth. University of Wisconsin Press.

Gladwell, Malcolm (2005) Blink : the power of thinking without thinking. Recorded Books, LLC.

Goble, Frank G. (1970) The Third Force : The Psychology of Abraham Maslow. Grossman Publishers.

Goewey, Don Joseph (2009) Mystic Cool : a proven approach to transcend stress, achieve optimal brian function, and maximize your creative potential. Atria Books, A Division of Simon & Schuster, Inc.

Goffman, Erving (1969) Strategic Interactions. University of Pennsylvania Press

Goldstein, Noah J., Martin, Steve J., Cialdini, Robert B. (2008) Yes! 50 Scientifically Proven Ways to Be Persuasive. Recorded Books.com

Gordon, Dick (1984) Boxer Billy Miske Put Up the Fight of His Life for One Last Christmas. Sports Illustrated Vault.

Gotlieb, Ian H. & Hammen, Constance L. (editors) (2002) Handbook of Depression. The Guilford Press.

Green, Joshua D., Nystrom, Leigh E., Engell, Andrew D., Darley, John M., and

Greenberg, Gary (2013) The Book of Woe : the DSM and the Unmaking of Psychiatry. Blue Rider Press.

Greenfield, Kent (2011) The Myth of Choice : personal responsibility in a world of limits. Yale University Press.

Hanh, Tich Nhat (2001) Essential Writings. Riverhead Books, Penguin Putnam, Inc.

Haller, John S. Jr. (2014) Shadow Medicine. Columbia University Press.

Hallowell, Edward M. (2004) Dare to Foregive. Health Communications, Inc.

Hanna, Thomas (1988) Somatics : reawakening the mind's control of movement, flexibility, and health. Lifelong Books, member Perseus Books.

Harlow, Harry (1958) Harlow, H. F. (1958). The nature of love. *American Psychologist, 13*(12), 673-685. http://psychclassics.yorku.ca/Harlow/love.htm

Harrington, Anne (1997) The Placebo Effect : an interdiscipinary Exploration. Harvard University Press. *

Harrington, Anne (2008) The Cure Within : a history of mind-body medicine. W.W.Norton & Company. *

Harris, Dan (2014) 10% Happier : how I tamed the voice in my head, reduced stress without losing my edge, and found self-help that actually works — a true story. it books, HarperCollins Publishers

Harris, Sam (2004) The End of Faith : religion, terror, and the future of reason. W.W. Norton. Crown Publishers.

Herbert, Wray (2010) On Second Thought : outsmarting your mind's hard-wired habits.

Higgins, Mary & Raphael, Chester M. (edited by) (1967) Reich Speaks of

Freud : Wilhelm Reich discusses his work and his relationship with Sigmund Freud. Farrar, Straus & Ciroux.

Hill, Robert J. & Castro, Eduardo (2002) Getting Rid of Ritalin : how neurofeedback can successfully treat attention deficit disorder without drugs. Hampton Roads Publishing Company.

Hill, Robert J. & Castro, Eduardo (2009) Healing Young Brains : the neurofeedback solution. Hadmpton Roads Publishing Company, Inc.

Hyman, Mark (2009) The UltraMind Solution: Fix your Broken Brain by Healing Your Body First. Scribner.

Isaacson, Walter (2011) Steve Jobs. Simon & Schuster.

Jackson Nakagawa, Donna (2015) Childhood Disrupted: How Your Biography Becomes Your Biology, and How You Can Heal. Astria Books, Imprint of Simon & Schuster.

Jamison, Kay Redfield (1993) Touched with Fire : manic-depressive illness and the artistic temperament. The Free Press.

Janiger, Oscar & Goldberg Philip (1993) A Different Kind of Healing. Putnam Book

Jarvis, Judith Thomson, Killing, Letting Die, and the Trolley Problem, 59 The Monist 204-17 (1976)

Jarvis, Judith Thomson, The Trolley Problem, 94 Yale Law Journal 1395-1415 (1985)

Johnson, Clay A. (2012) The Information Diet : a case for conscious consumption. O'Reilly.

Hallinan, Joseph T. (2009) Why We Make Mistakes. Doubleday Publishing Group, a division of Random House, Inc., NY

Hanson, Rick with Mendius, Richard (2009) Buddha's Brain : the practical neuroscience of happiness, love, & wisdom. New Harbinger Publications, Inc.

Hillenbrand, Laura (2010) Unbroken: A World War II Story of Survival, Resilience, and Redemption. Random House.

Iacoboni, Marco (2008) Mirroring People : the new science of how we connect with others. Farrar, Straus and Giroux.

Isherwood, Christopher (2001) A Single Man. University of Minnesota Press.

Kabat-Zinn, Jon. (1990) Full Catastrophe Living : using the wisdom of your body and mind to face stress, pain, and illness.

Kabat-Zinn, Jon. (2005) Coming to Our Senses : Healing ourselves and the world through mindfulness. Hyperion.

Kahneman, Daniel (2011) Thinking, Fast & Slow. Random House Audio, Books on Tape.

Kaufman, G.D. (1981) The Theological Imagination: constructing the concept of God. Westminster Press.

Kalanithi, Paul (2016) When Breath Becomes Air. Random House

Kandel, Eric R. (2007) In Search of Memory. WWW Norton &

Company, In

Keenan, Julian Paul (2003) The Face in the Mirror : the search for the origins of consciousness. Harper Collins.

Kessler, David A. (2016) Capture: Unraveling the Mystery of Mental Suffering. Harper Wave.

Kirkpatrick, L. A. (1995). Attachment theory and religious experience. In R. W. Hood, Jr. (Ed.), Handbook of religious experience (pp. 446– 475). Birmingham, AL: Religious Education Press.

Klein, Stefan (2002) The Science of Happiness. Marlowe & Company.

Kora, Takehisa, Peterson, with Gregory, Peterson & Reynolds, David (translators) (1995) How to Live Well : secrets of using neurosis. State University of New York.

Kramer, Gregory (2007) Insight Dialogue : the interpersonal path to freedom. Shambhala.

Kuby, Lolette (2001) Faith and the Placebo Effect: an argument for self-healing. Origin Press.

Larsen, Stephen (2006) The Healing Power of Neurofeedback : the revolutionary LENS technique for restoring optimal brain function. Healing Arts Press.

Kessler, David A. (2016) Capture: unraveling the mystery of mental suffering. Harper Collins Publishers.

Kotler, Steven (2014) The Rise of Superman: decoding the science of ultimate human performance. Houghton Mifflin Harcourt Publishing Company.

Kutner, Lawrence & Olson, Cheryl K. (2008) Grand Theft Childhood : the surprising truth about violent video games. Simon & Schuster.

Langer, Ellen (2009) Counterclockwise : mindful health and the power of possibility. *Ballantine Books.

LeDoux, Joseph (1996) The Emotional Life of the Brain : the mysterious underpinnings   of emotional life. Simon & Schuster.

Levin, Janna (2006) A Madman Dreams of Turing Machines. Alfred Knopf.

Levine, Robert V. (2016) Stranger in the Mirror: the Scientific Search for the Self. Princeton Press.

Lindstrom, Martin (2011) Brandwashed : tricks companies use to manipulate our Minds. Crown Business.

Luntz, Frank (2007) Words That Work : it's not what you say, it's what people hear.Hyperion.

Lysiak, Matthew (2013) Newtown: an American tragedy. Gallery Books, A Division of Simon & Schuster, Inc.

Lyubomirsky, Sonja (2008) The How of Happiness : A scientific approach to getting what you want. T he Penguin Press.

216

Macdonald, Glynn (2002) Illustrated Elements of Alexander Technique. Element, Imprint of Harper Collins Publishers Ltd.

Marchnt, Jo (2016) Cure: a journey into the science of mind over body. Crown Publishers.

Marita, Shoma (1998) Therapy and the true nature of anxiety based disorders (Shinkeishitsu); translated by Kondo, Akihisa; edited by Peg LeVine. State University of New York Press.

Maslow, Abraham H. (1962) Toward a Psychology of Being. Van Nostrand.

Maslow, Abraham H. (1964) Religions, Values, and Peak-Experiences. Arana, Penguin Group.

Maslow, Abraham H. (1993) The Farther Reaches of Human Nature. Arkana

Maslow, Abraham H. (2001) Toward a Psychology of Being. John Wiley & Sons, Inc.

MGilchrist, Iain (2010) The Master and his Emissary : the divided brain and the making of the western world. Yale University Press.

Mlodinow, Leonard (2012) Subliminal : how your unconscious mind rules your behavior. Pantheon Books.

Mooney, Jonathan & Cole, David (2000) Learning Outside the Lines. Fireside.

Morse, Melvin with Perry, Paul (2000) Where God Lives : the science of the paranormal and how our brains are linked to the universe. Cliff Street Books; Harper Collins.

Mukherjee, Siddhartha (2016) The Gene: An intimate History. Scribner

Mullane, Nancy (2012) Life After Murder : five men in search of redemption. Public Affairs, Perseus Books Group.

Murphy, Joseph (1968) The Cosmic Power Within You. Parker Publishing Company, Inc.

Murphy, Joseph (1973) Telepsychics: Tapping Your Hidden Subconscious Powers. Parker Publishing Company, Inc.

Murphy, Joseph & (2000) The Power of Your Subconscious Mind. Bantam Book(Revision Wilder Publications, LLC. 2007; Penguin Edition 2010 Penguin Group).

Murphy, Joseph & Revised by McMahan, Ian D. (2001) The Amazing Laws of Cosmic Mind Power. Prentice Hall Press, Adobe Digital Editions.

Nakazawa, Donna Jackson. (2015) Childhood Disruptied: How Your Biography Becomes Your Biology, and How You Can Heal. Atria Books

Nasar, Sylvia (1998) A Beautiful Mind. Touchstone.

Nease, Bob (2016) The Power of Fifty Bits: The New Science of Turning Good Intentions into Positive Results. Harper Collins Publishers.

Neill, Michael (2008) Effortless Success 6-CD Set. Hay House, Inc.

Netzley, Patricia D. (2013) How Does Video Game Violence Affect Society? Reference Point Press.

Newberg, Andrew. (2006) Why We Believe What We Believe: Uncovering our biological need for meaning, spirituality and truth. Free Press, A division of Simon and Schuster, Inc.

42. Newberg, Andrew B. and Wald, Mark R. (2009) How God Changes Your Brain. Ballantine Books.

Newber, Andrew B. Principles of Neurotheology (2010) Ashgate Publishing Company.

Nicholls, Carolyn (2008) Body, Breath & Being : a new guide to the Alexander Technique. D & B Publishing.

Nicholls, Carolyn (2012) The Posture Workbook. D & B Publishing.

Niehoff, Debra (1999) The Biology of Violence: how understanding the brain, behavior, and environment can break the vicious cycle of aggression. The Free Press.

Niven, David (2000) The 100 Secret Habits of Happy People : What Scientists Have Learned and How You Can Use it. Harper Collins Books.

Noe, Alva (2009) Out of Our Heads: Why you are not your brain, and other lessons from the biology of consciousness. Hill and Wang, A division of Farrar, Straus and Giroux.

Norem, Julie K. (2002) The Positive Power of Negative Thinking : Using Defensive Pessimism to Manage Anxiety and Perform at Your Peak. Basic Books, Perseus Books Group.

Norretranders, Nor (1998) (Translation). The User Illusion:Cutting Consciousness Down to Size. Penguin Books.

Offit, Paul A. (2013) Do You Believe in Magic : the sense and nonsense id alternative medicine. HarperCollins.

O'Hanlon, William Hudson; Martin, Michael (1992) Solution-Oriented Hypnosis: An Erikson Approach. WW.Norton & Company.

Ottaviani, Jim & Meconis, Dylan (2007) Wire Mothers : harry harlow and the science of love. General Tektronics Labs.

Panksepp, Jaak & Biven, Lucy (2012) The Archaeology of Mind : neuroevolutionary origins of human emotions. Norton & Company, Inc.

Partnoy, Frank (2012) Wait : the art and science of delay. Public Affairs, Perseus Books Group.

Pattakos, Alex. (2004) Prisoners of Our Thoughts. Borrett-Koehler.

Pauley, Jane (2004) Skywriting. Random House.

Pennebaker, James W. (2004) Writing to Heal : a guided journal for recovering from trauma & emotional upheaval. New Harbinger Publications, Inc.

Perlmutter, David & Villoldo, Alberto (2011) Power Up Your Brain: the neuroscience of enlightenment. Hay House, Inc.

Potter-Efron (2012) Healing the Angry Brain: Understanding the way your brain works can help you control anger & aggression. New Harbinger Publications, Inc.

Raine, Adrian (2013) The Anatomy of Violence : the biological roots of

218

crime. Pantheon Books, Division of Random House, Inc.

Rami, Rabbi (2011) Guide to Forgiveness : roadside assistance for the spiritual traveler.

Spirituality and Health Books.

Ramo, Joshua Cooper (2010) The Age of the Unthinkable: Why the New World Disorder Constantly Surprises Us and What We Can Do About It. Back Bay Books.

Rankin, Lissa (2013) Mind Over Medicine : scientific proof that you can heal yourself. Hay House, Inc.

Rappoport, Judith L. (1989) Boy Who Couldn't Stop Washing. E.P. Dutton.

Ratey, John J. & Manning, Richard (2014) Go Wild : free your body and mind from the afflictions of Civilization. Little, Brown & Company (Hachette Book Group).

Reich, Willhelm (1945) Selected Writings : an introduction to Orgonomy. Farrar, Straus & Giroux.

Reich, Wilhelm (1945) Character Analysis. Farrar, Straus & Giroux.

Reich, Wilhelm (1945) The Sexual Revolution : toward a self-governing character structure. Farrar, Straus & Giroux.

Reich, Wilhelm (1967) Reich Speaks of Freud : Wilhelm Reich discusses his work and his relationship with Sigmund Freud. : Farrar, Straus & Giroux.

Reich, Wilhelm (1974) Listen, Little Man! Farrar, Straus, and Giroux.

Rein, Adrian (2013) The Anatomy of Violence : the biological roots of crime. Pantheon Books, Random House, Inc.

Reynolds, David K (1980) The Quiet Therapies. University of Hawaii Press.

Robbins, Jim (2000,2008) A Symphony in the Brain : the evolution of the new brain wave biofeedback. Grove Press.

Robertson, Donald (Ed.) (2009). The Discovery of Hypnosis: The Complete Writings of James Braid, the Father of Hypnotherapy. National Council for Hypnotherapy.

Ronson, Jon (2008) The Psychopath Test : a journey through the madness industry. Riverhead Books, Penguin Group.

Rosen, Sidney. (1982) My Voice Will Go With You: the teaching tales of Milton H. Erickson. W.W. Norton & Company, Inc.

Rossi, Ernest L. & Cheek, David B. (1988) Mind-Body Therapy: ideodynamic healing in hypnosis. W.W. Norton & Company.

Sacks, Oliver (2010) The Mind's Eye. Alfred A. Knopf.

Saks, Elyn R. (2007) The Center Cannot Hold. Hyperion.

Sapolsky, Robert M. (2001) A Primate's Memoir: A neuroscientist's unconventional life among the baboons. Scribner.

Sapolksy, Robert M. (2004) Why Zebras Don't Get Ulcers. Henry Holt and Company, LLC

Sapolsky, Robert M. November 2004 The Frontal Cortex and the Criminal Justice System. The Royal Society Publishing.

Sapolsky, Robert M. (2005) Monkeyluv: and other essays on our lives as animals. Scribner.

Sapolsky, Robert M. (2005) Biology & Human Behavior: The Neurological Origins of Individuality, 2nd Edition. The Teaching Company.

Satterfield, Jason M. (2015) Cognitive Behavioral Therapy: Techniques for Retraining Your Brain. Course Guidebook. The Great Courses.

Scheeres, Julia (2011) A Thousand Lives : the untold story of hope, deception, and survival at Jonestown. Free Press, A Division of Simon k& Schuster, Inc.

Schermer, Michael (2011) The Believing Brain: from ghosts and gods to politics and conspiracies -- how we construct beliefs and reinforce he as truths. Times Books.

Schultz, Johannes H. & Luthe, Wolfgang (1969) Autogenic Therapy. Grune & Stratton.

Schwartz, Jeffrey M. (1996) Brain Lock. Harper Collins Publishers, Inc.

Schwartz, Jeffrey M (1997) Brain Lock. Harper Collins. Schwartz, Jeffrey M. & Begley, Sharon. (2002) The Mind and the Brain: neuroplasticity and the power of mental force. Harper Collins.

Schwartz, Jeffrey M. & Gladding, Rebecca. (2011) You Are Not Your Brain: the 4-step solution for changing bad habits, ending unhealthy thinking, and taking control of your life. Penguin Books Ltd.

Schwartz, Joseph (1999) Cassandra's Daughter : A history of psychoanalysis. Viking

Seligman, Martin E.P. (2002) Authentic Happiness. Free Press, Simon & Schuster.

Seligman, Martin E.P. (2006) Learned Optimism : How to Change Your Mind and Life. Vintage Books, A Division of Random House, Inc.

Seligman, Martin E.P. (2011) Flourish. Free Press, Simon & Schuster.

Seligman, Martin E.P. (2011) Flourish. Simon & Schuster Audio

Selye, Hans (1956) The Stress of Life. McGraw-Hill Book Company, Inc.

Selye, Hans (1975) Stress Without Distress : how to use stress as a positive force to achieve a rewarding lifestyle. Harper & Row Publishers, Inc.

Selye, Hans (1979) The Stress of My Life : a scientist's memoirs. Van Nostrand Reinhold Company.

Shafarman, Steven (1997) Awareness Heals : the Feldenkrais Method for dynamic health. Addison Wesley.

Sharma, Robin (2003) The Saint, the Surfer and the CEO : a remarkable story about living your heart's desire. Hay House, Inc.

Shapiro, Francine (2012) Getting Past Your Past : take control of your life with self-help techniques from EMDSR therapy. Rodale.

Shapiro, Rami (2011) Forgiveness : roadside assistance for the spiritual traveler. Spirituality and Health Books.

Sharot, Tali (2011) The Optimism Bias: A tour of the irrationally positive brain. Pantheon Books.

Sheiman, Bruce (2009) An Atheist Defends Religion : Why Humanity is Better Off with Religion than without it. Alpha, Penguin Group.

Siddhartha, Mukherjee (2016) The Gene: An Intimate History. Scribner.

Siegel, Dan (2007) The Mindful Brain:reflection and attunement in the cultivation of well-being. W.W. Norton & Company, Inc.

Siegel, Dan (2008) The Mindful Brain:The Neurobiology of Well-being. Sounds True Audio.

Siegel, Dan (2008) The Neurobiology of We:How Relationships, the Mind, and the Brain Interact to Shape Who We Are. Sounds True Audio.

Siegel, Dan (2010) The Mindful Therapist : a clinician's guide to mindsight and neural integration. W.W. Norton & Company, Inc.

Silva, Jose & Miele, Philip (1977) Pocket Books, Simon & Schuster, Inc.

Slahi, Mohamedou Ould (2015) Guantanamo Diary. Blackstone Hachette Audio.

Smede, Lewis B. (1984) Forgive & Gorget : healing the hurts we don't deserve. Harper One, Harper Collins Publishers.

Smith, Jeff (2015) Mr. Smith Goes to Prison. St. Martins Press

Southard, Susan (2015) Nagasaki: Life After Nuclear War. Viking

Southwick, Steven M. & Charney, Dennis S. (2012) Resilience : the science of mastering life's greatest challenges : ten key ways to bounce back from stress and trauma. Cambridge University Press.

Storr, Anthony (1972) The Dynamics of Creation. Atheneum.

Taleb, Nassim Nicholas (2012) Anifragile : things that gain from disorder. Random House.

Thaler, Richard H. & Sunstein, Cass R. (2008) Nudge: improving decisions about health, wealth, and happiness. A Caravan Book.

Thomson, Garner with Khan, Khalid (2008) Magic in Practice : Introducing Medical NLP : The Art and Science of Language in Healing and Health.

Thorton, Mark. (2004) Meditation in a Minute : Super Calm for the Super Busy. Sounds True, Inc.

Tough, Paul (2012) How Children Succeed : gift, curiosity, and the hidden power of character. HoughtonMifflin (book) Tantor Audio (CD).

Trivers, Robert (2011) The Foley of Fools : the logic of deceit and self-deception in human life. Basic Books.

Turner, Kelly A. (2014) Radical Remission: the nine key factors that can make a real difference. Harper Collins.

Wallace, Patricia (1999) The Psychology of the Internet. Cambridge University Press.

Wegner, Daniel M. (1989) White Bears and Other Unwanted Thought:

Suppression, Obsession, and the Psychology of Mental Control. Viking.

Wells, Adrian (1997) Cognitive Therapy of Anxiety Disorders: A Practice Manual and Conceptual Guide. John Wiley & Sons.

Wells, Adrian (2009) Metacognitive Therapy for Anxiety and Depression. The Guilford Press.

Wells, Adrian & Fisher, Peter (2009). Metacognitive Therapy: Distinctive Features. Routledge Taylor and Francis Group.

Wilson, Timothy D. (2011) Redirect : the surprising new science of psychological change. Little, Brown and Company.

Wise, Jeff (2009) Extreme Fear : the science of your mind in danger. Palgrave Macmillan.

Wittmann, Marc (2016) Felt Time: the psychology of how we perceive time. Massachusetts Institute of Technology (translation from German)

Wu, Tim (2016) The Attention Merchants: The Epic Scramble to Get Inside Our Heads. Knopf.

CREDITS

12669567R00141

Made in the USA
San Bernardino, CA
11 December 2018